D0432747

The Flying Hours

THE FLYING HOURS

THE COMPELLING MEMOIR OF SQUADRON LEADER ANDREW MILLAR, DSO, DFC, AND THE SECOND WORLD WAR BATTLE AGAINST JAPAN

ANDREW MILLAR

Published in 2015 by Fighting High Ltd
www.fightinghigh.com

Copyright © Fighting High Ltd, 2015
Copyright text © Andrew Millar, 2015

British Library Cataloguing-in-Publication data. A CIP record for this title is available from the British Library.

ISBN – 13: 9780993212901

Typeset in Adobe Minion 11/17pt
by Alex Szabo-Haslam, www.truthstudio.co.uk

Printed and bound in China by Toppan Leefung.
Front cover design by www.truthstudio.co.uk

Eheu, horae fugaces labuntur computanturque.

Alas! The flying hours slide by and are logged to our account.

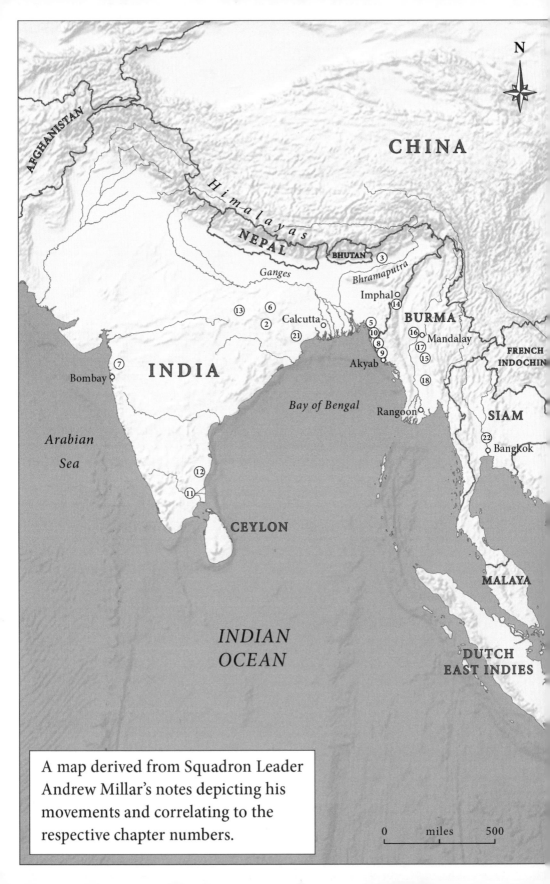

A map derived from Squadron Leader
Andrew Millar's notes depicting his
movements and correlating to the
respective chapter numbers.

Contents

by Andrew Millar (son of Squadron Leader Andrew Millar, DSO, DFC)

Our family house had a Japanese officer's sword above the kitchen door, a cigarette box with RAF wings in the living room and a carved model Spitfire in Dad's study next to two framed certificates with the King's signature. At Sunday teatime we would say: 'Tell us about the RAF Dad!' Dad, aka 'Dr Andrew Patrick Millar, DSO, DFC, MB, BS, DRCOG' (as addressed on some GP letters) would always oblige. One favourite (we children must all have been less than five) was how he parked his aeroplane in a cloud to escape some Japanese fighters.

Dad always recalled his wartime experiences easily and without any big deal. His respect and affection for many of his comrades was obvious. He liked to tell a story about a Kiwi flight lieutenant called Sandy McPhail and how he beat a large strong Scotsman in a wrestling match during a night's drinking by a bonfire. He told us about snakes in flying boots, racing rickshaws 'borrowed' from locals during nights out and about his extreme fevers and rigors with malaria. Mum would chip in to say he weighed 8½ stones when he returned from India and this was a man at over 6 feet tall. There was also a boxing match with a belligerent army officer. Unusually, I would say, for an Allied combatant against the Japanese, he had considerable respect for them and their fighting ability.

When I was a teenage schoolboy he started to write his 'memoirs' – sitting in his study and tapping his typewriter with two fingers while referring to his log book to see what memories he could conjure up. Doubtless a few of these were 'rose-tinted', with some omissions and a little misting twenty years on, but I believe they represent his most faithful recollections. Dad tried to get the collection published, without success. I read them when I was about seventeen and had not looked at them again until 2014.

However, in 2013 I was reminded of Dad's remarkable – in fact rather unbelievable – wartime experiences. From reading the memoirs, my niece Meg had worked out that there may still be film footage somewhere of 20 Squadron, shot by a War Office cameraman. This was because Dad described two specific incidents. Doggedly she tracked these down to the Imperial War Museum, who sent a DVD that I watched spellbound. It contained previously unseen film of Dad when he was younger than my son, climbing out of an aircraft; briefing his squadron; the squadron stripping and running into the Indian Ocean; aeroplane maintenance; and bartering with natives. There was also erratic flying a few feet above the surf and an attack on a target described in the memoirs, shortly before a shell hit his engine and he limped home short of oil.

We are very grateful to Steve Darlow for his initiative to track us down and publish this book more than thirty years after Dad's early death from colonic cancer in 1982. Steve's contact caused me to reread the memoirs now as a sixty-year-old, as opposed to my previous teenage view. It astonished me that Dad did all this when he was the same age as my children are now – their early twenties. The endurance, danger, resourcefulness, courage and extreme luck of the survivors are unimaginable by today's standards. To take off with a map on your knees, unreliable weather reports and negligible radio to explore unknown mountains above hostile terrain and judge the return flight to within a minute or two of fuel reserves, seems little more than foolhardy, but was a run-of-the-mill sortie. On top of this were the constant tropical skin diseases, the chronic amoebic dysentery and the recurrent bouts of rigors from malaria. This continued for four years.

Towards the end of the memoirs Dad keeps remarking that he must have gone round the twist; I find it amazing that he and his fellow airmen kept going at all. Dad told me that his squadron used to call him 'mad Millar' – and that could mean a number of things – but when, as a seventeen-year-old, I was hitch-hiking around New Zealand and called in to see Sandy McPhail, he treated me as if it was my father in front of him. I could see the greatest respect and affection in this man's eyes – who was scrum half and captain of the Wanganui Rugby Club – when he laughingly told me that 'Mad Millar used to make us all sing hymns on Sundays.'

There is a naïvety to some of Dad's writing and I think it is pertinent to reflect that he was brought up as a Scottish Protestant and not allowed to put his hands in his pockets or whistle on a Sunday. I suspect that the self-discipline and inner fortitude of his Christian belief carried him through, along with very large and recurrent slices of luck. He lost his belief in his forties, preferring instead a scientific explanation for the way things are.

When he died early from his colonic cancer, having been sprightly and fit until his final illness, he showed not a jot of fear or emotion on his deathbed apart from regret at leaving our mother alone. I suspect his wartime experiences had given him the necessary guts to set this example. He never forgot his squadron motto 'Facta non verba' ('Deeds not words'), and was fond of opportunities to say it. He had an enduring loving relationship with his wife Anne Elizabeth, whose motto might well have been 'Facta et verba'.

My sisters and I are delighted to see this going into print; it is written in the voice of the 1960s with a political incorrectness in places that I hope will be understood and forgiven.

Publisher's note: We would like to express our sincere appreciation to Vic Pheasant and the Hayling Island Branch of RAFA, who brought the manuscript to our attention and prompted the search for Andrew Millar's family. While editing the manuscript it has been clear that there are variations in the wartime and modern spellings of place names and we have decided to remain true to Andrew Millar's original manuscript. Additionally Squadron Leader Millar used numerous acronyms and for some it is now unclear exactly what these mean. They have been left in to protect the integrity of the story.

Preface

This is an account of my time on 20 Squadron in the Far East during the Second World War. While I was still in Madras, I wrote down some observations of a flight from Madras to Rangoon and back, which I have included unchanged in Chapter 20. Soon after the war I made some other notes, incorporated here in Chapters 1 to 5. Otherwise my only source of reference has been my log books in which are recorded all my flying hours. They have enabled me to place events in their correct sequence.

Chapter 1

Arrival in India – June 1942

The liner had arrived at Bombay during the hours of darkness. After breakfast the passengers filtered up on deck to find the ship anchored about 300 yards out in the bay. The trip from England had taken two months in convoy. The convoy had travelled at the speed of the slowest ship, zigzagging regularly every few minutes and taking a wide circuitous route to avoid the menace of U-boats and minefields. It was June 1942. Two ships had been sunk between Freetown and Durban, but otherwise the voyage had been uneventful.

Aged twenty-two, I was an RAF flying officer from an army cooperation squadron. I had been flying almost daily for nearly two years. The break had come just at the right moment as I had been getting stale; but now after two months of enforced idleness on the voyage, my zest and keenness for flying had been restored, and I was eager to get back on the job.

Although it was still early, the sun was already strong, exerting an almost physical pressure on the shoulders and heads of the passengers on deck. The knowledgeable pointed out the Gateway of India, a triumphal arch that stood out whitely beyond the glinting water of the bay.

At noon the liner docked. On shore, life had come to a standstill under the midday sun and there was little movement apart from the shimmering of the heat-laden air. High overhead large hawks wheeled and soared, occasionally swooping down to earth to scavenge food. On the quayside some coolies were playing cards, leaning or sprawling on bales of cargo. For them there seemed to be no other business of importance. Each card was played with care and an exaggerated dramatic gesture of despair or triumph due, it seemed, not so much to the state of the game as to a child-like pleasure that the pretence afforded them. There was none of the rush or activity associated with points of arrival and departure in England.

We were finally allowed ashore, and with one of my cabin mates I visited an air-conditioned cinema, which felt chilly when we entered. However, we soon became acclimatised and it was a considerably less pleasant sensation when we left the cinema and returned to the hot and humid atmosphere outside. In the evening we stopped by a restaurant with a good reputation. There was a wide choice on the menu, and feeling a trifle homesick I ordered roast beef and Yorkshire pudding. I was disappointed to find that it tasted of curry, but everything probably tasted of curry in India and after a few months I would not have noticed it. We returned to the ship for a final night on board before dispersing to our various destinations the next day.

Pilots were scarce at that period and I had received an individual posting from the Air Ministry to join 20 Squadron in India. My immediate instructions were to report to Air Headquarters (AHQ) at Delhi and I was given a railway warrant for the journey. In spite of the heat, the main railway terminus at Bombay was a more active and crowded scene than at the port, confusing to the newcomer. Hundreds of Indians dressed in a variety of ways were mixing in the great space between the platforms and the booking halls. Some formalities had to be observed at the booking clerk's office. Here one's luggage was weighed and the results noted on the ticket by an Indian clerk. A porter was hovering near and I signed to him to take the luggage. These railway porters were uniformly dressed in small red turbans and red shirts that hung outside a length of dirty white cloth worn around their loins. On the left side of each shirt was printed in English and in some Indian script: 'Official porter. Rate of hire 1 anna per article.' (An anna was the equivalent of 1½ old pence.) The porters appeared undersized and wasted, their spindly legs giving no promise of being able to carry any great weight. On their dark-skinned faces some had grown moustaches cut in different styles; others were hairless but for a few straggling black hairs growing from the chin. Some of the porters looked old and decrepit but they somehow managed to carry on their heads a load greater than the average white man would care to lift.

My porter now stood docilely while two others lifted my trunk and placed it on his head. To this they added my bedroll. This did not seem to perturb the porter who grasped my last article of luggage, a suitcase, in his hand and waited for instructions.

''Itch tren sahib?' asked the coolie.

'Um. I want the train for Delhi,' I replied, speaking with the slow distinctness that an Englishman feels must be understood by a foreigner.

'Sa'b?'

'Delhi … Del-ee,' I tried again.

'Theek hai, sa'b.' (Pronounced 'teak high', this phrase is universally used and is the equivalent of our 'OK'.)

The coolie turned and led the way with the trotting gait that Indians use when carrying loads. Soon I was installed in one of the standard first-class compartments on Indian railways. There was one other person in the compartment. This was in marked contrast to the rest of the train, which was bursting at the seams with Indian passengers. They were not only crammed together in the carriages but were hanging on to the running boards and also sitting on the roofs of the carriages. Our compartment had leather bench seats along its two sides extending as far as the entrance door at the front of the compartment. The benches were pulled out from the wall at night to form beds. There were two additional bunk beds available near the ceiling, which were folded against the wall during the day. At the forward end there was a door leading into a smaller compartment, which contained a shower bath and toilet. The windows had three layers that could be used singly or in combination: they were glass, mosquito net and shutters. The glass and shutters were used in the daytime to keep out the hot outside air and the sun's rays. At night the windows could be opened and the mosquito netting came into use. Electric fans and lighting were fitted.

Doing some mental arithmetic, I now offered the equivalent of 6d in Indian currency to the coolie who had carried my luggage. Instead of accepting it, he shook his head, dissatisfied. I was feeling in my pocket again when there was an interjection from the other occupant of the carriage. 'Here, don't give the beggar any more.' Taking the coin from my hand, he pushed it on to the coolie. 'Cha annas, bus!' he said, adding 'Now jow, go on, jow!' as the coolie showed signs of lingering. 'You want to watch these black devils,' he directed at me, 'they'll take as much money off you as they can get.' The coolie made off with a mutely protesting expression while my companion watched him threateningly.

As the train pulled out, I lay back full length on one of the seats. The fans were going but the heat was intense. Through inexperience, I had bought for the journey a couple of Indian magazines printed in English.

After reading a few paragraphs it was obvious that they catered for readers of very simple taste. I put these aside and turned to my newspaper. This proclaimed the hottest of hot seasons for many years. Cases were reported of natives dying from heat exhaustion. In one column was printed some easy phrases in Hindustani for the benefit of soldiers newly arrived in India.

Soon the train was crossing the bridge over the channel that separated Bombay from the mainland of India and after a time we were winding our way over flat country with a view of high hills in the distance. Everywhere the land was hot and baked dry. Along dusty tracks through the fields, carts moved slowly, drawn by bullocks whose skeletons were clearly framed beneath their skin.

My travelling companion was a young man in his early twenties, dressed in the khaki shorts and shirt that was the common uniform of the services. On his shoulders he wore the rank of an army lieutenant. Observing my newness, he decided to give me the benefit of his experience. He had spent the last six months in Malaya. Fighting was hard, he implied, and the conditions physically exacting. Our numbers were still hopelessly inadequate for our defensive position and he expected the Japanese through again, this time into India. He himself was off to Kashmir on leave and was only stopping at Delhi to collect a wife. This last phrase struck me as odd, although subsequent conversation showed that he really was married.

When the conversation flagged, my interest was captured by the strangeness of the country. The train had climbed to some 2,000 feet above sea level and the air was somewhat cooler. Occasionally the train would halt at a wayside station and along the cinder track would come beggars, perhaps a woman or an old man, always emaciated, often with some deformity, and usually swathed in a grey-white sheet that seemed the common article of Indian clothing. They would stand looking up from the railway line, distracting the occupants of the train with importunate cries that reached a crescendo as the train began to move out of the station. The train sped by villages whose huts were mud-walled, with roofs of bamboo thatching. Wild-looking men standing close to the railway line, naked except for a loin cloth, and young children, their little black bodies completely exposed, watched stolidly as we raced by. As dusk fell, we carried on our way inland towards the central capital. Now the air was cool and twilight had replaced the blinding glare of day. The glow from a cooking fire would throw a friendly light on some primitive dwelling as the train continued to travel into the darkness.

I slept fitfully, without blankets, my rest interrupted by intermittent stoppings throughout the night, when the air would be filled with high-pitched nasal cries of Indians on the railway platforms, followed by the clanking of heavy metal and jolting as our train again took up its journey.

Another day followed. Cool in the first light of dawn, the first of many I was to see in this land, the temperature soon rose as the day began to unfold. Unaccustomed scenery flashed past our train. Flat semi-desert country, uninhabited, with scrub-carpeted sand would give way to rocky slopes covered with trees through which monkeys swung or clambered over boulders. Always at each station a few beggars would collect below the carriage window, their cries for money mingling to form an incessant and irritating wail. At certain times of the day the train would stop for a longer interval at a station to enable the passengers to have a meal, as there were no facilities for this on board the train itself. I discovered there were one or two others on the train who had been on the ship with me, including Sutherland who had been one of my three cabin mates. Flying Officer Sutherland was a plump, sleek older man, who had been in the RAF before the war and who had already done a tour in India in peacetime. He did not like the heat and often said that he would have preferred to be posted to some icy country as he could always warm himself up but could not cool himself down. Fortunately I preferred to be too hot than too cold. On his previous tour, Sutherland had been a corporal armourer and he wore the ribbon of the Indian general service medal. I met him once again, two years later, when we were both squadron leaders and we spent an evening together at a club in Calcutta, but I did not see him again after that. He now joined the lieutenant and myself in our compartment.

At one point on the journey, the train slowed down to a halt before crossing a long bridge over a river. I put my head outside the window to investigate and experienced a blast of hot air that could well have come from a furnace. The air in our carriage was cool by comparison with the heated air outside, which was filled with particles of dust. These penetrated into our carriage and at many of the stops it was necessary for a sweeper to enter and clean the carriage. The sweepers of the untouchable caste had generally a most abject appearance and seemed to regard themselves in as low esteem as did the rest of their community. Almost leper-like, they drew out of my way, lest by touching them I should defile myself.

Our journey to Delhi took us past the Taj Mahal, which was the one and only time I saw that edifice. It was nightfall when we arrived in Delhi, and

Sutherland and I sought out the railway transport officer (RTO) to help us find billets for the night. At that time General Sir Archibald Wavell was commander-in-chief and the RTO told us that he and Lady Wavell had offered to put up any two officers who happened to be stranded overnight in Delhi. Accordingly the RTO phoned through to the Wavell's residence, but the two beds were already taken. Eventually we were billeted in a comfortable hotel in Delhi.

The next day I reported to AHQ. In England we had been told that the shortage of new aircraft was due to supplies being diverted to the Far East. Visions of flying up-to-date aircraft in India were soon dispelled, however. I discovered that 20 Squadron was flying Lysanders and that there were two squadrons of Mohawks: 5 and 155 Squadrons. No. 20 Squadron had in fact only recently been converted from biplanes. A visit to HQ provided a chance to short-circuit the normal official channels and I resolved to try and arrange a switch to one of the Mohawk squadrons. I had had my fill of Lysanders and as I had flown Tomahawks, a later version of the Mohawk, this seemed to strengthen my chances.

I was directed to a squared cloister with screens of bamboo strips hanging from the ceiling on its inner side, which faced into an open square exposed to the sun. An Indian was engaged in throwing water on to the screens in order to lower the temperature in the cloister itself. Offices led off from the outer sides of the square, and I was directed to the office of the senior personnel staff officer (SPSO). Inside were two desks. At one sat a rather bald, grey-haired wing commander, with a dried-up sallow face and dyspeptic expression. The other desk was empty.

'Good morning, sir,' I said and saluted smartly. 'I've just come from Bombay.'

'Yes, yes, I know who you are,' the wing commander interrupted contemptuously. 'Come back at two o'clock.'

I returned at the appointed time. Now there was also a squadron leader with a pleasant expression sitting at the second desk.

'Good afternoon sir,' I addressed the wing commander. 'You told me to be here at two.'

'Mm,' said the wingco. 'Let's see. You're an armourer.'

I felt this called for a contradiction. 'No sir. I'm GD – a pilot.'

This brought an obstinate glitter into the man's eyes and it became obvious that the interview would not be fruitful.

'Very well. You can do aerodrome siting.' He ceased to regard me and turned to the younger man at the second desk. 'He's just come from England and should know the requirements for runways and modern aircraft. He can have his own plane.'

While this may sound reasonably attractive, I should explain that I had just spent over a year on a squadron in Northern Ireland, which had been sent there as part of the defence against a possible German invasion through southern Ireland. Fortunately this never happened, but as time went on I felt more and more that I was not making a worthwhile contribution to the war and so I started putting in a monthly application for a posting to a fighter squadron. This annoyed the squadron commander and I was finally given this posting to the Far East. Finding that I was in danger of losing my place on a squadron, I abandoned my plans for a switch to Mohawks and concentrated on keeping my place on 20 Squadron! The wingco handed me over to the younger, more alert-looking squadron leader, whose name was Friend. He took me out into the cloister where I declared that I wanted to join a squadron and not do aerodrome siting.

'Are you ready to go on operations at once?' he asked me, studying me closely. However much one may have decided on a course of action, a sudden question of this sort can act like a blow in the ribs. After all, I thought, that is what I am aiming to do. A moment later I said yes. I think he had had a discussion on this subject with the wing commander, who had probably maintained that most pilots would extemporise and ask for a few weeks' reprieve. At any rate Squadron Leader Friend returned to the office and said in a pleased tone that he had found someone who was willing to go on operations right away. The wing commander was not impressed. With his jaundiced eye he gave me a withering look.

'Have you ever been under fire?' he asked, seeming to italicise the last two words.

'No sir,' I had to admit.

'Then how do you know you will be any use in action?'

My determination was not proof against discouragement and I felt one could not do more than offer to go on 'ops'. I said politely but firmly that I had a posting by the Air Ministry specifically to 20 Squadron. Eventually I left the office feeling lucky that I was still posted to 20 Squadron and not assigned to aerodrome siting.

I boarded the 'Calcutta Mail' train the next day and was shown to an empty first-class carriage by a tall, pleasant Indian wearing a clean white uniform and turban and a coloured belt. He advised me to have some ice in a tin bath to keep the carriage cool. When I agreed to this suggestion, he got the ice for me at a very small cost and placed it beneath the large rotary fan that hung from the ceiling, so that the air cooled by the ice would circulate throughout the carriage. I reached Jamshedpur early the next morning. This was west of Calcutta and was where 20 Squadron was then based. From the station I rang the adjutant and asked for transport to take me to the camp. I was to remain with 20 Squadron for the rest of the war.

Chapter 2

Jamshedpur – 16 June–17 July 1942

No. 20 Squadron was in the gradual process of moving from the North-West Frontier Province, where it had spent the inter-war years, towards the present war in Burma. It had got as far as Jamshedpur, a small town of moderate influence by Indian standards, about 150 miles west of Calcutta and still well clear of the fighting zone. The town owed its prosperity to the large steel works nearby, owned by a company called Tatas. At the edge of the town the concrete stopped and, apart from a metal road, earth footpaths through the fields connected the town with the neighbouring villages. I watched young Indian men walk hand in hand along these paths. It seemed an innocent demonstration of friendship, although today people would probably think of other connotations. Most of the shops in India were open fronted, without the shop windows of their European counterparts. This probably made for coolness as air conditioning was only to be found in some cinemas in the big cities.

The squadron was using a grass airfield belonging to Tatas. Two schools had been requisitioned for the sergeants' mess and the airmen's quarters. The hotel in Jamshedpur had been taken over as the officers' mess, and each officer had a room to himself with a bathroom attached. The hotel was on the main road in the town centre. Continuing along the road to the airfield, one passed a house on the right that was the squadron sick quarters. There was a turning to the left that led to the airfield. If instead one carried straight on, the road reached the squadron headquarters (SHQ), which was in a large house set back from the road on the right. It seemed a rambling disorganised place where an assortment of admin officers did very little work.

On the morning of my arrival my luggage was dropped off at the mess and I was taken to SHQ. It was very early, about 6am, and although some airmen and the squadron warrant officer were present, no other officer had yet put in an appearance. The first one to arrive was the adjutant, Flying Officer Bailey, a crisp little man with sandy hair and trim moustache, who would have fitted in well as secretary of a golf club. He told me that the CO was away on leave and that the senior flight commander was acting as squadron commander in his absence. While I was waiting for the acting CO to appear, a flight lieutenant walked into the office and introduced himself as Jamie Milne. He had crinkly fair hair and a fair moustache with pale blue eyes and a wide smile. His quick movements tended to conceal his muscular frame.

Later, Flight Lieutenant Fletcher arrived and called me into the CO's office. He was a small man in his late twenties with acne spots on his face; he had dark hair and a moustache and was neatly dressed. He seemed in good spirits and would break out in an explosive laugh after most of his remarks. He had a northern accent and was the only officer at the time with a Distinguished Flying Cross (DFC) on 20 Squadron. He had been awarded this while flying Lysanders in the desert. After some chit-chat, he told me that I would be joining A Flight.

On my first morning, I walked around the aircraft and spoke to the ground crews. I was struck by the washed-out appearance of their eyes and the reluctance with which their eyes converged on near objects. The climate seemed to affect most people this way, after a couple of hot seasons.

The squadron was divided into three flights situated at different corners of the grass aerodrome. Each flight had four Lysander Mk IIs. For identification, the hubs of the propellers were painted red for A Flight, yellow for B Flight and blue for C Flight. The Lysanders had been sent out to the Middle East in 1940 when the army cooperation squadrons in England were re-equipped with Mk III Lysanders. In 1941 the Mk III Lysander was dropped and army cooperation squadrons were converted to Tomahawks, an American fighter. After service in the Middle East with Wavell, the Lysanders were moved on to India and given to 20 and 28 Squadrons. Many of the squadron pilots had had very little flying experience generally, let alone on Lysanders.

The three flight commanders were widely different characters. Flight Lieutenant Milne, in command of A Flight, was a strongly built South African who had had some experience of operations in the Middle East. A natural pilot, Jamie had a strong head for liquor and was a self-confident

active individual. Flight Lieutenant Peter Moulding who was in charge of
B Flight, was 'tour expired' and due to return to England. He had worked
in a bank before the war. His place was taken by Flying Officer Neville
Rowson. Neville was a plump, jovial young man who had spent several
years in India before the war. His outlook was devoid of aggression and
most of his flying had been done on transport aircraft. This very different style of flying possibly helped to develop a different temperament in
Neville but, whichever was cause and effect, he was more cut out to be
a transport pilot. To the ground crews he was affectionately known as
'Granny' Rowson. The third flight commander, Fletcher, moved off to
Delhi and was replaced by Peter Joel, who had been on the same squadron
with me in the UK for over a year.

Joel had gone out to the Middle East and from there to Ceylon. Soon
after the fall of Singapore, the Japanese had put out a feeler in the direction
of Ceylon to assess our defences. There had been a motley collection of aircraft there at the time, and every available one was put in the air to give the
Japanese, from an aircraft carrier, a warm reception. The ploy was a success
and probably gave the Japanese a wrong impression of the strength of our
defences. At any rate they made no further attempt to invade India. Joel
was slightly built and small and although not an outstanding personality,
he had the knack of getting his men to work together as a team.

I had joined A Flight and, apart from Jamie Milne, there were only three
other pilots in the flight: an Australian, Pilot Officer McMillan, an Indian,
Pilot Officer Krishna, and a pre-war pilot, Warrant Officer Innes Smith;
a warrant officer pilot was a rare bird in those days.

Krishna was quiet and pleasant and from him I learned a little of India
and her ways. There were four Indian pilots on the squadron, all so poor-
ly trained as to be of little practical value. In the mess they were left to
themselves. Mehta was the most sophisticated of them; a Parsee from
Bombay, he was prepared to spend an evening in the club with the other
officers and was a good conversationalist. Hussain was a stolid type of
Indian. There was a small Madrasi, Pilot Officer Rammuny, who had a
much darker skin than the other Indians and who was cheerful and lively.
Krishna told me how his wife had been selected for him by his father and
brother, and in accordance with his religious customs he had not seen her
until the wedding ceremony.

Peter McMillan was a sturdy good-looking youngster, overconscious
of his home country and subjected to a certain amount of baiting on this

account. The CO was a Canadian in his late twenties called Freddie Lambert, who had an affected English accent. His apparently inconsequential and inane manner caused some amusement on the squadron. He celebrated his twenty-ninth birthday about this time, and in the club by the end of the evening he was quite certain he did not look his age! Certainly twenty-nine seemed a great age to us in those days.

Other pilots included a large impressive-looking Scot, Pilot Officer MacPherson and another Australian, Pilot Officer J.P. Thompson, a tall saturnine man, older than Peter Mac. There were several NCO pilots: Les Hill, J.I. Thompson and Carmichael. We also had a complement of air gunners and wireless operators/air gunners of whom Armstrong, Lyons, Trust, Murray, Carruthers and Calcutt come to mind.

Early mornings at Jamshedpur were bright and clear, with the temperature like an English summer's day. By mid-morning the likeness had disappeared and we were searching for shade. At noon work stopped for the day, having begun at 6am. The sun was already overpoweringly hot. Jamshedpur was surrounded by hills and some thought this contributed to the feeling that one was in an oven during that hot spell. The afternoons were spent resting in our bedrooms. At sundown, social activities began and the officers would visit the club, which remained open until the small hours.

There was a white population of twenty or thirty people in the town, employed in advisory or executive positions in the steel factory or its subsidiaries. These people gave the squadron a very warm and hospitable welcome. It is worthy of record that the club threw its premises open once a week to the entire squadron, which was over 200 strong – an unusually generous effort.

One midday in the club, I had had a drink when Jamie Milne appeared and wanted me to take up a Lysander for some reason or other. I told him that I had imbibed and therefore could not fly. Jamie Milne insisted, so I said that I would have liked nothing better but having had a drink I felt I should not take to the skies. Finally Jamie did the flight himself, obviously angry with me. There were no definite rules about drinking and flying then, but I felt I was on safe ground in refusing to fly.

During the morning, many of the officers would be found in the medical officer's (MO's) office drinking tea, a common past-time in the Far East. The squadron MO was a ginger-haired Scot, Flight Lieutenant R.J.A. Morris, generally known as the quack. Occasionally Fletcher would pull his leg laboriously in the mess, which the quack took with good humour. Fletcher made jokes that nobody else could fathom at times, but we joined in politely when he laughed. Now that time has rolled by and our destinies are known, of the officers in the mess at that time, only Doc Morris was to reach high rank in the RAF.

In support of our claim to be an army cooperation squadron, an Army Liaison Section was attached to us, consisting of an Indian major, two British captains and their clerks. Major Vir Singh was a Sikh, trained at Sandhurst. He was a handsome man of about thirty with a very gentle and scholarly manner. Sikhs come from north-west India. Their religion forbids them to cut or trim their hair, so that not only do they grow beards, but the hair on their head when long is rolled up into buns, which are covered by their turbans. The name of a Sikh always ends in Singh, which I believe is added to the surname when the young Sikh is fully initiated into his religion. Unlike many religions of the East, this one embraces monogamy and lays great stress on the fidelity to be practised by man and wife.

The two English Army officers were Captain Pearce (known as Captain Teapot because of his liking for tea), and Captain Pitcairn, who had a stroke and died at a railway station a few months later. It was a large section for a squadron and subsequently we operated with a single army liaison officer and an RAF intelligence officer.

The hotel, which was our mess, was built above a line of shops. Our meals were taken at a long table in the dining room. Each officer had a bearer or personal servant, or shared one with another officer. The bearers stood a short distance behind their officers and catered for their needs according to their ability. Each wore a white uniform with the RAF colours wound into their turbans and round their waist belts. Their pay at this time was about £2 a month. Flight Lieutenant Fletcher's bearer was a tall, handsome Pathan with a natural dignity who treated the officers with respect and commanded respect in return. The other bearers obviously regarded him as their leader.

After tiffin, the midday meal, we retired to our rooms for a siesta. My room was supplied with its own shower and toilet and had a fan suspended from the ceiling above the bed, worked by a variable rheostat. The hot-water storage tanks were on the roof, heated by the sun without benefit of any modern solar-heating equipment. The water was piping hot, but I was not there in the cold season to see how it functioned then. Supplies of ice were kept in the airmen's quarters where there had been cases of heat exhaustion occurring during the night, when the minimum temperature was still above 100°F. At 5pm I was awakened by my bearer with a tray of tea and sandwiches. At 6pm I had a shower and changed into bush shirt and slacks and then went into the ante-room to await the appearance of other members of the squadron. Jamie Milne was one of the first to appear. He gave me to understand that by tradition I would not be allowed to pay for any drinks on my first night and it soon became clear that I was expected to make the most of the opportunity. The prospect did not appeal to me as I was not a heavy drinker and I think Jamie Milne was disappointed.

After dinner at the hotel the officers would go to the club, where there might be two or three white civilians, and stay there drinking until the small hours. Around midnight the vocalists would be sufficiently primed to burst into song. Neville Rowson had a repertoire of songs that could be sung in harmony, such as 'The Bells of Aberdovey' and one about a clock that ticked away throughout a man's life, stopping permanently when the man died. Pilot Officer Ferrier Jones, a pleasant, cheerful, bucolic ground defence type, was fond of 'The Farmer's Boy' and a pornographic song with the words set to a hymn tune, which with my Presbyterian upbringing, seemed to me blasphemous. The two Australians, Tom and Peter Mac, enjoyed singing 'Waltzing Matilda'. We would finally retire to our beds for a short sleep before work, with the prospect of a longer rest in the afternoon.

I had vaguely assumed that I would remain in India for a year or so, and it was a shock to learn that the overseas tour for a married man was three years and four years for a single man. These were very important years for a 22-year-old, especially as I still wished to become a doctor.

Before leaving England we were given a sheet of notes for guidance as to clothing suitable in the Far East. This came from the Air Ministry. As the war had been running for less than three years, the notes still related to peacetime conditions. We were advised to take a dinner jacket in our luggage. It did not need much deliberation to ignore that advice, but we would have been well advised to disregard the notes altogether. The clothes that were sold in England for use in the Far East may have been fashionable in the time of Queen Victoria, but they stuck out like a sore thumb in India in 1942. The topees sold by Moss Bros were helmet shaped and heavy, in marked contrast to the lightweight pith topees with flat tops worn in India. Similarly, the material and cut of the garments were very different from what was generally worn. Most new arrivals summed up the situation and got a new stock of clothes from the local tailor or dherzi, but our armament officer, Flying Officer Brown, who was married and having to economise, continued to wear the outlandish kit he had acquired in England. This gave him a distinctive appearance. With a tall angular figure, Flying Officer Brown was a sober, serious and sensible type who was friendly when approached, but who felt out of place at Jamshedpur and, fortunately for him, he was soon posted.

Our equipment officer was a large smooth chap called Evans who was exceptional in that he was accompanied by his wife. Presumably they had moved out to India in peacetime or in the early days of the war. He was posted to Delhi soon after I joined the squadron and was replaced by a Pilot Officer Culverwell, a cheerful, plump man with a large moustache, who was something of a caricature of the RAF type.

On 18 June, after a gap of three months off flying, I had my first flight with 20 Squadron. The Mk III Lysander had a stubbier engine than the Mk II, but the only real difference in appearance lay in the state of the windscreens of the Mk II Lysanders. These were yellow, scratched and opaque. Other differences became obvious when I opened the throttle for take-off. First of all, I received a blast of hot air from the engine into the cockpit, which was very unpleasant, and I was next appalled by the lack of power as the machine trundled sluggishly along for take-off. Over the next few months, we had to reconcile ourselves to the fact that this was all we had, and we used the aircraft on operations against the Japanese even after they had begun to fall apart.

The squadron was carrying out flights of a general nature, doing none of the photographic work, artillery shoots or reconnaissances that had been our routine at home. On 23 June I was flying in formation with the CO when my engine lost power and failed to respond to the throttle. This lasted for half a minute before picking up again. I reported it to Sergeant Simpson of A Flight, a little man with a large moustache. Later in the morning I was detailed to fly the same machine on an air-to-ground firing practice, using the two peashooters that were housed in the spats around the front wheels of the Lysander. A large hill near the airfield had been selected as the air-firing range and targets were put up on the hillside. One of the Indian pilots, Pilot Officer Hussain, was in a station wagon at the foot of the hill, watching the exercise.

I made a dive at the target, firing my guns, and pulled up steeply to my right. To my horror, the engine failed to sustain the climb and the aircraft rapidly lost speed and stalled. I quickly did a stall turn to the left so that I was facing down the mountainside. The words of my instructor, Flying Officer Hole, during my first days of flying came to my mind: 'If your aircraft is stalled, you must push the stick forward. If you don't, the aircraft will remain stalled and continue to sink until it hits the ground.' I pushed the stick forward but I could see that I had insufficient height to regain flying speed and that I was going to crash. So this was it! 'God receive my soul!' As I prayed, I could feel the engine begin to recover, but not in time to avoid the crash. There was the shock of impact and, for a moment of time, trees and undergrowth flashed by on either side. The next instant the plane had bounced off the side of the hill without getting tangled up with a tree and the engine was behaving normally. I held her straight and level very carefully and then looked round to assess the damage. The starboard wheel had staved in; some of the undersurface of the fuselage had been ripped away; and the tip of the starboard wing had been damaged. I gently tested out the controls and found they responded as usual. To restore my nerve, I decided to do one more run on the target before returning to the aerodrome. I did a shallow dive and a horizontal turn away from the target very gingerly. My air gunner now passed me a message: 'We have hit the hill. Tail badly damaged.' He thought I did not know!

We were not out of the wood yet, though, as we still had to land. I planned to come in as steadily and as slowly as possible, with the left wing down to keep the damaged wheel off the ground as long as possible. Everything went according to plan. As soon as the starboard wheel touched down it acted like an anchor, but by that time we had lost enough speed not to ground loop. Even so, the plane was pulled round to the right towards the boundary fence, coming to a halt with just a few yards to spare. My air gunner exited the machine almost before it came to a standstill. I thought there was no particular danger of fire and got out in a more leisurely manner. Apart from the damage already mentioned there was a large smear of blood on the starboard wingtip. Presumably we had hit a vulture or a kite in a tree on the hill.

This flight was laconically recorded in my log book as follows: '1942. June 23. Lysander II. R1991. Pilot Self. Airgunner Sgt Calcutt. FXGP. Aircraft damaged but landed safely. 20 minutes' (flying time). (FXGP was an abbreviation for: Front guns only. Ground target. Practice firing.) Sergeant Simpson was in a tizzy when I reported what had happened as he should not have let the aircraft fly until the fault had been rectified. At lunchtime Jamie Milne told me that Pilot Officer Hussain said that I had hit the mountain while making a dive attack on the target, and my account was not believed.

As a sequel to this story, the squadron moved a short time later to Assam. Squadron Leader Lambert was flying this Lysander on the squadron move. It had then been repaired and he was on the last leg of the journey, when he decided to have a dogfight with Jamie Milne who was flying with him. The Lysander behaved in exactly the same way as before, with loss of power, and Freddie Lambert decided to force land. In doing so he crashed the aircraft and broke an arm. While he was sitting on the wing of his crashed aircraft waiting to be picked up, he smoked a cigarette and managed to set fire to the Lysander. Later in the war, we once tried to set fire to a Hurricane and found it was not so easy! Had it not been that his luggage and that of his air gunner, Flight Sergeant Carruthers, were lost in the fire, I would have wondered whether the fire was deliberate, to get rid of a bad machine.

On our way to flight dispersals at Jamshedpur one day, I heard the sound of bagpipes and, looking round as we drew level with the sound, saw a group of Indian soldiers instead of the expected Scots. Indian music at first sounds strange to Western ears, but one can acquire a taste for most things and in the end I learned to appreciate Indian music. Bagpipes are not solely a Scottish instrument, and other nations have their own form of bagpipes, but I did not hear them played again during my time in India. I believe the bagpipes were invented by the Greeks in about 50 BC.

The erks, sprogs or AC plonks, as the airmen were called in air force slang, used the mystic combination of figures 'two-six' in the Far East to extract maximum effort from themselves and others. They responded to this call and I often used it myself, if, for example, an aircraft wheel was bogged down in the mud and had to be lifted clear. Some Urdu words and phrases appealed to the airmen, perhaps having vague associations with English words. Subcheese was a popular word meaning 'the whole lot', and would be used in a sentence in which all the other words were English. Kiswasty meant 'why'. Jow, to rhyme with cow, translated as 'go away!' Chiprow meant 'shut up!' Karab was used for 'bad', karab wallah, a 'bad man'. Atchay baht meant 'well said!' Bunderbust signified an arrangement or bit of organisation. It was probably spelt 'bandobast', but as I am unaware of the correct spelling, I have spelled the Urdu words phonetic-ally. Jildhi meant 'hurry!' Karroh indicated 'make' and was often added to an adjective to form a verb. Saf denoted 'clean', while saf karroh was to 'make clean' or 'to clean'. There were no words for please or thank you. Nay was 'no' and jee was 'yes'. The most commonly used phrase was theek hai meaning 'OK'. A commode was known to both the officers and their bearers as a thunder box, while scrambled eggs were rumble tumble unda, unda being eggs. The airmen larded their language with Urdu and air force slang, and so after a time did most of us.

There were some favourite slogans among the airmen. 'Get your knees brown' would be addressed to a newcomer from the UK who was guilty of giving unwanted advice. 'Roll on the boat!' was the exclamation of an airman longing for his repatriation.

The Lysander Mk II was capable of flying at speeds ranging from 45mph to 160mph. As it slowed down to 90mph, automatic slots came out from the leading edge of the mainplane, increasing the flow of air over the mainplane and ailerons. At 85mph automatic flaps were lowered. With these two devices and the inherent stability of a high-winged monoplane, the Lysander could fly safely at very low speeds.

On one Lysander at Jamshedpur, I noticed there was a time lag of nearly 2 seconds before the engine responded to the throttle. An unconventional way of landing the Lysander was to trim it to fly at 45mph, position oneself over the downwind boundary of the airfield at 500 feet and then close the throttle. The machine would come down like a lift and then a slight burst of throttle near the ground would check the fall and the Lizzie would run gently along the ground on a short landing run. I decided to do one of these landings and fortunately remembered the machine's peculiarity. I opened the throttle a couple of seconds sooner than usual so that the engine picked up just in time to make a smooth touchdown. Jamie Milne happened to be watching the landing. He had not seen this kind before and if I had not opened the throttle early, I would have made a big hole in the ground and he would not have realised what had gone wrong.

On another occasion I was climbing to fly over the hills out of Jam-shedpur, when I experienced a sudden severe pain over one eye. It was incapacitating and lasted about half a minute. In retrospect, one of my frontal sinuses may have got blocked by dust but, whatever the cause, fortunately the pain never recurred.

The monsoon moves up steadily from the bottom right-hand corner of the map of the Far East towards the top left. It arrived in Jamshedpur about the beginning of July. We were playing football in the late afternoon. It was my first game since I was a boy of fourteen and it was pleasant to be participating in a game that I thought I was finished with. Jamie Milne was playing on the right wing and showed surprising energy considering he had had several pints of beer at lunchtime. I was over on the left side when clouds filled the sky and rain came down in sheets on the right-hand side of the pitch. Where I stood the ground was still dry and dusty. The shower was short-lived and did not stop the game.

A few days later, I was airborne near the aerodrome when I saw a dark monsoon storm forming on the far side of the airfield about a mile away. Flying nearer the airfield, I could see the windsock pointing horizontally towards the storm, which seemed to indicate that a strong wind was blowing the storm away from the airfield. Reassured I continued my flying practice, but the next time I looked at the airfield, the windsock was hanging limply and the storm was centred over the airfield. The monsoons, though, brought a welcome fall in temperature that particular summer at Jamshedpur.

There must have been some knowledge of an impending squadron move, as Jamie told Peter Mac and myself to have twenty-four hours in Calcutta, saying that we might not get another opportunity. On a previous occasion we had flown in wide formation to Calcutta through a monsoon storm and I had seen lightning playing around his aircraft, a phenomenon that I only saw on that occasion. This time we took one aircraft, which we each flew one way. It was my first visit into the heart of Calcutta. In mid-1942 it was a pleasant city and there was no difficulty in getting a room at either of the two big hotels. For taxis there were either horse-drawn gharries or open tourer cars driven by turbanned Sikhs. The taxis had horns with rubber bulbs, which the Sikhs used non-stop while driving. From my hotel room I could look down on the taxi rank in the middle of Chowringhee, the main thoroughfare. The taxi drivers did not put on the handbrake while in the taxi rank, and it was the habit for the newest arrival at the end of the queue to bump the taxi in front of him. The bump was then transmitted from one taxi to the next, edging them all forward.

Nine days later I was sitting in the adjutant's office, when Jamie came out of the CO's room. 'We're being moved forward,' he said, 'and one of our kites is needed immediately for a special job. Can you get your kit and be off in half an hour?' I was glad to do so and Jamie, seeing this, said: 'I would have gone myself but I have to stay to look after the flight. Freddie and I will be following with A and B Flights. Joel is stopping here to look after HQ while Freddie's away.' There was not really anyone else suitable to go off alone. I was suddenly excited. Jumping into the station wagon I drove down to the aerodrome and warned the ground crew to get my machine ready. 'It's ops at last!' I could never refrain from showing off to the ground crews. Next I drove off to find my air gunner and then get our kit packed. Soon we were on our way.

There were no Met reports or radio facilities then and the pilot navigated the machine by dead reckoning. The pilot communicated with his air gunner by written messages and with other aircraft by visual signals. A cord attached to each shoulder strap of the pilot's harness led back to the rear cockpit. A system of tugs on these strings by the air gunner gave the pilot warning of aircraft approaching from the rear. Long steady pulls meant that aircraft were drawing near from below, short tugs denoted that aircraft were diving from above. Pulls on one side indicated that enemy aircraft were advancing from that side, while pulls on both strings meant they were attacking from astern. My air gunner was a tall, gaunt young man called Calcutt.

We got as far as Calcutta on the first day (1½ hours' flying) and made an overnight stop there. We spent the rest of the next day in the air and reached our destination at nightfall.

Chapter 3

Tezpur – 17 July–31 August 1942

The main aerodrome at Calcutta was called Dum Dum. It was quite civilised, with permanent buildings on the airfield and such comforts as a canteen for aircrew. There were a few American transport pilots about and one or two English Hurricane pilots. At that time one could ring the motor transport (MT) section and ask for conveyance into Calcutta, although later on in the war, when there were more people about and things had tightened up, this was no longer possible.

Our first leg on 18 July was to Cooch Behar, about 270 miles north of Calcutta. One of the Lysanders had a brown blind that could be pulled forward from above and behind the pilot's head to screen him from the sun, but which reduced his field of vision for other aircraft. The sun was soon directly overhead and my knees became uncomfortably burned, as I was wearing shorts and had to remain in a fixed position while flying. I would have appreciated the blind then. As we flew north, I noted that we were flying out of the tropic of Cancer. Our course lay parallel with the lower reaches of the Brahmaputra; at Cooch Behar the river bent at a right angle. A speck on the aerodrome grew larger as we approached and then resolved itself into an elephant; on its head sat an Indian with the inevitable umbrella used as a parasol. When we landed I taxied up to some wooden buildings at the edge of the airfield. These were rest rooms for travellers to stay overnight but there was nobody about. I forget how we managed to get the aircraft refuelled, but before taking off again we noticed there was a puncture in the tailwheel. This was not a rare event and we carried a spare in the rear cockpit. To jack up the tail of the Lysander, we would run a strong bamboo rod through a hole in the rear fuselage, lift the tail and rest the rod on any suitable pair of objects that we could find, such as two large 40-gallon petrol drums. Then would follow the arduous task of changing the wheel.

From Cooch Behar the rest of the journey was to the east, still along the banks of the Brahmaputra. I noticed that several railway bridges over rivers had been swept away by the monsoon floods. On either side of the Brahmaputra were flat tea estates. Further north were the foothills of the Himalayas, and mountains could also be seen to the south. Near the end of the day's travel eastward the flat ground on either side of the river diminished and gradually the mountains converged to block the eastern end of the valley. The Brahmaputra originates in the mountainous country of Tibet, running from west to east before turning south into Assam – still wild from its journey through sombre uninhabited valleys – but then flowing west for 400 miles, its banks widening out and its surface appearing smooth and placid. At Cooch Behar it once more veers south towards Calcutta and the sea, where first it joins the Ganges and, unlike other rivers, it splits up again to enter the sea as a number of different waterways.

I had no information as to the exact whereabouts of Tezpur airfield and spent some time flying around the outskirts of the town and even on the south side of the Brahmaputra. I finally found it a few miles north of the town. Apart from the main landing ground, there was a wide avenue cut through a wood, which was evidently used as a runway, with Mohawks parked on either side. On arriving I was told that I was to fly on to Dinjan right away, so that after refuelling I took off, flying once more in an easterly direction. By now the weather was different from the strong sun of the earlier part of the day. There was 'ten-tenths' cloud, as it was then called, which at times looked very dark. There were strong up-currents just below the cloud base and I had to put the nose down to avoid being drawn up into the cloud. I found the Lysander was flying at 160mph without losing height. Later I learned that the up-currents increased in strength and violence inside a storm. Two years later, all the Spitfires of 615 Squadron were lost in such a storm.

On parts of the journey, I flew just above the water of the river, and the scenery was so wild that it would not have been surprising if a rhinoceros or some other wild animal had appeared on the riverbank. I had been briefed to follow the river until a certain landmark, an island, was reached and then turn south-west and fly on a given course for a set distance, when with luck I should be able to spot the aerodrome. First of all I passed over a dummy aerodrome with models of Mohawks picketed on it. It was hoped that the Japanese would be persuaded to spend their ammunition on this mock-up instead of on the real airfield not far away.

Dusk was falling as we arrived at our destination in the eastern corner of the Brahmaputra valley. We had been flying most of the day and felt tired and dirty. A staff car containing two officers approached our aircraft. One was a small, very alert wing commander called Chater, whom I was to meet in various places in the future. The other officer was a squadron leader called Pitt Brown, who proved to have been a contemporary in our preparatory schooldays. He was then Bill Stephens and I believe he had changed his name in accordance with the terms of a will. I recalled he had gone on to Cranwell after his public school. A jeep also drove up containing another well-known character on that front – Gus Alder, a South African pilot with a large moustache. He drove me round to a dilapidated bungalow on stilts (which was the nearest Far Eastern equivalent to a damp-proof course). There I dumped my luggage and carried on to the 5 Squadron mess. Pitt Brown was the squadron commander and was engaged in a discussion with Wing Commander Chater on the most important qualities needed in a fighter pilot. Pitt Brown was in favour of precision in flying, while Chater advocated guts and determination. The debate went on for a long time.

I found I was sharing the bungalow with two officers of the A & SD branch – or admin wallahs – and a medical officer, a quiet long-faced man called Flight Lieutenant Kelly. The admin officers were in their thirties, with clerical backgrounds before joining the service and probably originally from one of the big industrial centres. The present conditions must have required considerable adjustment on their part. Flight Lieutenant Kelly must have found the place very depressing.

It was bad enough spending just a couple of days there, but longer would have taxed the most philosophical disposition. In 1942 there was a high incidence of suicide among service medical officers in the Far East. This tendency is higher in the medical profession than in other groups of the population, but it was more evident at that time. The MO at Tezpur was another Flight Lieutenant Kelly, but he was a dapper little man with a Ronald Colman moustache, and very different from the gentle, melancholic MO at Dinjan.

The muddy ground beneath the building was used for washing and there was not much in the way of facilities other than a bucket of water. The evening meal, eaten by the light of a hurricane lamp and served by a collection of jungly villagers posing as bearers, consisted of tinned food and dehydrated potatoes. From their meagre stocks, the officers succeeded in fixing me up with a makeshift bed and mosquito net on the verandah, which was luckily protected by an overhanging roof from the torrential thunderstorms that were let loose during the night. In the morning I put on shirt and shorts that were still wet from the sweat of the previous day. The atmosphere was extremely humid and during the morning I sat motionless in the shade watching incredulously while the sweat dripped from my fingers as from a tap.

There was a single-storey building on the airfield that contained an office at one end for Group Captain Clarke, with a sign saying 'O.C. Air Forces in Assam' and another for Wing Commander Chater at the other end. Chater was a small, vital buccaneer of a man, who wore his peaked cap at a jaunty angle and whose speech was larded with Americanisms. Clarke on the other hand had a plump, smooth face, oily black hair and a precise way of talking. There was some friction between the two.

The job for which the Lysander had been requested was a reconnaissance of the Japanese aerodrome at Myitkyina. British agents near the aerodrome would pass on information to me by means of ground signals. Group Captain Clarke explained this to me in his office. Apart from being a very vulnerable aircraft, it looked to me as though the Lysander would not have the endurance to fly over the range of mountains that separated Dinjan from the Burma plain. This problem of distance was to be a constantly recurring factor in this theatre of war.

It was still early morning but cumulus clouds could be seen piling up on the mountains to the south. The hills averaged 6,000 feet in height, while the cumulus clouds by midday would be towering up to 20,000 feet. This was much higher than the Lizzie would go and it was obvious that we should start at once. We took off and headed south for Myitkyina. Soon we were over the high hills, jungle covered and apparently uninhabited. Around the bases of the hills muddy rivers wound, sluggish and lifeless, with no movement in their black swamp-like depths. This type of country continued as far as the eye could see, although I was suddenly surprised to spot a solitary bamboo hut on stilts in a clearing, with a man sitting on the platform at the entrance to the house.

I was using a small-scale map and soon found it impossible to identify each river or even the general contours of the country, some of which was marked on the map as 'unsurveyed'. My air gunner, Sergeant Calcutt, asked permission to test his guns, the twin Brownings in the rear cockpit. It soon became evident that he would not need to use them as our petrol was one-third gone by the time we were halfway to our objective. I therefore abandoned the mission and returned to Dinjan.

I had no change of clothing and the next morning my clothes were not only damp and uncomfortable, but also had an unpleasant cheesy smell. I was glad to hear that I was to return to Tezpur, some 200 miles west of Dinjan and north of the river, where the squadron had now arrived and where my luggage was. We arrived at Tezpur in the late afternoon. At the small wooden hut on the airfield used as an HQ, somebody was carving up a beautifully juicy pineapple. There was a bowlful of juice and the slice I was given was delicious.

The various sites of our new station were pleasant but inconvenient. The tea planters had presented us with their club at Thakiburi for our officers' mess. This was about 15 miles from the aerodrome at the end of a narrow dirt road full of potholes and ruts, so that 10mph was the top speed on the journey. The airmen's quarters in the town were placed a similar distance away in another direction. It was dusk as I reached the mess and the air was beautiful with countless fireflies. They were so numerous it was a simple matter to catch one. Their light was due to some phosphorescent matter in the undersurface of their tails. The glow appeared to flicker when this surface was turned away from the observer. If a firefly was squashed underfoot, the glow remained, smeared over the ground.

Freddie Lambert was sitting on the verandah of the club with his arm in plaster, having broken it as previously described. Other 20 Squadron officers who had recently arrived were there together with pilots from 5 and 13 Squadrons, both units having detachments at Tezpur. The club had a dining room, billiard room and bar, all facing on to a wide verandah. There was a very large room that had once served as a ballroom and cinema but this was now filled with beds for the officers. Completing the club's facilities there was also an open-air swimming pool, where the water was at times uncomfortably warm; a changing room with showers; and tennis courts.

Freddie returned to the squadron base, leaving Jamie Milne, the senior of the two flight commanders, in charge of the detachment. On 24 and 25 July I flew to Dinjan in the morning and stood by all day, returning to Tezpur in the evening. At Dinjan there were also some American B25s and a few Kittyhawks. Some months later the Japs raided Dinjan and destroyed most of the aircraft on the ground, including one of our Lysanders.

On 26 July, two aircraft from 20 Squadron were required to fly a colonel and his Burmese aide to Fort Hertz, a small town near the Chinese
border. Here the colonel was to organise a resistance movement. It was
uncertain whether the town had yet been occupied by the Japanese, so the
Mohawks and B25s were going to create a diversion at the north end of the
town while we slipped in to the landing ground at the south. The plan was
unusual and doomed to failure by the lack of attention to detailed planning. The colonel insisted that he would not bale out under any circumstances as he 'blacked out even off a diving board'. The cumulus clouds
piled up steadily over the mountains from midday onwards, and it was
obviously important for us to start as early in the day as possible. In spite
of this, the trip was planned for the afternoon, but for some reason was
delayed until I thought the attempt would be postponed.

One of the Lysanders was supposed to consume petrol more heavily
than the other and, as this was a factor to be considered, Jamie and I tossed
a coin as to who should fly it. For once in quite a while I won the toss. It
was far too late in the afternoon when we took off. Although I was the
more experienced pilot I had not the rank to interfere with the decisions.
Jamie Milne lifted off first with the colonel in his rear cockpit. I followed
him, starting a climbing turn to the left before I was properly airborne.
As a result the Lysander stalled and hit the grass alongside the runway. I
hastily straightened out and waited until the aircraft had gained enough
speed before turning to follow Jamie. The Lysander was a remarkably
well-behaved machine and recovered without trouble. I took up a position wide out on Jamie's starboard side and we started to climb because
of the mountains ahead. I made no attempt to map-read myself and could
see that Jamie was following valleys between hills rather than flying high
on a set course. He was also proceeding too slowly. There were two opti-
mum economical speeds for the Lysander; the slower of the two used less
petrol and kept you in the air longer, while the slightly faster speed had a
heavier consumption but carried you a greater distance even though the
time airborne was less. The increase in consumption was relatively less
than the increase in speed. We were now travelling at a rate calculated to
give maximum endurance rather than maximum range.

For some time we threaded our way through valleys with cloud-covered
mountains towering on either side. I was watching the clock, comparing
our progress with the passage of time and estimating whether we could

get back before sundown. Soon we had gone beyond the point where this was possible. On we went and I saw we were approaching a pass, itself some 7,000 feet high, with cloud-covered mountains on either side. But there was a gap through which we could fly. I assumed this was the pass leading into the Fort Hertz valley and brought my aircraft close to Jamie's. He looked at me quizzically and I nodded, feeling that we should at least investigate what lay further on. We flew through the gap and then the leading Lysander rolled over on its side and dived away through the layers of cloud that covered the valley. The distance between us rapidly increased and then my plane too was diving after his. The valley was narrow, with clouds forming a lid to the hills surrounding it and had barely room to turn an aircraft. There was a realisation that this was the wrong valley and we now had neither time nor petrol to complete the original plan. Indeed, the question was whether the old Lysander would be able to regain the height required to clear the hills around the valley.

I broke off the dive and started to climb. Jamie Milne must have made the same decision. I was climbing in broken cloud, occasionally catching a glimpse of the mountains that encircled us, which enabled me to turn inside the valley as the Lysander slowly gained height. I finally cleared the ridge and continued to ascend on an approximate course, through layers of cloud, miserably aware that the map showed mountains in this area at a greater height than I had attained. I had set the airscrew to fine and used full throttle short of the maximum power available for take-off only, as I had scaled the valley sides. This had increased the fuel consumption. The petrol tank was sited behind the pilot and had a float with a vertical extension to show how much fuel was left. It now showed nearly empty. But the mountains and the clouds passed and now the sun was dropping low in the west. The land became dark and indistinct, yet the dying rays of the sun reflected on the waters of the rivers and I could make out the Brahmaputra in the distance and could pick out the island where we turned on a set course for Dinjan. I projected this course from the island and turned my aircraft to the west to intercept the line before it met the mountains. Some minutes later, I saw Dinjan directly ahead of me in the dusk.

Until then I had kept to a height of 6,000 feet in case the petrol had run out and we had had to use our parachutes. I now did a glide approach and landing. We had been airborne for 2 hours 40 minutes. In England 2 hours 15 minutes was taken as the endurance of a Lysander. In the next 15 minutes it became clear that Jamie's aircraft could not still be airborne.

Some time later a phone call came from a tea plantation to say that a Lysander had crashed there. The plantation was only 15 miles short of the airfield, but Jamie Milne was unable to rely on a parachute descent if he had run out of petrol (because of his passenger) and he had decided to make a precautionary landing. The tea estate had a long, straight but narrow track running through it. Jamie had tried to land on this, although it was not really possible. He had managed to touch down on the track but had skidded off after a few yards and the Lysander had turned a cartwheel. Jamie's head had hit the gunsight, killing him, while his passenger had broken his back. Ironically, there was enough petrol left to have got them back to Dinjan. The colonel's refusal to bale out had contributed to the accident and this knowledge caused him great distress. 'He was such a fine chap!' he wept over and over again. Jamie Milne was buried at Dibrugarh, the nearest town to Dinjan, on the south bank of the Brahmaputra. A small number of us travelled by road to form the funeral party. No other 20 Squadron pilot killed subsequently in Burma received a burial, so far as we knew, as their bodies were never recovered.

Some changes now took place on the squadron. Freddie Lambert was posted and Fletcher became CO in his place; Neville Rowson as senior flight commander became OC Detachment and I took over command of A Flight in place of Jamie. Life was very pleasant at Tezpur, away from the boozy conditions at Jamshedpur. Not that we were entirely sober; at Tezpur there was a flight of Mohawks from 5 Squadron under Flight Lieutenant Cunliffe and a flight of Blenheims from 113 Squadron under Squadron Leader Penney, a well-built man with a florid complexion and an enormous moustache. We had quite a party celebrating his twenty-first birthday, or so he claimed it to be.

At that time promotion was slow to come through, and one day we heard that Neville Rowson's overdue promotion to flight lieutenant had arrived. The news came simultaneously with a case of Highland Dew Scotch whisky and a sackful of beer bottles. Neville threw a party that went on for hours. Towards the end I have a curious but distinct recollection of seeing a frog halfway up a pole, which Neville grasped, saying that he liked frogs. He then walked down the steps into the pool, disappearing below the water. He could next be seen swimming along the bottom flashing a torchlight under water, apparently looking for the frog. Strangely enough the torch still worked the next day.

The journey between the club and the airfield took a slice out of the day. The detachment had a large station wagon, which was not in good condition and was not capable of going fast, even if the state of the road had permitted it. We worked in the mornings and had a siesta in the afternoons. Tents were erected and clearings cut for aeroplane dispersals. On the inside of my flight tent, an insect parked itself, shaped exactly like a leaf. It did not move and in more natural surroundings, it would have been perfectly camouflaged. A tall tree nearby had a colony of beetles in its branches, which periodically sent down a jet of liquid. The airmen called them piss beetles. Near the flight tent someone had nailed the skull of a cow to a tree with a sign below which stated: 'There are some mad pilots and there are some old pilots, but there are very few mad, old pilots.' The heat and humidity were oppressive and we were glad to relax on our beds in the afternoons. We had been unable to bring our bearers with us and now employed local men who were untrained and 'jungly'. This was an epithet applied to anyone who was rough and unkempt in appearance – jungly wallahs! Two airmen were in charge of the mess, helped by a tall Indian. Once I saw him pick up a chicken, place its head under a wing, and then move it around through the air in circles. After a few such movements, he placed it on the ground where it remained motionless.

My main companions were the plump and affable Neville; Macpherson, a tall well-built Scotsman of the best type; Ferrier Jones or F.J., our ground defence officer; and Major Vir Singh, the Sikh liaison officer. Vir Singh would get up early each morning and go for a cross-country run. The club had two tennis courts placed on high ground that commanded a good view, where Vir Singh, myself and others used to play. One evening after a strenuous game I was lying prone on the grass when I felt a pricking sensation down the centre of my chest. Sitting up I found there was a rash of red spots over my sternum. This was diagnosed as prickly heat, and although it was of acute onset, it remained with me for years.

The swimming pool was further down the hill on which the club was built. It was the end of July and the water was too hot to swim in before the evening. We were well away from the beaten track. In these surroundings we became careless of our dress, swimming naked in the pool, and thus we were in this state when the tea planters arrived one Sunday to play tennis with their wives.

On another occasion I was swimming the crawl in the pool, when I heard a muffled report as my ears were in the water and found that a

South African pilot had taken a shot with his revolver at a snake that
was swimming near me. I do not know how bullets behave in water, but
I would have thought there was some risk of ricocheting. However, he
had actually managed to shoot the snake in two. I have a photograph of
Captain Pearce from our ALO section holding the remains of the snake on
a stick, with myself and the South African standing beside him and Lulu
Penney aiming the revolver at the snake. The others had wound towels
round their waists for the photograph, while I just folded my hands in
front of my undercarriage. Subsequently, in a fit of modesty I blacked
out this part of the picture, which rather spoiled the photo. F.J. was in the
background, wearing pyjama trousers and evidently just awakened from
his siesta. Flight Lieutenant Kelly, the MO, can be seen on the springboard
at the end of the pool.

In the dormitory our beds were arranged in three lines at regular intervals. This was in the large room that had been the club cinema. Major Vir
Singh's bed was in one corner. One afternoon when he was at HQ some of
us suspended a coil of rope in the air beside his bed by means of a thread
attached to the ceiling. This was supposed to represent the Indian rope
trick and beside it we placed a note saying 'Back in 5 minutes'.

The foothills of the Himalayas formed the northern border of the valley. I
tried flying over them in a Lysander, but they were higher than they looked
and the old aircraft could not get above 10,000 feet, so I had to give up
the attempt. The mountains were covered with jungle and rose steadily
as one went northwards. Somewhere below was a track used by hillfolk
from Tibet, when once a year they made their way through the foothills to
Tezpur with furs and trappings for the bazaar. After we had been at Tezpur
for a week or so, the visibility improved so that we could see the tall peaks
of the Himalayas 50 miles away, impressive in their vastness, with blue
shadows on their covering of snow.

Tezpur was about 30 miles from our mess. It resided beside the river,
which at this point was wide and placid on the surface but with a swift
current flowing to the west. Some squadron equipment had been sent by
rail and had not arrived and several visits were made to the local railway
office in an effort to trace it. On these trips we caught glimpses of the
town, which seemed a clean place with good shops and a large native
bazaar. In the market there were vegetables for sale that I had not seen
before and we spent a morning looking around. With Major Vir Singh's

help, I bought an odd-looking vegetable that I took back to the mess to examine! Fruit was plentiful in Tezpur in the form of limes and pine-apples. The latter were larger and juicier than any others I had seen and could be bought for a few pence. A fascinating sight was the giant bats or 'flying foxes', which hung, suspended, from tall palm trees during the day and could sometimes be seen flying at dusk. We occasionally went to the cinema at Tezpur, where there was room for about half a dozen people upstairs with their individual armchairs.

Once, a holy man passed us, dirty, unshaven and in rags. With one hand he continuously shook a small bell. His incessant ringing was apparently his claim to holiness. Other varieties of this type could be seen in the big cities of India. Sometimes an Indian would hold one arm vertically above his head until it became fixed in that position. Luckily the Indian did not have to put on a shirt!

On Sundays most of the officers on the detachment went to the small chapel in the town and swelled the size of the congregation. There would be two or three middle-aged English ladies in front and some Indian con-verts sitting at the back of the church. I found evensong services in churches in the Far East were spiritually satisfying and restful, and I remember enjoying singing such hymns as 'Lead Kindly Light' in that little church, as darkness fell outside. Macpherson, who had been inspecting the men's billets as orderly officer, came striding into church late, still wearing his revolver and belt, bringing with him a reminder of the war.

The distance between billets and the aerodrome involved long drives, which were made less tedious and even enjoyable by Neville's habit of singing in a fine tenor voice as we drove along. Soon the rest of us would join in the chorus and sing other songs of our own.

Tea planting was the main job for whites in that area and the planters' biggest club was in Tezpur itself. They were friendly and hospitable, glad of the chance to meet somebody new. During war the staff on a tea estate was generally reduced to a single individual who would consequently be overworked and lonely. There was a greater consumption of alcohol in India than at home and the planters were not backward in that respect. We spent some pleasant evenings with them and on one occasion visited a tea factory. A large number of coolies, men and women, were employed to pick the leaves from the tea plants. These coolies were paid a few shil-lings a month on which they managed to live. The leaves they gathered were dried, ground and after one or two other mechanical processes, were boxed to be taken away for blending. Each factory had its own side track leading to the main railway line.

There were big cats in the area, although I never saw any. The minister of the church told us that they had once had a tiger in their house and a panther was seen on one occasion by one of the RAF officers.

A trip to the dentist involved a week's journey by paddle steamer down the Brahmaputra to Calcutta, for any of the ground crew who needed treatment.

I was puzzled to see an Assamese person sitting on the bund or wall of a paddy field fishing in what had been dry cracked earth prior to the coming of the monsoon, and learned that he was fishing for mudfish. These fish buried themselves in the mud during the dry season and came to life again with the return of the monsoons. They were a bony tasteless type of fish to eat. We caught sight of a wader bird engaged in a similar occupation, which someone identified as an adjutant bird.

On 4 August, nine days after Jamie's death, a request came through from Dinjan for another Lysander. The British Army were retreating out of Burma and a group had got as far north as they could before being halted by the Naga hills, which separated them from the Brahmaputra valley. A Lysander was needed to pick up a message from them. For this sort of operation the Lysander was equipped with a long rod hinged anteriorly to the belly of the Lysander, having a coiled hook at the free end of the rod. The rod could be lowered down by unwinding a reel in the rear cockpit. The message bag had about a yard of coloured cloth attached and some lead in it to weigh it down. A long loop of strong string was fastened to the bag and the string was then loosely fixed to the top of two poles set about 15 feet apart, with the message bag lying on the ground between them. The aircraft would then fly between the poles, catching up the string by the pick-up hook and the message would be retrieved by the air gunner winding up the rod.

The group were at a spot called Shinbwiyang close to the hills, which ran more or less east–west and on the east side of the river. There were thirty or forty people, mostly white, and when they saw me they started to erect the poles for the message. The approach to the pick-up site was interrupted by a shoulder of hill extending southwards from the range of mountains, and there was another mountain on the other side of the river at the end of the pick-up run. Before retrieving the message, I threw down to them a bag of silver rupees, which I had been given for this purpose. I then lined up, got the air gunner to lower the rod and flew at 85mph between the poles. As soon as I was past, I signalled to my air gunner to wind up the rod and started to turn steeply to the left to avoid the mountain, which was close ahead of us. I was disappointed when my air gunner told me that the message had not been collected. We were again unsuccessful on the next attempt. In fact the coiled pick-up hook was faulty but this did not occur to me at the time and on my third run I went down so low that I picked up the string on my airscrew. It was rapidly wound in and in no time the message bag with its coloured cloth was rotating round behind the boss of the propeller.

I was afraid now that all the material might make the airscrew jam, but fortunately it did not and I was able to climb and fly back over the mountains to Dinjan. I could not help thinking how close I was to that isolated group and yet at the same time completely separate. I did not see the Japanese who were further downriver and in pursuit. When I got back to Dinjan, the South African, Gus Alder, was staggered to see the message bag wound around the airscrew. We finally untangled the string and the bag, only to find that the centrifugal force had torn the lead weight through the bottom of the bag, taking the message with it.

So far our operational sorties had not been productive. Back at Tezpur we tried out the Lysanders to make sure that we had one with a pick-up hook that worked. Pilot Officer McMillan took the machine to Dinjan and succeeded in picking up the message. It stated that they had cholera in their camp and asked for medical aid. A medical officer volunteered and was dropped by parachute, knowing that conditions were terrible and that he must ultimately become a prisoner of war. We heard that he broke his leg on landing.

About this time, Neville Rowson flew south to test the strip at Imphal, which was just completed, thus becoming the first of many pilots to land in the valley. At about this time, too, 5 Squadron shot down a solitary Jap fighter. I think Pilot Officer Tovey was the chap who did it.

No. 4 Corps HQ was stationed at Jorhat, south of the Brahmaputra, and Squadron Leader Fletcher was asked to fly in to have a talk with them. However, he found that the landing site consisted of a polo ground, 320 yards long, so he decided not to land and asked me to go instead! I found that there were trees, some 150 feet high, on the downwind boundary. In order to land I had to come in at 45mph over the trees, cutting the throttle as soon as I was past them so that the machine sank quickly to ground level and then giving a touch of throttle to catch the machine before it hit the earth.

On taxiing back, I noticed an RAF officer walking towards me from the perimeter. It turned out to be a Flight Lieutenant Greenfield, whom I had met earlier in the war at Speke, Liverpool. At that time he was in the MSFU. His job consisted of flying a Hurricane – catapulted from a merchant ship in the event of an attack by a Focke-Wulf Condor – in mid-Atlantic. After the action, the Hurricane was regarded as expendable and the pilot hoped to be picked up after baling out. Greenfield was a wild irresponsible type, who had a motto hanging above his bed at Speke saying 'Work is the curse of the drinking classes'. He took me to a mess tent where I talked with him and an army officer over lunch and a drink of beer. After lunch I took off and did one of the rapid climbs peculiar to the Lysander, doing a 180-degree stall turn at the top of the climb, finishing with my nose pointed down towards the mess tent. I did not have enough height in fact to do a 'beat-up' of the mess, as I had overlooked that my take-off run was shorter than usual and I had not built up enough speed. This was the last time I took a drink before flying, as I felt the beer had made me that little bit too careless, where I might have killed myself.

On one of my trips back from Dinjan, I dived the Lysander to a speed of about 180mph prior to doing a loop. At that point there was a repeated banging noise and one of the panels broke loose from the fuselage!

The Lysander was equipped for aerial photography and on 30 August I did a mosaic photograph of Tezpur aerodrome.

By the end of August, activity in Tezpur had died down. The Mohawks and Blenheims had moved off and I was not sorry when Joel flew up from Jamshedpur to relieve me as OC A Flight. On 31 August I left with F.J. as passenger en route for Jamshedpur. We broke our journey at Calcutta. The city was not yet packed with troops and we secured rooms without difficulty at the Great Eastern Hotel. For the first time we found that additional appreciation of our soft surroundings that was experienced by men coming out of Burma. The noise of water flushing from a cistern could be music in the ears! F.J. was a man in his mid-thirties, happily married, with the complexion of a country man, cheerful and popular with the rest of the squadron. We decided to reconnoitre Karaiah Road, the celebrated red-light district in Calcutta, and so we took a gharry after dinner in that direction. The houses were built in a comfortable English suburban style.

The first house we entered was correspondingly comfortable inside. However, the two women in the house were pasty and pudgy in appearance. At that time I had not experienced sexual intercourse and felt I did not want to have that kind of encounter with one of these for a partner. We accordingly bought a round of drinks at an inflated price and moved on. F.J. said he knew a house further along, lived in by one woman who was half French. We rang at the front door, which was opened by a servant. The lady was engaged upstairs with a client, so we were shown into a drawing room, where we settled down and waited. Finally the lady appeared and pretended to remember F.J. Apart from being much older than I was, she was thinner and livelier than the two previous prostitutes. She was wearing a long evening gown, and as she walked over to F.J. she suddenly lifted it up as though she was going to dance the cancan, showing that she had dispensed with such refinements as underwear. F.J. grinned widely at this, but with my strict upbringing, I averted my gaze! Once again we bought drinks at a price that reconciled the lady to our lack of activity in her main line of business.

We finished up at a nightclub near the Grand Central Hotel called the Porto Rico. There were less than a dozen people there, a few merchant seamen and a girl with an artificial leg who nevertheless managed to act as one of the two dance hostesses. Later in the war, the Porto Rico became crowded with army officers and lost its character. I experienced an interesting hang-up with regard to the club. For some time in Calcutta, I was able to find it at night after a few drinks, but I was unable to locate it by day! Possibly the landmarks were different in artificial light but I was reminded of the drunk millionaire in *City Lights* who only recognised Charlie Chaplin when he was intoxicated. We returned to Jamshedpur on 2 September.

Chapter 4

Jamshedpur and Bhopal Detachment – 2 September–26 October 1942

Back at Jamshedpur I took over C Flight, which was mainly composed of pilots recently posted to the squadron. Apart from Sergeant Parr, a Rhodesian who had already been on a fighter squadron, they were badly in need of flying training and their attempts to land a Lysander were thrilling to watch.

Gandhi and other Indian politicians were casting favourable glances at the Japanese, so they were put in detention, and Sir Stafford Cripps flew out to spread diplomatic oil on troubled waters. Some of the Indians captured at Singapore acceded to the Japs, but the great majority fought loyally on the side of the Allies for the rest of the war.

There was a scare that Gandhi's supporters would sabotage the railway lines, so we had to stooge along the lines in our area, looking for suspicious activity by Indians wearing the little white hats of the Congress party. One of our new inadequately trained pilots had been flying low along a stretch of railway line; wishing to climb and return home, Sergeant Beadle opened his throttle and pulled the nose of his aircraft up. The increase in engine power was, however, insufficient to cope with the additional drag of the plane's new attitude and instead of climbing the aircraft gradually lost speed and height. At this point he should have changed into fine pitch and used full throttle. For some distance the Lysander flew along, getting closer to the ground, and finally finished ingloriously beside the railway track.

Other new pilots were Pilot Officer Burton, Pilot Officer Stilliard, Sergeant Wallace and Sergeant Brittain. They had all been in India before the outbreak of war, including Sergeant Beadle.

On 20 September I flew with another Lysander to Ranchi where 28 Squadron was stationed, and with two Lysanders from that squadron we flew on to Bhopal in central India, where Brigadier Wingate was preparing for his first expedition into Burma. A Flying Officer Dunford from 28 Squadron and an NCO pilot from each squadron made up the detachment, of which I was in charge. The mess at Bhopal was a single-storey brick building with a verandah. One of the officers had a baby leopard, whose claws and teeth looked capable of causing injury, even though in play, and none of the other officers was prepared to take the risk of petting it. The kitten had been found after its mother had been shot. The CO had told the officer that he would have to get rid of his pet. The CO, Wing Commander Hammerbeck, was described as pathologically bad tempered, which was how a tour in India affected a lot of people! Another officer, Teddy Dyson, had a remarkable likeness to the Duke of Windsor as a young man. He also was near the end of his tour, which he had mainly spent in the North-West Frontier Province.

Air observer is an aircrew category which may well no longer exist. The brevet was a circle under a half wing. There were two observers attached to Wingate's HQ as air liaison officers, who had flown with Sir Alan Cobham's Air Circus before the war. They had been given the task of finding a suitable landing ground near the HQ for the Lysanders. I took one of them in the back of my aircraft to try out the landing grounds. The first strip had involved clearing a landing run through a wood. A road ran along the downwind boundary and the second observer was in a car to one side of the strip to watch the Lysander touch down. After a precautionary run over the strip, I decided to try a landing, avoiding some stumps that had not been cleared from the strip. The ground was soft and at the end of the landing run, the port wheel sank into the earth. On walking back over the ground the Lysander had covered, I found several stumps and obstacles that would have caused the Lysander to crash if it had hit any of them. The strip was obviously unsafe. After we had collected together enough Indians to help lift the Lysander's wheel out of the mud, we flew away to test out the alternative landing ground. This turned out to be a field with a pronounced downhill slope. Halfway along its length, the field bent sharply to the left, and there was a pond straight ahead at this point as an added hazard! The observers had nothing else to offer, so I decided that the second site was possible to use.

I was not familiar with Wingate's name at that time and the observer, Flight Lieutenant Longmore, told me that he was the Englishman who had led the Abyssinian patriots against the Italians. I then remembered seeing pictures in the papers of a bearded gentleman, who was Wingate, taken during the Abyssinian war. He was getting over an attack of malaria at the time we tested the landing ground at Dhana, and was consequently shaky and not very impressive. I was standing with a group of army officers of varying ranks when another army officer appeared, now clean shaven and not looking very well, but walking briskly nevertheless. I was surprised to see all the other officers stiffen smartly to attention as he passed through them and entered a tent. They followed him in for a briefing while Long-more and I flew back to Bhopal. The next day General Wavell arrived at Bhopal in his DC3. Inside, the cabin had been converted into an office to enable Wavell to work during flight. This was as close as the DC3 could get to Wingate's HQ and it became clear that one of our tasks was to fly Wavell in, to confer with Wingate, in the back of my Lysander. It was about an hour's trip to Dhana, with very few landmarks on the journey. His pilot had told me at Bhopal that the previous month Wavell had been involved in a forced landing when he was flown by a pilot who had lost his way. It was remarkable how very important people were often entrusted in wartime to RAF pilots without any check of the pilot's ability. A stricter supervision might have avoided the loss of men such as Wingate.

Flying Officer Dunford took General Wavell's aide-de-camp (ADC), and one of the sergeant pilots carried a third member of the party. The trip went off without incident, although the 40-degree turn during the landing was a little hair-raising with Wavell in the back. We were briefed to do a tactical reconnaissance of Wingate's troops and to drop bags of flour on them in lieu of bombs. First of all we had to fly back to Bhopal to collect our air gunners. After the tactical recce we landed at Dhana and spent the night there. We visited an old club that had not been much affected by the war, apart from the influx of Wingate's army officers. The older servants had put henna on their greying hair, presumably to disguise this sign of age. Red hair was a much prized physical attribute among the Pathans on the North-West Frontier, who were often more pale skinned than other Indians.

The plan was to sleep out in the open that night as we had no tent, but by midnight we found that a heavy dew was falling and to keep dry we moved our bedrolls under the tailboard of a nearby lorry. In the morning we were ready to transport Wavell back to Bhopal. Flying Officer Dunford asked me if he could fly Wavell on the return trip and I agreed to this.

General Wavell rolled up with his ADC. An Australian air gunner from
28 Squadron called Butcher had a camera, and for the first time I observed
the effect of a camera on a celebrity. The slight sag disappeared as Wavell
tucked his tummy in and puffed out his chest. Butcher took a snap of
Wavell standing beside me but unfortunately he was repatriated to Australia the following month and I never saw the print.

'Well, my boy!' Wavell said to me. 'Ready to aviate?' As he made his way
to my Lysander, I intercepted him and asked him if he would fly in another
machine, indicating the Lysander where Dunford was already strapped
in, eagerly awaiting his passenger. I should have been more forthcoming,
explaining that we all regarded it as a great privilege to be allowed to
fly him and that this was the reason for the change of planes, but alas, I
was never eloquent. A more mundane consideration was the prospect of
having Wavell's name in one's log book! Wavell frowned but climbed into
the Lysander as requested. His ADC was my passenger and at Bhopal I
landed first as the formation leader. I taxied up to where I could see the
welcoming committee, among whom were the station commander and
the maharajah of Bhopal. When Wing Commander Hammerbeck saw
it was the ADC in the back of the aircraft he nearly had a fit, and waved
my aircraft brusquely away. Dunford then rolled up with Wavell and the
reception proceeded according to plan. However, they decided to have
lunch at the maharajah's palace and not on the aerodrome as originally
proposed.

Two large adjoining tents had been erected, with Persian carpets covering the grass and with the walls hung with tapestries. One room was fur-
nished as a lounge and the other as a dining room. The pilots and air
gunners were left to enjoy an unexpected and luxurious luncheon. When
a mosquito settled in Sergeant Parr's glass of lime juice, it was removed
and a fresh glass substituted. At the end of the meal, the keeper of the
household came forward and apologised for the humble fare!

At Bhopal we saw many Italians, who had been taken prisoners of war
by Wavell in the desert, and who were now providing labour in the fields.
They may have been working for the maharajah, who was on good terms
with Wavell.

The next day we returned to Jamshedpur via Allahabad and Ranchi.
In Allahabad we noticed camels being used for transport. Back at Jamshedpur the air was full of flying ants, which the villagers down near the
flight dispersal were busy catching. Pilot Officer Krishna told me that the

villagers made them into a soup.

Each morning we would beat the roof of the flight tent, to dislodge any snakes that had taken residence on the tent overnight. There were some very large but harmless tree snakes about and I saw one about 9-foot long. On one occasion my attention was attracted by some squeaking and, looking down, I found that a frog had been caught by a snake, which had its jaws clenched on one of the frog's hind feet. The snake was only about 18 inches in length, and each time the frog jumped, it dragged the snake along with it. However, the snake was steadily swallowing the frog's hind leg, and when it reached the frog's pelvis, it opened its jaws wider and started to engulf the amphibian's body, causing the other hind leg to flex at the hip. At this point neither animal could move and I intervened to break the snake's back with a stone, after which the frog dragged itself out of the snake's mouth and limped off into the bushes.

The field telephones in the flight tents were provided for us by the army, and were very inefficient. Some maintained that it was the actual shouting one could hear coming from the flight tent on the other side of the aerodrome and not the voice relayed along the telephone wire itself. These phones did not improve and were still remarkably poor when the war finished.

In England part of our work consisted of aerial photography. The Lysander could take either vertical or oblique photographs; the former through the floor and the latter through the side of the machine. By making parallel runs and taking a series of photographs on each run with a calculated amount of overlap, one could make up a composite picture called a mosaic. This involved an exact calculation of one's height, course, speed and the time interval between exposures. All these could be worked out from formulae and the camera could be set to take the exposures at the right interval. The chief technical difficulty was to maintain the exact height, course and speed required. There was a small panel that could be slid out from the floor of the pilot's cockpit, leaving a pane of glass that had two wires running along it from front to rear and a circle in the centre of the glass between the two wires. This was the viewfinder for the camera and the pilot could see it by looking down between his knees. When the aircraft was trimmed to fly at the calculated speed, the air gunner levelled off the camera to point vertically downwards. One had to concentrate on the camera sight while photographing, so that one was a sitting duck for enemy aircraft, while the steady course, height and air speed made one vulnerable to gunfire from the ground. During October I did mosaics of Ranchi, Ramgarh (near Ranchi) and Jamshedpur.

One of the characters at most RAF stations in India was the 'char wallah'. He would appear at the time of the tea break with tea and an assortment of cakes iced in lurid colours. These would be carried in a large black tin trunk similar to those used by the servicemen. Ordinary trunks were vulnerable to attacks by white ants, who would eat their way in from the bottom. The tea would be contained in an urn, which was sometimes carried by an assistant.

Any store of sugar attracted ants, and apart from coming in a colour range of red, white or black, they were also available in a wide range of sizes, the biggest ones being about an inch long and capable of covering the ground at high speed. In addition to ants in the sugar, weevils in the bread were an inescapable feature of life in the Far East. Even in the best hotels, one still found weevils in the bread, albeit on a reduced scale.

Seemingly unmindful of the war, Squadron Leader Fletcher had plans for an RAF pageant. Each flight and section had to organise a stand or stall, whose objective was to entertain but also to make a profit to help pay for the pageant. I decided that C Flight would run an Aunt Sally. This was easy to arrange – canvas screens at the back and sides with a netting behind which the Aunt Sally walked. The netting had a lower piece in the centre to give the customers a better chance of hitting their target when 'she' passed the spot. One of the riggers, a Cockney Jew called Reynolds, managed to find an old top hat and proved to be good at clowning and persuading others to pelt him with tennis balls. On the day, the Aunt Sally stall was a success both as entertainment and financially – the latter because we had no outgoing expenses.

The Donkey Derby was one of the highlights of the afternoon. Sergeant Wallace, I think, produced a cluster of small donkeys and a similar number of coloured jockey uniforms. There were spirited races, with the riders having to hold their legs up to clear the ground. Three Lizzies flew by, leaving coloured trails from smoke canisters and that was about it, as far as a flying display was concerned.

The sideshows and races were followed by boxing and dancing at sundown. The evening finished up with a squadron Jirga. This was an Indian word that I imagined meant a get-together of tribal warriors on the North-West

Frontier, but which was possibly merely Urdu for 'piss-up'. There were a couple of senior NCOs sitting at a table on the airfield during the evening, who drank beer steadily until empties were piled up around them. The beer had no discernible effect on them and they continued to sit quietly as though they had been drinking tea.

Prize-giving took place rather late in the proceedings, by which time pretty well everybody was drunk and some of the men had to be supported as they went up to receive their prizes from Mrs Evans, the wife of our former equipment officer.

Most people driving at night will have noticed the light reflected from an animal's eyes and this phenomenon is all the more noticeable in the case of a large animal. I noticed this first at Jamshedpur on the long road sloping down from the station to the town. Bullock carts coming up the slope would give a light at a distance equal to a car's sidelights, solely due to the light reflected by the bullock's eyes.

One morning I was called into the CO's office and shown a signal. It was a request for two Lysanders to work with the 14th Indian Army Division. Joel and I were the only trained army cooperation pilots on the squadron. Peter Joel was still at Tezpur and was determined to stay there as long as possible, as he did not get on with Fletcher. Accordingly, I was detailed to be in charge of the detachment. I chose Sergeant Carmichael to fly the second aircraft. He was a quiet man in his mid-twenties, with a precise way of speaking, who had worked in India as a chartered accountant.

Chapter 5

Chittagong – 26 October 1942–7 January 1943

Leaving Jamshedpur, we stopped at Calcutta for lunch and made our destination, Feni, in the late afternoon without any further stops on the way. Feni, at the top of the Bay of Bengal on its east side, was well behind the fighting line, but Japanese planes had penetrated even further north than this and group had ordered that no aerodrome nearer to the front line than Feni was to be used in order not to expose aircraft to the risk of attack while on the ground. There were no anti-aircraft defences at that time. As a safety precaution one was not meant to fly due east from Calcutta to Feni as this would involve crossing many miles of desolate waterways and a portion of the Bay of Bengal. Instead the corridor, as it was called, followed a route over more inhabited regions north of the bay. Any pilot forced-landing on this route stood a better chance of being picked up. Furthermore, aircraft proceeding direct across the bay to Calcutta could be positively identified as hostile. The former reason did not carry much weight and it became the custom to fly direct to Calcutta, giving 'ops' prior notice.

With the aircraft dispersed and picketed down, we had to sit back and wait the arrival of Major Vir Singh. The domestic site was some distance away in the native town. Feni had had an entirely Indian population in peacetime and consequently lacked the improvements supplied by a European community in the way of metal roads and sanitation. I have never seen more dust than on the roads around Feni. It was very fine and was about 4 inches deep, so that one was ankle deep in dust, which rose in a cloud when disturbed. There was a railway station at Feni where one could get a meal and we were advised to order the meal in the morning, which we did. We told the man in charge that we wanted a chicken dinner that evening. Later in the day we passed the railway station restaurant and found a headless chicken jumping around in the road. This was to be our dinner later.

I stayed in a red-brick house that had been abandoned by its owner. There were a couple of 'ground types' in residence, who were in charge of the 'R & R' party or rearming and refuelling parties. One was a half-mad Australian flying officer and the other a tough, unintelligent English pilot officer. Living conditions were at a low level. The day after our arrival we were joined by Major Vir Singh and five ground crew, who had been transported by Dakota; about the first air lift on this front. Major Vir Singh wished to establish contact with divisional headquarters at Chittagong and on the following day we set off together in a Lysander, flying low down the coast to avoid enemy air attack. I was glad to get away from Feni, which was a boring place.

Chittagong aerodrome had originally belonged to the Burmah Shell Company and was situated near the coast, while the town lay several miles inland on a broad winding river, which reached the sea just south of the airfield. The aerodrome seemed deserted; there was one short runway available and another longer one under construction, crossing this at right angles. We landed and parked at the top of the short runway beside a burned-out Blenheim. The day before, forty Jap fighters had strafed the area, claiming the Blenheim as a victim. A solitary Hurricane, piloted by Wing Commander Frank Carey, was ready to take off as the Japanese fighters circled the aerodrome, and in fact proceeded to do so, keeping low and flying north. He was pursued by two Jap fighters, one of whom flew into the ground, probably concentrating on getting the Hurricane in his gunsight. Carey said he could see their bullets passing him, presumably tracers, and when they became too close he would do a violent turn through them. I heard Frank Carey tell this story on a couple of occasions and passed it on to the official historian after the war, so that it is recorded in the RAF history.

One of the 'R & R' party now came up to me. 'You're Mr Millar, aren't you, sir?' he asked. I recognised one of the mechanics who had been on 231 Squadron in Ireland, named Beveridge. After some difficulty with the phone at the watch hut we got in touch with divisional HQ, who sent out transport to pick us up. The riverside road leading to town had a bad surface and it was about 45 minutes before a staff car arrived. We were greeted by an army captain who had had previous acquaintance with 20 Squadron on the Frontier and who now drove us to divisional HQ at Chittagong. I took little part in this first meeting with the divisional staff and waited while Major Vir Singh discussed matters.

We then went on to the RAF mess. This had been the district commissioner's residence and was situated on a hilltop. It was the end of October and the climate was now very pleasant. A drive swept up to the DC's bungalow, finishing as a large forecourt. Some steps led up to a wide verandah, roofed over but with open sides. The view from here overlooked the town and beyond to the headland where the aerodrome was located. Past the verandah the bungalow opened on to a sizeable lounge, and several bedrooms led off from this main room. The number of officers in the mess was small and the house was large and comfortable, the more appreciated because of our recent sojourn at Feni.

Life would obviously be more pleasant operating from here, but there were no dispersal points yet ready on the airfield. Besides, there was an explicit order from group that aircraft should not remain on site. The routine planned for the detachment was that the planes should fly up from Feni as required and be refuelled while the pilot was briefed for his task; after the sortie the pilot would return to Feni. This was an unsatisfactory scheme from my point of view, mainly perhaps because it meant living at Feni. It also meant stretching the distance the Lysander had to cover, thereby reducing the time available for staying in the target area. The extra flying would also make the Lysanders more rapidly due for their periodic overhaul. This occurred on a cycle of forty flying hours and necessitated their return to base. A third argument against the proposed scheme was the poor state of communications between Chittagong and Feni. I envied Major Vir Singh's decision to remain at Chittagong to be in close touch with the army, and was glad to hear that the dispersals would soon be completed. They were in fact ready two days later, so I ignored the group order and moved the complete detachment to Chittagong. Great pains were taken to conceal the Lysanders, and these were dispersed nearly half a mile from the runway and covered with nets to which bits of green and brown fabric were attached, so as to be invisible from the air.

It was clear early on that a good deal of help and cooperation could be expected from the RAF CO at Chittagong – a young flight lieutenant named Bingham Wallis, who had been a flight commander on 67, the Brewster Buffalo Squadron at Rangoon, which had later converted to Hurricanes at Calcutta. He was now given a non-operational job, officially in charge of the R & R party, but actually filling an important role as officer commanding RAF Chittagong. His excessive initiative and zeal accomplished much during this time, but were too pronounced for the tastes of higher authority and he received no credit later for his work.

His adjutant was an older, white-haired aristocratic-looking man with the rank of flying officer called Craig Adams. His son had been killed as a pilot and, although well over age, he had managed to join the air force and was now serving in a climate that was probably undermining his health. Goddard was the only other flight lieutenant in the mess. It was still a fairly rare rank. A tall, slightly built man with a gentle manner, Goddard checked on the operational activities around Chittagong and had a giant chart in his room at HQ whereon he plotted movements of friendly and enemy aircraft. His information was largely derived from a young pilot officer with a shock of fair hair and spectacles called Brookes, who ran a radar station close to the aerodrome. At that period radar was in its early days and we knew little about it. Goddard was in the process of setting up radar posts inland among the hills, where dwelt the Naga headhunters, and he or Brookes would be away for several days at a time.

A necessary part of any wartime station was the cipher section and ours was run by two officers: a small, shy but cheerful Australian named Woolcock and a tall, thin and serious Northcountryman called Cornish who was by vocation a schoolmaster. All messages coming or going had to pass through the cipher section and these officers were kept working long hours over the monotonous system of figures that the cipher involved. A young Irish second lieutenant with a snub nose and fair hair called Paddy English, looked after our system of communications and was subjected to a deal of good-humoured criticism on that account. Two elderly and solid ground defence types completed the mess occupants.

Bingham Wallis had good taste in buildings and had chosen another attractive structure for his HQ, with a bougainvillea growing against the wall of the house, while for the sergeants' mess he had commandeered the bishop's residence, complete with billiard room and library. We were amused to find some risqué books there. All the local worthies had moved off at the threat of the Japanese approach. Chittagong was a port situated near the wide mouth of a river. Further from the port itself, the flat land gave way to a number of small hills and the residences were built on these, each on its own hill. The airmen were billeted in what had been a school for the children of tea planters run by Indian women.

On 29 October, the day after we arrived at Chittagong, two generals had to be flown down to Cox's Bazar, about the same distance down the coast from Chittagong as Chittagong was from Feni. Many years before, Cox's Bazar had been a trading post. There was a grass landing strip that had been dug across at regular intervals to make it unusable by the Japs. These ditches had subsequently been refilled when it was realised that we needed the strip ourselves. I flew the general with a crown and crossed swords on his shoulder, thinking he was the senior of the two, and asked Carmichael to take the other general, who had a pip and crossed swords, and who turned out to be the higher ranked. The latter was Lieutenant General Irwin, probably a corps commander, and the former was Major General Lloyd commanding the 14th Indian Army Division. On the return journey in the late afternoon, as we climbed out of the aircraft at Chittagong, I confided to the general that I hoped to use the Lysanders for dive-bombing. He appeared a bit critical when he heard this.

The next morning Major Vir Singh and I were summoned to divisional headquarters. Singh had already been briefed that the Lysander was unsuitable for operations and was to be used by the army for transport and communications only. Understandably, as a result, they were thinking of us as air taxis. On the other hand I was a fully trained army cooperation pilot and had no intention of acting as a taxi driver.

There were lots of army officers milling around at HQ and there were no other RAF officers to be seen. Eventually we were ushered into the general's room, and he proved to be the man I had flown in my Lysander the previous day, which was a pleasant surprise as we had got on well together. Major General Lloyd was a tall, thin good-looking man with clear blue eyes who had won the DSO and MC during the First World War. Also present at the meeting were the second in command, the GI, Lieutenant Colonel Warren, and the AQMG, Lieutenant Col Creffield.

Creffield had a supercilious air, with a sharp face and thin moustache; he wore red tabs on his shirt and a red band round his hat. He was older than the other army officers and was probably not going to get any more promotion before he retired. At the meeting he made it clear that he hoped to use the Lysander quite a bit, and specifically wanted a trip to Calcutta. Major Vir Singh kicked off by saying that he realised that the Lysanders should not be used for offensive action. Fortunately, he acted as a devil's advocate in putting forward the official viewpoint, and the general took him up on this, agreeing with my contention that we should be allowed to do some operational flying. I explained that the Lysander required a periodic inspection for every forty hours of flying, and that every third inspection was a major procedure, putting the Lysander out of action for a considerable time. The squadron had a limited number of Lysanders and it was essential for us to use the flying time available in the best possible way. As Colonel Creffield wished to stay in Calcutta, the general compromised by accepting that he should be flown to Calcutta, but should find his own way back. 'And that', said the general, 'is better than a slap in the belly with a piece of wet fish!' To this unexpected piece of facetiousness Creffield smiled rather sourly. The general also concurred that we should be given some operational jobs.

On 31 October – the following day – I carried out my first operational flight on the Arakan. It was uncertain what response this would arouse from the Japanese, so the arrangement was that I should take off from Chittagong, do the tactical reconnaissance, and drop my findings in a message bag at Chittagong. I would then fly straight on to land at Feni, so that if the Japanese strafed Chittagong they would not catch the Lizzie on the ground. Not much flying had been done south of Chittagong and there was a report that the Japanese were using a system of smoke fires for signalling the route of our aircraft. Certainly columns of smoke were to be seen down the valley of the Mayu river, which was a natural route to follow, but it soon became clear that these were fires made by individual Burmese for domestic purposes and had nothing to do with signalling. For my first few trips, I avoided the more obvious routes to the front in case the Japs had look-out posts to warn and direct their fighters, but the Jap fighters were used for offensive sweeps rather than on interception duties. Our main source of trouble was from machine-gun posts, which were more effective against the slowly moving Lizzies than against faster aircraft, but even these did not trouble us a great deal and were ineffective above heights of 1,300 feet.

On my first operational trip, I found myself trembling, which interfered with my flying. I told myself that this reaction was of no value as there was no one to observe it and take pity on me, and that it was impairing my performance as a pilot, which was vitally important. This actually worked and I settled down to fly properly. On this first flight I flew down the Mayu river inspecting the land on either side, including the settlement of Buthidaung, which was held by the Japanese. I returned and dropped my message bag with my report inside, as arranged at Chittagong, and flew on to Feni. This sortie did not provoke any immediate reply from the enemy. I returned to Chittagong later in the day, and did not use Feni again after that.

The front line was 25 miles south of Cox's Bazar, more or less along a road which ran east–west, joining the towns of Maungdaw and Buthidaung. Maungdaw was on the coast and had a small harbour, being separated from the Bay of Bengal by a narrow peninsula that was attached to the mainland at its northern end. It was divided from Buthidaung by a range of hills which traversed north–south. Buthidaung was on the west bank of the Mayu river, which flowed in the valley between these hills and a range of mountains to the east that blocked off the Arakan from the main plain of Burma. The valley in which Buthidaung was sited, and the coastal region to the west, were to be the main scene of operations on the Arakan front.

The nature of the country made it difficult for the Japanese to pursue a military offensive. Rivers and mountains had to be crossed to transport supplies. There was jungle both on the plains and in the hills. The Burmese side of the Bay of Bengal contained mountain ranges running in ridges from north to south, gradually converging with the coast in the south. There, one or two mountain passes formed a restricted means of communication with the rest of Burma. To the north, the British did not have these geographical difficulties.

On 2 November I flew Lieutenant Colonel Creffield to Cox's Bazar, returned alone to Chittagong, and then flew a visiting brigadier down to Cox's Bazar, finally arriving back at Chittagong once more, with Creffield. My next flight was a recce around Cox's Bazar on 8 November. I think this was to enable the army officer in the rear cockpit to survey the road, which was to be heavily used in the future. The next day I carried out an attack with two 250-lb bombs on enemy positions. Before that, Sergeant Carmichael had carried out a bombing raid at dawn on a Japanese camp near Maungdaw. This was the first of its kind and reports came through later that he had caused more casualties than the whole army on the front up to that date! An escort was provided by three Hurricanes from 615 Squadron, 'Churchill's own'. During the sortie a Junkers reconnaissance plane flew past to the south and was unsuccessfully pursued. This recce plane paid several visits to Chittagong either before or after Japanese air raids. Our fighter squadrons were most cooperative and willing to provide escorts, but these were only requested rarely. The Lizzie could carry either eight 20-lb bombs or two 250-lb bombs under the stub wings that projected from the wheel spats. Later, an 18-inch rod was attached to the nose of the bomb, causing it to detonate before burying itself in the ground. This produced a more horizontal blast and were called 'anti-personnel' bombs.

On 11 November Colonel Creffield got his trip to Calcutta, on the pre-scribed route via Feni. I picked up a 20 Squadron air gunner at Dum Dum and flew back with him the next day to Chittagong. Sergeant Carmichael returned to Jamshedpur with a Lysander that was due for inspection, and was replaced by Warrant Officer Innes Smith. On 13 November I spotted two river steamers on the Mayu, moored to the bank. The army turned down my request that we should be allowed to dive-bomb them. That evening Flight Lieutenant Bingham Wallis took me round to the naval mess at Chittagong. The senior naval officer was a Captain Hallet. He was near retirement age, and pleasant if somewhat regal in manner. Bing-ham Wallis knew him and they obviously got on well together, despite the differences in age and rank. There was a pleasant bunch of about four junior officers in the naval mess. With them on this occasion the general commanding the division was having a quiet drink and I took the oppor-tunity to point out that the Jap steamers would make a good target for the Lysanders' bombs. He agreed and said that his staff was wrong in not letting me attack them. Accordingly, the next afternoon the two Lizzies took off, each carrying two 250-lb bombs. One of the tactics we used to employ was to vary the times of our sorties, so that the enemy would not expect us. This was Vir Singh's suggestion, although in retrospect we did tend to arrive over our target at first light in spite of his advice. I had in fact done a dawn recce that morning, to check that the steamers were still there. Unfortunately we scored no hits on the steamers. Our bad result was partly due to inexperience and partly to the weapons at our disposal. Two years later, with better aircraft and armament, we were accurately hitting very much smaller targets.

The following day I was asked to do a mosaic photograph of some Japanese-occupied villages, and was provided with a fighter escort of three Mohawks from 5 Squadron. I do not remember what the three Mohawks did while my Lysander stooged backwards and forwards on a set course and height carrying out the photography. I had taken the opportunity of loading my Lizzie with eight 20-lb bombs, and when the mosaic was completed dive-bombed the steamers once again, still without sinking them! I imagine that group sent some Hurricane IICs or Blenheims to do the job properly.

My air gunner, Sergeant Trust, was tour expired and due for repatriation, so on 17 November I took him back to Jamshedpur in a Lysander that was due for inspection, returning the next day with Flight Sergeant Armstrong in another Lysander. On one of these inspections, a German bullet was found embedded in the main spar of the Lysander and had presumably been there since its spell in the Middle East. Armstrong was getting bored with life at Jamshedpur and was drinking a fair bit. On a previous occasion, I had finally tracked him down to his billet at the school, which was serving as the sergeants' mess. He was in a drunken stupor, oblivious to a fly crawling over his face. I gave up the attempt to arouse him and took Sergeant Trust instead. There were plenty of volunteers among the air gunners, eager to come on the detachment. For some reason we were once sent a Sergeant Keilly, a plump, smooth-faced, soft-spoken Irishman. Just before we were going to take off on a sortie, he would complain of earache or some other ailment, and was obviously intent on avoiding operations. He was the exception among a fine lot of air gunners. No disciplinary action was taken against him and he was eventually posted from the squadron.

The Japanese were extremely good at concealment and were hardly ever to be seen from the air. Their dug-in positions were usually underground and covered with foliage so as to be unnoticeable even at close range. Flying towards the front line our own forces and equipment could be easily spotted from a distance; columns of dust rising from the road revealed the presence of mechanised transport moving in an endless stream to and from the front. It is surprising that the Japanese never took advantage of the targets, thus offered at a time when air superiority was theirs. A very different picture presented itself when we looked down on Japanese territory. There was never any sign of Japanese equipment or even a single soldier. Occasionally tracer bullets would fly past as an assurance that the enemy really were there but it was obvious that they had nothing like the materiel used by our forces. This was continually pointed out to the divisional staff through Vir Singh, and we would feel disheartened by the failure of the army to take advantage of their opponent's weakness. In being briefed for sorties we would be given unbelievable figures for the strength of the Japanese infantry in the area. This faulty intelligence was possibly part of the Japanese design to mislead our army. On many occasions during this phase of the war, the Japs, with inferior numbers and equipment, were able to outmanoeuvre us and hold their ground. Their great asset was their familiarity with that type of country and their ability to live off the land, whereas the British were dependent on food supplies being brought up from the rear. As might be expected from this, the information we brought back from reconnaissance sorties was fairly meagre and yet seemed to give divisional HQ satisfaction.

The British were steadily building up a large force on the Arakan front. In the middle of November, divisional HQ left the comforts of Chittagong and moved forward to Cox's Bazar, a small coastal town still 25 miles from the front. Nevertheless, there was an atmosphere at 'advance divisional HQ' of awe at their own daring. Cox's Bazar possessed a grass aerodrome, which had been ploughed up during the retreat, exposing a subsoil of sand, but it had been sufficiently repaired to allow the Lysanders to land. Dispersals were prepared some distance from the strip, where the Lysanders could be refuelled and await requirements. Although the position was once again unsatisfactory in that we were based at Chittagong and operating from Cox's Bazar, I made no attempt to move the detachment forward and leave the comforts of Chittagong. Divisional HQ were satisfied, as our arrangements did not interfere with our commitments. Operating from Cox's Bazar gave the Lysanders an additional range for reconnaissance, always a factor in a land of vast distances. Apart from the grass strip at Cox's Bazar, there was nothing else. Divisional HQ was some miles away. Next to the narrow runway was a sandy beach where we bathed when we had time. At the north end of the strip there was a small stream that flowed into the sea. The first time I saw it, I thought the banks on either side of the stream were covered with shells and shingle, but as I moved forward they disappeared, revealing a sandy beach, and I realised there were countless hermit crabs who had popped down holes in the sand. The effect was like a magical transformation.

The sand on the main beach became so hot that it would burn the soles of one's feet. The tide went out about 100 yards on this beach, leaving a long pool parallel to the sea edge with a sandbank separating it from the sea. On 21 November we decided to swim in the early morning before going off on a recce. I took the jeep, which had been lent to me by the army and, accompanied by Flight Sergeant Armstrong, I drove down the beach, around the edge of the sea pool and along on to the sandbank beyond. We were just enjoying our swim when I realised that the tide was coming in and that we would have to move quickly to get away. Jumping out of the water I started the jeep, but could not retreat immediately because of the sea pool. I was forced to drive along the sandbank to get to the end of the pool. The waves were now running over the bank and into the pool. Soon a wave hit the side of the jeep and splashed up, stopping the engine. We were unable to push the vehicle – which was now settling into the sand – and as the tide was rising we were forced to abandon the vehicle. Flight Sergeant Armstrong made a futile attempt to shift the jeep by putting it in gear and trying to move it on the self-starter. As we later took off on our sortie, only the roof was visible, and it could not be recovered until low tide – by which time it had been seriously damaged by the salt water. Luckily I was in good standing with the army, and escaped retribution for the mishap.

Returning from my recce on that morning, I was flying north up the Mayu river at about 100 feet; the river ahead turned at right angles to the left and then after a short distance took the same degree of turn to the right. As I approached the stretch of river with the two right angles, I saw moored to the northern bank a large river steamer, and around the bend a second steamer. I decided to maintain my course so that the people on the ground might hope that I had not spotted the steamers. Looking over my left shoulder, I saw about 100 men in white shirts on the opposite bank, heading west for the hills north of Buthidaung. I returned to Cox's Bazar and gave Vir Singh the information. It gave Lieutenant Colonel Warren a useful indication as to the Japanese plans and the river steamers were sunk the next day by a Hurricane squadron.

On the evening of 22 November, my bête noire, Lieutenant Colonel Creffield, rang up to ask me for a trip to Cox's Bazar the following morning and also to ask if I would train him as an air gunner! Unfortunately he took a childish delight in flying in the back of a Lysander and this would be his fifth flight with me. I could not refuse his first request but declined him permission to fire the twin Brownings in case he shot my tailplane away. On this occasion I was determined to discourage him. At dawn the next day we were waiting by the Lizzie when Colonel Creffield's staff car appeared. We were going to fly to Cox's Bazar and then do a recce from there, so I insisted that he would have to share the rear cockpit with my air gunner. I warned him that if we met with an enemy air attack, that my air gunner would not have room in which to work his guns and, having been primed beforehand, my air gunner was going to do what he could to make the colonel uncomfortable! But Creffield wished to travel alone and after some argument ordered Armstrong from the Lysander. Armstrong got out. This annoyed me, as RAF teaching makes it clear that the pilot is captain of the aircraft. I pointed this out to Creffield and ordered my air gunner to get back in. Flight Sergeant Armstrong, who was good at clowning, did so with an exaggerated air of bewilderment. Things were getting tricky. Creffield, threatening to report me to the air officer commanding (AOC), general officer commanding (GOC), Air Ministry and anyone else he could think of, climbed in with Armstrong. Luckily the AQMG was largely unpopular and I heard nothing further on the matter, but I took the precaution of seeing the second in command and explaining the situation to him. From my log book I see that Creffield managed to get in two more flights at the beginning of December, and probably others in the second Lysander. I then carried out a reconnaissance of a small island off the coast, St Martin's, which the army feared was being used by the enemy. In fact it was definitely uninhabited. I took some low oblique photographs and returned to make my report.

On 24 November we carried out a dive-bombing attack on some Japanese military huts, using both Lysanders. Between us we dropped fourteen 20-lb bombs; presumably two bombs refused to leave the bomb rack as each Lizzie could carry eight 20-lb bombs. Two direct hits were scored but Warrant Officer Innes Smith's Lizzie was hit by a .303 in the front of the radial engine so that smoke was curling out from a bullet hole in the cowling. Innes Smith took the machine back to Jamshedpur and the replacement was flown out by Sergeant Parr. Parr was a tall, thin young man who had already had some action on a fighter squadron. In a dogfight a Japanese bullet had hit his throttle and his hand, bending the throttle so that it was in a fixed position and nearly severing his little finger. In landing he had to control his engine by switching it on and off. He was picked up beside his machine, and as the ambulance came up, he pulled off the left little finger and threw it away, saying 'I won't be needing that any more!'

On 25 November Lieutenant Colonel Warren wanted to be flown to Calcutta, and I had first to pick him up at Cox's Bazar. We stopped at Feni, which had already developed since we had stopped there three weeks earlier, and which was now the base for a Hurricane fighter squadron. Warren wanted to empty his bladder, and when I assured him that General Wavell had done so beside the aircraft, he did not hesitate, saying: 'Who am I to differ?' The Lysander battery was flat and would not start the engine, so a slave or starter battery was brought up, twice the voltage of our usual ones. The airscrew spun round furiously and the engine sprung into life without its usual preliminary hesitations. We stayed overnight in Calcutta and rendezvoused the next day at Dum Dum. Here I met Nick Thompson, who was then a wing commander at AHQ, Delhi, and who had been in the Battle of Britain, getting a bullet in his buttock over Dunkirk. Our families were friends in London, and we had an amiable chat without commenting on the strangeness of finding ourselves together in Calcutta. This sort of meeting seemed to happen every now and then in wartime. Colonel Warren next appeared with a case of spirits for the army mess at Cox's Bazar, while I had bought a case of rum on the instructions of Bingham Wallis for the mess at Chittagong. The mess would occasionally be filled overnight by some fighter squadron – usually 615 Squadron, who flew Hurricanes – who would leave the following dawn on an offensive sweep of some Japanese aerodrome. These brief visits would cause a big drop in our bar stocks. On one occasion I joined them, but my flying performance was so impaired by my hangover a few hours later at dawn, that I never again had a drink if I was in the air early the next day.

In order to save flying time on the return trip, I cleared it with the duty pilot that I would travel back from Dum Dum straight across the Bay of Bengal, over the Sundarbans as the islands in the delta are called. It only made a difference of a quarter of an hour in the actual flying time, and we had to hang around at Chittagong for a staff car that was laid on for the arrival time, as if we had flown via Feni.

Colonel Warren had some messages to deliver before journeying on to Cox's Bazar. We chatted while we waited at Chittagong. I gathered he had an estate in Ireland or at least that he used to spend time on such an estate, and that he was a keen fisherman. He was a placid, comfortable man and the general seemed to leave much of the operational planning to him. Warren was rapidly promoted over the next year or two, but unfortunately was killed in an air crash in Burma in 1944, by which time he was a major general.

Reaching the target at dawn the next day, I located and dive-bombed three machine-gun posts, using eight 20-lb bombs. In that light, the tracers from the enemy guns could be easily seen, like sparks that rapidly lost their velocity and curved away in a dying fall. Tracers from a cannon were more unpleasant, going by on a straight track at a higher velocity.

At that time, an R & R party stationed at Dohazari, not far from Chittagong, made an excursion into the neighbouring village and raped the women. There had been no officer in charge and a letter had been sent to Bingham Wallis as CO of the nearest RAF station by a civilian administrator who was still in the area, pointing out very mildly that this was a bad show. On 28 November I flew Peter to Dohazari so that he could investigate the incident. We were both horrified, as the propaganda had led us to expect this sort of behaviour from the enemy and not from our own side.

The following day I carried out a mosaic photograph of a Japanese landing ground at Aleythangyaw, together with a 'vertical line overlap' of the road from Aleythangyaw to Maungdaw. For this job I was given fighter cover by three Mohawks.

There were five ground crew in the 20 Squadron detachment: Shipman, Brockes, Edge and Humphries, with a Corporal Stevens in charge. They all worked hard and well during the detachment, and as the Lysanders were usually away during the day, this often meant toiling at night by hurricane lamp. Edge was the electrician. He was a smallish chap with a large head and a large nose. The batteries of the Lysanders were in a poor state and required recharging every night; this was Edge's responsibility and he would remove the batteries each evening and charge them up overnight at the station headquarters. To fire up the aircraft we used a starter battery if one was available. The aircraft's own battery was capable of igniting the engine about three times before going flat. If one was careful and followed the correct procedure exactly, the engine would start first time. If it did not, a lot of electricity could be used up in trying. When there was no starter battery, as on a forward strip, one could not afford to make a slip of this sort.

On the aerodrome a body of some thirty men formed the R & R party. Their job was to service aircraft, calling at the 'drome, and they were wholeheartedly in favour of their CO, Flight Lieutenant Bingham Wallis. As I had his backing, I also derived plenty of cooperation from the R & R party. An unexpected source of help came from the Calcutta Communications Flight. Two Lysanders were held by this flight and they were well equipped with Lysander spare parts. Their CO, Flight Lieutenant Parry, in an uncommonly helpful spirit, more or less placed these at my disposal, thereby greatly improving the maintenance of our aircraft. His reason was that our Lizzies were engaged on operations, and it was all the more creditable to Parry in that his assistance naturally reacted unfavourably on his own unit's serviceability.

Much as I enjoyed the company in the mess, I saw little of the other officers. Nearly every morning I would be awakened by a Bengali servant at 4.30am, and after a solitary breakfast would pick my way in the dark down the wide stone steps to the 15cwt van that Bingham Wallis had allocated to the detachment. Then down the hill on which the DC's residence was built, along a dusty, bumpy road with headlights on and up another hill that led to the bishop's house where the sergeants now resided. Here I would pick up the other pilot and the two air gunners. At first we would collect the ground crews also. Initially they were billeted in a school, which later became group HQ, but they were subsequently billeted on the aerodrome and then we would proceed direct from the bishop's residence to the airfield. It was the time of year in India known as the cold season and as the end of 1942 approached, these early morning drives became progressively colder. None of the detachment had come prepared with warmer clothing and we were all shivering until the sun came up, when the temperature rose rapidly to a comfortable level. After a few mornings like this, Major Vir Singh announced that a pile of army jerseys had been found, oddly enough just the right number for the detachment. The unit's name on the parcel was indecipherable, but included the number 20, which was Vir Singh's explanation of how it had got to us. We took them gladly, without question, but Vir Singh may well have organised it and chose this way to do it, in order not to hurt anyone's feelings at being offered extra clothing.

The drive from the town was pleasant. First the 101 smells of the Indian bazaar and then the cool fresh air of the country as the road followed the wide flowing river leading to the sea. At dawn, one's appreciation of the scene was not diminished by the dust and heat of midday. It was the time of year when the sun permitted the flowers to grow. At the airfield the Lizzies were picketed down in the shelter of some woods 500 to 600 yards from the runway. A dirt track led to the runway and there was a tendency for the engines to overheat in taxiing this distance, especially if one of the wheels sank into the mud. Sometimes the only way to extricate the Lysander from this situation was to round up a large number of coolies who by their combined efforts would lift the wheel and, aided by

the engine, the Lizzie would move on. The Japanese were making periodic attacks on the airfield and this deterred the coolies from turning up
for work. An increase in their pay provided sufficient incentive, just as
labourers on some fighter aerodromes in the south of England had to be
paid 'danger money', which brought their pay up to more than that of the
fighter pilots!

One had to climb up some 8 feet to reach the cockpit of a Lysander and this was done by a series of footholds taken in a set sequence.
The parachute was either left in the pilot's seat or put on before climbing
into the aircraft. Once strapped in, I always got the rigger to polish up
the windscreen, as these were discoloured, scratched and opaque. Priming the engine was a critical part of the firing-up procedure; one soon
learned the right number of strokes of the priming pump. The throttle
would be positioned for starting. Mixture set to rich. Airscrew tuned to
fine pitch. Both magnetos were turned on, and there was a third switch
for the starter magneto. When all was checked and ready, one would sing
out to the mechanic by the starter battery: 'All clear?' and to his reply 'All
clear', 'Switches on, contact.' With luck the engine would pick up first time,
and then one would run it at a fast idling speed while the engine warmed
up and one did the cockpit drill. An essential part of the drill was to set
the elevator trim. This involved several turns of a large wheel, on the left
side of the cockpit. It could not be done during take-off and if it had been
overlooked, the result could be frightening, causing a steep climb, which
the control column could not govern. Fins around the engine had to be
opened fully for take-off. This was done by turning a long rod, connected
to the fins anteriorly, which extended back to the cockpit. At the cockpit
end was a small wheel that could be reached by stretching forward and
downwards with the left hand. When airborne, the fins had to be closed
again. When the engine had warmed up, the throttle was opened to make
sure the engine developed the right amount of revs and that the revs were
sustained when the magnetos were tested individually.

Sometimes we were airborne before dawn, so as to be over the target
area at first light. We would take off by moonlight or by the light of goose-
neck flares. These were like watering cans with long spouts and were filled
with paraffin with a wick up the spout. They were generally used in night
flying during the war and could be quickly laid out along a landing path.
There was no ambulance or fire tender on the aerodrome. Having taken
off, I would climb to 6,000 feet and set course for the target. The sun her-

alded its appearance by a faint light in the sky to the east, while pools of darkness remained in the hollows of the ground. I enjoyed watching the transformation from night to day while making this part of the journey.

Apart from bombing sorties, the work consisted of photography and reconnaissance. We would land at Cox's Bazar afterwards, finally return-ing to the mess at Chittagong after dark, dirty and tired. The permanent duty pilot at Chittagong was a sergeant air gunner called Yorkie Smith. His face could have been hewn out of a rock, with straw-coloured hair and moustache. He was always ready to chat and was full of good humour. I wondered what misdeed had landed him with this job. His watch office was a small hut on the aerodrome. 'You know,' he would say, 'when I first came out here, I noticed something strange about the other guys in the camp, but after a fortnight, bless me if I could see anything wrong with them!' He had washed-out blue eyes that seemed to have difficulty focus-ing on near objects, and most of us were affected in this way eventually. 'See Burma and die?' I asked him. 'Hey!' Yorkie Smith chuckled, 'You're not half right there, sir!' One morning he told me that a bird on one side of the airfield had been going 'Tuctu' all night, while another bird on the other side kept saying 'OK! OK!' The first animal would have been a tucktoo lizard, but the second one was probably mythical, a product of Sergeant Smith's inventive mind. After hearing this cry for several nights, Yorkie Smith reckoned that he would eventually be taken away crying 'Tuk you too!'

For a time there was an air-sea rescue launch at Chittagong, and I was taken for a trip in it. It was powered by an aircraft engine that had been used in the Schneider Trophy air race.

The Lysanders were showing distinct signs of age. On several occasions I flew on operations without an air-speed indicator (ASI). The auto-matic flaps and slots that came out at set speeds were a useful guide when there was no ASI. Very often our meagre armament of two forward-firing .303s would be reduced to one or even none by the presence of dust or sand in the firing mechanism. When I was later replaced by Peter Joel at Chittagong, the Lysander he was flying crashed as the result of engine failure, causing Peter a severe head injury, which probably contributed to his death a few years later, from a subarachnoid haemorrhage.

At the end of November and the beginning of December 1942 I car-ried out three lots of photography for the army. With the help of the

command photographic officer and, again, Peter Bingham Wallis, we had
established our own Photo Section at Chittagong. At this stage there was a
Photo Reconnaissance Unit Flight at Dum Dum under Wing Commander Wise. He learned of the army's requirements for photography and took
over that task, using high-flying Mosquitoes and oblique cameras. On
3 December I took Colonel Creffield on the round trip from Cox's Bazar
to Chittagong and return. I also took up a Lieutenant General Goddard
for 'air observation' at Chittagong.

There were two operational groups in this theatre: 221 and 224. One
looked after the bombers while the other controlled the fighters. Both
group HQs were stationed at Calcutta, although 221 Group moved even
further back to Asansol for a while. Now with the gathering offensive
of 14th Division, the fighter group showed signs of coming forward to
Chittagong. This they did later, while 221 Group, following their example,
moved to the northern sector of the front at Imphal. In these two relative
positions the groups remained until the end of the war, changing their
roles to look after all aircraft in their own area.

In the meantime, we received news that the AOC 224 Group was going
to visit us. Peter Bingham Wallis decided to parade all the officers at RAF
Chittagong to meet the AOC and we were all lined up on the runway when
his plane arrived. It drew up some 25 yards from us. I think it was a Hudson. A stepladder was let down and as we stiffened to attention, a pair of
female legs came into view, followed by the rest of a slinky-looking popsie.
Air Commodore Wilson and his senior air staff officer (SASO), Group
Captain Moore, appeared next. They had had a good party in Calcutta the
night before and had promised this girl a trip with them to Chittagong.
Hank Moore was a Battle of Britain pilot and one of the first DFCs in the
war. Soon after he arrived at Chittagong he went off on strikes with the
fighter squadrons and in one of these was shot down and taken prisoner
of war. He was seen leaning against his crashed aircraft smoking a cigarette and I heard later that he had been taken to a special Japanese POW
camp because of his seniority. The authorities were embarrassed by the
event as officers of his rank were not supposed to partake in operations
without special permission. I did not hear whether he survived his time
as a POW.

On the day after his arrival, I took Air Commodore Wilson to Cox's
Bazar to have talks at divisional HQ. We were met on the strip by Lieutenant Colonel Warren and the air commodore did not go much on

this at all. He made it clear that he expected to talk with somebody of equal rank to himself. It was explained to him that Warren was in fact the second in command of the division. Group Captain Moore was flown down by Sergeant Parr to join in the talks. By midday the AOC was ready to fly back to Chittagong and asked me before take-off to do some low flying on the return journey. He was also eager to fire the twin Brownings in the rear cockpit. Being the AOC I did not argue with him but showed him how they worked, merely warning him not to fire directly astern as this endangered the integrity of my aircraft's tailplane.

At that time, a normal take-off had a very shallow angle. The Lysander had a somewhat short take-off run, and if it was held down until the speed built up, it could be made to climb steeply, startling anyone unaccustomed to the sight. I did this variety of take-off for the benefit of Air Commodore Wilson, doing a stall turn to the left towards the sea at the end of my climb. At that moment I saw a turtle swimming northwards in the sea only 100 yards from the shore. As I dived towards it, the turtle disappeared below the surface and I did not see it again. I gave the air commodore a chance to fire his guns and then pointed the Lizzie towards Chittagong, weaving between the trees, so that I think we both enjoyed the trip! As we drew near Chittagong I gained height and did a copybook approach and circuit of the aerodrome. There was a small group of people waiting at the inter-section of the runway, with the strip still under construction. I could see them as I covered the circuit most sedately, as befitted the arrival of the AOC. I brought the Lysander in very carefully, doing a three-point landing after holding off a few inches above the ground. The machine rolled to a halt at the intersection and I turned off to the left to leave the runway clear for Sergeant Parr who was due to arrive next with Group Captain Moore. Parr was still fairly new to Lysanders and did not settle down on his first landing attempt and had to go round again. However, he was more skilled than a number of the squadron pilots who would have been unable to cope with operational flying at that time.

A Group Captain Nominy was among the entourage who had arrived with the AOC on the previous day. He now detached himself from the others and came up to me. He was a thin, grey-haired man with a fair moustache. He asked me if I would take him up after lunch to inspect the landing grounds in the area. I explained to him that we had to restrict the flying hours on the Lysanders as they would soon be due for major inspec-tions. He turned towards Air Commodore Wilson – rather like a child who had been told he can't have a toy to play with – protesting that he had come all this way for this purpose. Wilson came up to me with plenty of charm and requested that I take the group captain on his pursuit. I knew when not to argue and was also flattered by the AOC's approach. I said I would certainly oblige and the AOC turned to Group Captain Nominy with his hands raised and the palms apart as if to say: 'There you are. No problem.' Nominy told me he wanted to inspect the surfaces of the landing strips as well as to see their locations, so we came down low over them and I can remember running my wheels along the ground at Dohazari without losing flying speed. It turned out to be an enjoyable trip and the group captain was delighted.

The next morning at dawn I took off with two 250-pounders to bomb the courthouse at Buthidaung, which was reported to be the Jap HQ in that area. Although our bombs landed near the building, we had to return twice more before a direct hit was scored that blew away the roof and one of the walls – by which time, of course, the Japs would have moved elsewhere. The AOC left instructions with Bingham Wallis to requisition and prepare a suitable building for the group's move to Chittagong.

The Japanese air force used to operate as a concentrated force, moving all its fighters and bombers to one particular area, in order to deliver an attack with the greatest possible impact. Our own air force was dispersed over a front that stretched from Assam down to the Arakan. The nearest fighter base was at Feni, about 30 minutes' flying time away, although a fighter squadron would often arrive at Chittagong in the late afternoon in preparation for a dawn take-off. Sometimes Japanese fighters came over without bombers, looking for combat with the RAF. On these occasions the advantage was evenly divided; the score might one day favour the Japs and the next time benefit the British. On several days I had a grandstand view of these dogfights, which took place at heights of a few thousand feet.

One afternoon I was driving along the road from Chittagong to the aerodrome; this ran along the north side of the river on which the harbour was based. Looking to my left, I saw a formation of a dozen bombers sweep across the mouth of the river from the south-west, flying at about 100 feet. Above them we caught a glimpse of single fighters escorting them. I stopped my lorry and, as we watched, the bombers went into line astern and headed for the dockside. I could see the bombs released from the aircraft, some falling short in the water and sending up large spouts, while others found their target. Several seconds later the sound of the explosions reached us. At first I thought the bombs had delayed fuses, but then realised the delay was merely due to the distance the sound had to travel. The bombers continued in an easterly direction inland, climbing as they went, leaving the fighters to cover their tracks.

Some of our fighters were already in the air, others were taking off from the aerodrome, climbing and turning steeply towards the direction of the engagement, inland east of Chittagong. For what seemed a long time we watched the battle spread out into individual combats. Once, high up, we saw a Jap with a Hurricane on his tail turn so sharply that the position was almost immediately reversed. Then there was the high-pitched whine of overrevving engines and the staccato rap of the machine guns as the Hurricane dived vertically to the earth with the Japanese fighter in pursuit. The enemy broke off the chase within a few hundred feet of the ground and the Hurricane continued to fly low out of the battle area.

As my air gunner and I stood there, transfixed, a single Hurricane flew towards the aerodrome at about 2,000 feet with a white trail of glycol coming from the engine. There was a battery of heavy ack-ack on the air-field boundary, and one of the guns let off a single round that exploded just in front of the Hurricane, rocking it. However, the plane continued to fly straight and level and as there were no more shots it had presumably been identified by the gunners. The Hurricane made no attempt to circle and land, but continued to fly straight out to sea. At the end of the day one Hurricane was unaccounted for, piloted by a pleasant chap called Monks, who had become a flight commander that day. Possibly he was already dead as his plane approached the aerodrome, or he may have been killed by the shell from the ack-ack gun.

The Japanese fighter pilots who were brought down over Chittagong would resist capture and fight it out with a tommygun to the death. One enemy fighter pilot was knocked unconscious as he crashed, and was taken to the hospital at Chittagong with a bullet wound in his leg. I was taken there to see him, and my respect for the Japanese as fighters was only increased by the sight of him. Even with a damaged leg he looked as dangerous as a gorilla. Nobody could interrogate him as there was no interpreter and it was said that there were only two or three people in England then who could speak Japanese.

On another occasion, we could see the Japanese bomber formation flying back south towards their own lines at about 8,000 feet, pursued by a single Mohawk of 5 Squadron, captained by Pilot Officer Tovey. He was some 2,000 feet below them and 200–300 yards behind and gradually closing the gap. Suddenly we noticed a silvery object in the sky above and behind the others, swooping down at high speed. As it closed in on the Mohawk, the latter suddenly rolled over and dived towards the earth. After a time the sound of machine-gun fire reached us. Fortunately the Jap did not pursue the Mohawk, which eventually made its way back and landed safely, but the plane was riddled like a sieve with bullet holes. When it was patched up a month later, I offered to fly it back to 5 Squadron, as I was always interested in flying new types of aircraft, and I was already familiar with its successor, the Tomahawk. However, when I got into the cockpit there was an unfamiliar control marked 'supercharger' and I did not know in which position to set it for take-off, so regretfully I abandoned the trip.

With the influx of the fighter squadrons for overnight stays, the mess lost some of its cosy intimacy. One of the squadrons was 615 – 'Churchill's own' as the crews were proud to tell me. When they first arrived they gave me the impression of being rather tough guys, a perception not dispelled by further acquaintance. The two flight commanders wore battle-dress jackets and carried revolvers. The senior one, McCormack, had a Distinguished Flying Cross (DFC) ribbon and the other, Paul Louis, who had been at flying school with me, possessed the Distinguished Flying Medal (DFM). Both were well-known fighter pilots. McCormack was an Australian with a scar on his face. Neither of them was very voluble but what they said was to the point. The CO was a good-looking chap called Duckenfield, who had the Air Force Cross (AFC). On one of their morning fighter sweeps he was shot down over the Japanese airfield at Magwe and taken prisoner of war. I did not see him again for thirty years, but read that he had been released from the POW camp at the end of the war. The POWs were expected to bow their heads whenever they saw a Japanese. The newspaper report quoted Duckenfield as saying that eventually all the prisoners did this, although some refused initially and had to be beaten into submission.

Another colourful character whom I saw occasionally was Athol Forbes, who had been a Battle of Britain fighter pilot and was now a wingco in the area, reputedly doing 'cloak and dagger' work. He was a tall, good-looking man who was popular and respected among the pilots.

Other squadrons to visit Chittagong were Nos 5, 155 and 136, the Woodpecker Squadron. The latter used the woodpecker song as their signature tune. Their CO was Squadron Leader Ridler. One Sunday morning he was on an operational trip with one other aircraft. It was a beautiful, sunny, day and they were flying low over the sea off Akyab island, which was held by the Japanese. The sea was dead calm and mirror-like, when suddenly the number two saw his CO fly into the sea. There were many warning tales about flying low over calm water and misjudging one's height and this had evidently happened to Ridler. His number two flew around for a while but saw no sign of anything coming to the surface. The CO's belongings were gathered together and the usual letter of condolence dispatched to the next of kin. However, a rare 'possession' was a popsie in Calcutta, and the two flight commanders were said to have tossed up for her!

A few weeks later I was sitting on the verandah having tea as dusk fell. I was by myself and glancing up I saw Squadron leader Ridler standing at the top of the steps looking over at me with dirt ingrained in his face. For a moment I thought I was seeing a ghost, and he had probably intended to startle me. But he was real enough, and he had an interesting story to tell. When his aircraft disappeared into the sea he must have temporarily lost consciousness, and the first thing he was aware of was swimming in the water. He was picked up by a Burmese country-boat and taken to a village south of Akyab, where he was hidden from the Japanese who patrolled there. Once the settlement was strafed by English fighters and the villagers showed Ridler a cannon shell from one of our planes. Finally he was taken up the coast by boat to a British-held territory and from there had made his way to Chittagong. He was given a job at Delhi after that, as he probably needed a rest to recover his nerve.

At the aerodrome they were working on the second airstrip, running approximately east–west. At first they built the westward, or seaward, end of the runway up to the intersection with the existing one. Once this was complete it lessened considerably the taxiing distance for the Lysander, whose take-off run was short enough to use the piece of runway that had been completed, even though fighter aircraft were often picketed down along its edge. Gradually we became accustomed to the sight of two squadrons at readiness on the airstrip – which we had previously had to ourselves – or on which a visit from a PRU Hurricane or a Communications Flight aircraft was an event. At one stage there were so few planes around that one could often tell the pilot by his plane. Communications Flight had a Yale, the forerunner of the Harvard, and in fact identical except for a fixed undercarriage. This was piloted by a man named 'Burma' Isaacs, one of the few Jewish pilots I met. There was a Communications Flight twin-engined Hudson, captained by a chap called Aaronsen. He had the misfortune to run into a formation of Jap fighters who shot him down north of Chittagong, destroying the plane, but apart from a black eye, Aaronsen looked none the worse for his experience.

All operational stations had to submit a daily return of ammunition used and operational sorties flown, to AHQ, Delhi, although I do not remember having to do this later in the war. On some days in November, the only ammunition expended in that theatre of war were the bombs and .303 bullets of the Lysanders.

Maungdaw and Buthidaung were separated by a mountain range, which ran from north to south. The road that connected the two towns traversed a mountain pass and it was tempting for aircraft to use this route also. The Japanese were quick to notice this and stationed a machine gun on the pass, which succeeded in hitting a Blenheim as it flew over. On its return I walked up to the Blenheim, which had parked at the end of the runway at Chittagong. The pilot was standing by his aircraft and he pointed to a small hole in the nose of the fuselage. Unfortunately, the bullet responsible for this had finished up in the navigator's abdomen and I was shocked to learn that the wounded man was still inside the plane. Despite the absence of an ambulance or a fire tender we somehow got the navigator on his way to hospital in a short space of time. I heard later that the wound was only superficial. When the British took over the two towns, again the Japanese caused havoc by placing a machine gun in the pass, shooting up convoys that were crossing the mountain and then quickly retreating into the jungle before they could be caught. In this way a few men managed to disrupt a much larger number.

One morning before dawn I called at the bishop's residence to pick up another pilot and two air gunners. I found three very young aircrew drinking char in the dining room. They had been briefed to strike Akyab in their Wellington bomber, but according to them had been attacked by a Jap night fighter. Having fled the scene, badly damaged, they had tried to land at Chittagong, but the runway was so short that a night landing was difficult. The pilot was further handicapped by his aeroplane, which caught fire when the flaps were lowered for landing. The plane crash-landed and burned out completely. All the crew but the rear gunner had escaped, and the rest agreed that he was probably dead already as the result of the Japanese attack. When we saw the Wellington, only the framework was left and the engines were still glowing with red heat. Many aircrew wore a belt containing silver rupees at that time, which were to be used to pay natives for helping them return to our territory if they were brought down behind enemy lines. The ground was strewn with silver rupees around the remains of the Wellington and that was the only trace of the rear gunner. As the wreckage was strewn across the runway, the take-off of our two Lysanders was delayed until dawn, by which time we had intended to be over the target area.

One of the functions of an army cooperation pilot was to carry out aerial observation and direction of artillery. Vir Singh contacted an artillery regiment at Chittagong and arrangements were made for a 'puff shoot'. This was a dummy practice that involved considerable preparation. The army produced a landscape modelled mainly out of canvas, which occupied most of a room and was raised above floor level so that a soldier could move easily below it. The pilot and the army officers sat on a platform looking down on the model landscape. The pilot would then select a target, identify it by giving a map reference, and call for a round of gunfire. The soldier under the model would then produce a puff of chemical smoke through the canvas to simulate the fall of shells, and the pilot would call out the appropriate correction to bring the guns on to the target. For example, 'Add 200' would mean to increase the range by 200 yards. The lateral error was usually less than the amendment needed for range. The pilot would then call 'Fire' and watch out for the fall of shot, repeating this procedure until the guns were on target. It was necessary for the pilot to give the command 'Fire', as he had to manoeuvre himself into a position to observe the fall of the shells. In spite of the 'puff shoots', the CO of the artillery unit decided to direct the exercise himself from a forward observation post. His guns actually scored a direct hit on the OP, which killed him, and I never did carry out a live shoot with that unit.

On one occasion I was driving a 3-tonner back to the mess from the aerodrome. I was in a line of traffic moving fairly slowly and we were passing some coolies who were jogging along at the side of the road, when my front nearside mudguard hit one of them. I hastily came to a halt, but before I could jump out to see how he was, the coolie had appeared at the nearside door, apologising profusely! 'Sahib! Very sorry, sahib. Sorry, sahib.' My relief was mixed with amusement and astonishment.

I recollect driving in Chittagong later one evening and passing Lyons and Armstrong in a rickshaw. They were smoking cigars and evidently enjoying themselves immensely, Armstrong with an expansive smile and Lyons chuckling happily.

In the town, beggars would parade physical deformities as an inducement to giving them alms, and I remember a small boy who appeared to have a bunch of thumbs on each hand and who seemed happy to have this distinguishing feature.

Our own air offensive was carried out by Blenheims from 60 and 113 Squadrons. Much of the Japanese supplies were brought up the coast by sea to their main base for the Arakan front, which was the seaport town of Akyab on the island of the same name. A British-built aerodrome, complete with runways and hangars, was located beside the town and alongside the coast. The Japs used this as a refuelling point on their raids. The whole place, town and aerodrome, was well defended by heavy anti-aircraft batteries. Word would be brought back by one of our high-flying PRU aircraft that ships were in Akyab harbour and then Blenheim bombers would fly south from bases near Calcutta and inflict what damage they could. Often they met with a hot reception both from ground defences and from enemy fighters. Sometimes the Mohawk squadrons (now 155 as well as 5 Squadron) would be chosen to escort them, on account of their longer range compared with the Hurricane. After the raid, we would see the Blenheims flying north past Chittagong, singly or in small ragged formations, some flying low, some out to sea, returning to their base aerodrome. A few, unable to make the distance owing to damage, would land at Chittagong, then the nearest available airfield.

From 6–8 December we were ferrying General Lloyd around, between Cox's Bazar, Chittagong and Feni. Having returned him to Coxs Bazar on 8 December, I flew back to Chittagong; then with both Lysanders we bombed a Japanese position north of Kwazon.

One of the trips I recall with enjoyment was flying from Cox's Bazar up the coast to Chittagong one evening. We were flying at about 200 feet in formation over a dead-calm sea, broken only by scattered rocks jutting above its surface. The still evening air made the flight very smooth, while the setting sun imparted delightful colours to the scene.

Some of the officers attached to group HQ had moved into Chittagong and were staying in the mess. Among these was Flight Lieutenant Guy Marsland, who had been a flight commander on one of the fighter squadrons based at Calcutta. He was a bit crazy and got it into his head that he would like to come up in the back of the Lysander with a sackful of hand grenades, which he proposed to throw at the Japanese. He appeared on the verandah of the mess one afternoon while I was partaking of the sandwiches provided at teatime, dived his hand into the sack he was carrying and produced a hand grenade. English, the army subaltern, pointed out that by doing so he could have pulled out the firing pin from one of the other bombs and if that were to happen in the rear cockpit of the Lysander, it would destroy the plane. In the end I agreed to take him provided he rationed himself to half a dozen bombs. As the grenades exploded a few seconds after the pin was pulled out, they would only have time to fall a short distance before exploding, so consequently would need to be dropped from a low height.

I loaded up with eight 20-lb bombs under the stub wings and we arrived over Maungdaw at dawn, to attack some Japanese field-gun positions. I indicated to Guy where he should drop his grenades. I flew low so that they did not explode in mid-air, and used my two machine guns, which fired forward from the wheel spats. Marsland thought the sound was coming from machine guns on the ground, but although there was some small-arms fire, this was not audible in the aircraft. He managed to loose off some bullets from the twin Brownings and we both returned feeling that we had not wasted our time. After the war I was contacted by the official RAF historian and all I could tell him was this story and the one of Frank Carey taking off from Chittagong pursued by fighters. Both the stories appeared in the RAF history.

On the evening of that day, I flew Bingham Wallis to Calcutta, where he joined his wife. I stayed at the Great Eastern Hotel and at dinner the two of them entered the dining room. At their invitation I left the other officers with whom I was dining and joined them at their table. Women were so rare in India that it was a great pleasure to have a chance to talk to one, especially as Peter's wife was very attractive. After dinner we went on to the Calcutta Club, which was still relatively empty of service officers. Most of the clubs extended honorary membership to serving officers and no doubt later on in the war this club became just like any other officers' mess. It was cold enough, being 13 December, to wear a proper uniform, but as I had come from Chittagong I had only my bush shirt and khaki slacks with me. I can remember shivering during the evening, but managed to survive.

Peter's wife was a pretty girl whom he had met at Rangoon. Her father was the head of what had been a big company out there before the Japanese had captured the place. So far they had not succeeded in having a family and Peter told me that he had been in a flying accident when his testicles had been injured and he feared that this was the cause of their failure to have a child. Earlier on, his wife had come to Chittagong for a short stay and Peter moved out of the mess to another requisitioned house while she was there. There seemed to be no shortage of appealing, yet abandoned, houses at Chittagong. We returned to that city on the 14th, flying straight across the Bay of Bengal, as on the outward journey. On the following day we carried out a raid near Buthidaung with two Lizzies landing afterwards at Cox's Bazar.

Divisional headquarters were moving from Cox's Bazar to Bawli Bazar, a village some 20 miles inland and south-east of Cox's Bazar. A landing strip had been made at Bawli Bazar and Major Vir Singh and I went over to test the strip and visit the HQ. We took off from Cox's Bazar from south to north. Unknown to we two, the Japanese had been bombing Chittagong with a mixed force of fighters and bombers. The raiding party was now on its way back to its base and their route would take them close to us at Cox's Bazar. When divisional HQ received a message about this, the Lysander was getting ready for take-off. Sergeant Lyons, my air gunner, jumped into the jeep to warn us and raced down to the strip just in time to see us take off in the path of the Jap force, which was flying fairly low and with the fighters above the bombers. Fortunately the fighters did not notice our Lysander, but one of the bombers lagging behind the others, and already damaged, appeared to see the aircraft and possibly mistook it for an intercepting fighter. It turned unsteadily to port, lost control, and crashed a few miles inland, where we observed it later that day. I was blissfully unaware of the presence of the Japs (consisting of six '97s' and six '01s') until I returned from Bawli Bazar. Chittagong was bombed twice that day and again the following day. When we got back to the airfield at Chittagong, we found our transport had some bullet holes in it and so had Yorkie Smith's watch office at the south-east corner of the aerodrome. Yorkie Smith looked solemn but no real damage was done.

As I returned to Chittagong aerodrome on another occasion, I saw a large concentration of fighters and bombers flying southwards down the coast, at much the same height as myself. I immediately dived towards the ground where I would be less easy to see. However, one of the fighters had spotted me and was flying in my direction. I felt some short, quick tugs at my left shoulder, which was Sergeant Lyons signalling the approach of an enemy aircraft from above on the port side. I went into a spiral dive to the left and, straining my neck round over my left shoulder, I got a head-on view of a fighter making a diving quarter attack. At that point my air gunner 'Chunky' Lyons let off a short burst with his twin Brownings. The aircraft pulled away and I could see it was a Hurricane! My air gunner's bullets had hit the engine and the pilot had to force-land, fortunately without further damage. He came along to the mess that night, thinking it was highly amusing. The sympathies of the authorities were with the Lysander crew and we received no blame for the incident. As far as I knew it was the first time the RAF had imitated the Japanese tactics and sent a concentrated force to challenge the enemy over their own territory.

Although in England we had worked on the assumption that the Lysander's endurance was 2¼ hours, I had been making flights in the Arakan of up to 2¾ hours' duration. As a safety measure I would return to Chittagong at 6,000 feet, not reducing height until I was within gliding distance of the aerodrome. That this measure was needed is shown by the fact that I once ran out of petrol as I taxied away from the runway.

On 16 December I returned to raid the courthouse at Buthidaung and finally demolished it. It was unlikely to have been of any military value, but it had improved my bombing accuracy. The steeper the dive, the more precise was the bombing. On the trip there were flames coming through the stub exhaust of my engine. While at Jamshedpur, we once had to wait a fortnight for a spare exhaust to be delivered from the Middle East. The army were planning their offensive for the following day and when I told Colonel Warren my problem, he arranged for the army workshop at Chittagong to make an exhaust, which they did, and the ground crew had it fitted on to the aircraft in time for the dawn take-off next day.

Colonel Warren had told me the plan of attack, which seemed simple enough. Our job in the Lysanders was to carry out contact reconnaissances, marking the progress of our own troops. We now had three Lysanders, as our usefulness was established. On these recces our troops would display ground signals in response to white Very lights from the aircraft. I spent

the afternoon searching for white Very cartridges at Chittagong. I had set
off originally with Flight Lieutenant Goddard, the fighter ops controller,
but an air-raid alarm had sent him hurrying back to RAF HQ. Then I was
taken by an army warrant officer to the main army ammunition dump.
As we stood there talking, a formation of some fifteen Japanese bombers
appeared, flying quite low in good formation. It was the second and last
time in the war that I went down an air-raid shelter. It was a steep descent
but I lost no time in following the warrant officer down into the depths.
Fortunately no bombs were dropped and we were able to finish our business.

I carried out the first contact recce and Sergeant Parr and Sergeant Hill
followed during the morning. I let off various signals as planned and saw
some troops ahead of our own positions whom I strafed with the two
fixed machine guns in the wheel spats. I was horrified to learn later that
they had been our own troops. The offensive was taking place on the eastern side of the Mayu range. The Japs had already evacuated their position
and our advance continued unchecked, until an infantry platoon entering
an apparently deserted town 20 miles further south were ambushed and
never heard of again. I took off from Bawli Bazar in the afternoon for
another contact recce. As I was flying down on the west side of the range,
I looked out to the coast and saw four radial-engined fighters flying up
the coast at the same height as myself, about 4 miles away. They noticed
me at the same time and turned in my direction. Luckily there was plenty
of cloud cover and I had to ascend only a few hundred feet to disappear
into it. However, the Lysander II climbed very slowly and it seemed a
long time before I was hidden in the clouds. That evening in the mess I
mentioned nonchalantly to Group Captain Singer from group HQ that I
had seen four Jap fighters on the Mayu peninsula that afternoon. I could
see his brain ticking as soon as I told him this bit of information, and
then he said that four Mohawks (radial-engined fighters) had reported
sighting a Jap bomber in that area that had escaped into cloud. At least
the Mohawks looked more like Jap fighters than my aircraft looked like
an enemy bomber!

Four pilots who were with me at Chittagong were Carmichael, Innes
Smith, Parr and Hill. Sergeant Hill was a level-headed chap who refused
to be overawed by superior rank. He came from London and had been a
policeman before joining up, and had done some flying on twin engines
before joining 20 Squadron. While Bingham Wallis was definitely on the

side of the establishment, Sergeant Hill was somewhat irreverent. I can remember Peter and myself directing withering glances towards the back of the station wagon where Hill and the air gunners would be riding, in response to some interjections from Sergeant Hill during our conversation! My air gunners were Sergeant Trust, Flight Sergeant Armstrong, Sergeant Lyons and Flight Sergeant Murray. They were all very different and all first-class men. Lyons was a dark-haired stocky, cheerful Jew. Murray was a slim, dark quiet man, with whom I flew on my last few trips at Chittagong.

On 19 December, Air Commodore Wilson paid another visit to advance divisional HQ at Bawli Bazar, flown in by one of the other Lysanders, but transported back to Chittagong by myself. His staff car and chauffeur were waiting for him at the watch hut and did not come immediately to the aircraft. I therefore took him in the front seat of the 20cwt truck to his car, where he somewhat unnecessarily ticked off his chauffeur for not having attended to him more closely. He then told his driver to follow the truck and, climbing up beside me, rode into Chittagong with me. I was a bit mystified by his behaviour and thought perhaps he was using a roundabout way of assessing me as he had seemed favourably impressed by my flying. However, a week later – at Christmas – he got drunk at the officers' club and embroiled the senior naval officer (SNO) in a scrap, standing at the top of the steps and barring the naval captain's way. The report was that he threw him down the stairs. In addition to this, he was said to have made a drunken appearance at a commander-in-chiefs' conference at Delhi. He finally left for England under a cloud, and was replaced by Air Commodore Alec Gray, MM, whom I first met at divisional HQ at Maungdaw.

On 21 December I tested out a landing strip evacuated by the Japs four days earlier. It was a small grass aerodrome at a place called Aleythangyaw. When we landed, villagers started to gather on the small airfield. I told Sergeant Lyons to remain in the cockpit with his guns ready in case we were subjected to a sudden attack, while I alighted from the plane and surveyed the airfield. The Burmese stood around quietly and without any display of feeling. The strip was within a few yards of the sea, separated only by a sandy beach. The landing ground was in good condition but too small for anything other than a Lizzie or light aircraft. Aleythangyaw was south of Maungdaw and it was strange to be landing there after having known it as Japanese-held territory.

About this time we had two visitors. First was Squadron Leader Fletcher, who arrived with Corporal Hudgell in the rear cockpit. This was a wise choice of passenger as Hudgell was one of the best mechanics on the squadron and was qualified on both engines and airframes, so that if anything went wrong he would probably be able to fix it. I offered Fletcher the chance of an operational trip, which he declined. I introduced him to Bingham Wallis and the others at the mess and the next day he continued on his way towards Imphal where another 20 Squadron detachment was operating. The second visitor, on 21 December, was a Wing Commander Yorke, who was the new CO of the wing into which 20 Squadron was posted. He was newly arrived from England and wore the DSO ribbon. He was quite young, probably in his late twenties, good-looking and alert. He was favourably impressed by the keenness of the men on the detachment. Again, I took him back to the mess, where one could have a comfortable bath and remove the traces of the day's work, before putting on a well-laundered bush shirt. Evening life was a contrast to the sweat of the day. The next morning I flew Yorke and my air gunner Sergeant Lyons to Cox's Bazar, where some men belonging to divisional HQ still lived, and then to Bawli Bazar to meet the rest of them. I left him there while Lyons and I flew off to drop messages on the advancing British troops. Later that day we returned to Chittagong in the Lizzie and Wing Commander Yorke went back to his wing HQ at Ranchi the following day.

On 23 December I carried out the reconnaissance of a place near Akyab, which had a large aerodrome used by the Japanese. For this sortie I was provided with a fighter escort of two Hurricanes. It was getting near Christmas and the pilot of one of the Lysanders at that time was Sergeant Wallace. He was a Scot who had worked in a bank in Calcutta before the war. Knowing his way around, he arranged for a DC3 to fly a pig out to us at Chittagong for Christmas. Problems arose as nobody in the mess had experience of killing or butchering a pig. Luckily I was not involved.

On Christmas eve, Chittagong was treated to a magnificent but unintentional firework display. During the afternoon we noticed a sudden column of flames and smoke rising rapidly from a wooded area and at first thought that the Japs were attacking us. We discovered later that the R & R party had just got a new petrol bowser and one of the men was filling it at the petrol dump while smoking a cigarette! He had dropped the cigarette, which set fire to the petrol and the bowser. The fire then spread to the dump itself.

Next to that was the ammunition store and this too was soon ablaze. Hundreds of rounds of .303 popped merrily while the heavier bombs exploded under the intense heat and distributed shrapnel over a wide radius.

With some of the 20 Squadron detachment, Bingham Wallis and I drove round to find out what was happening. At a clearing in the wood in sight of the blaze, Bingham Wallis told me to stop the van and called on us to take shelter on the side away from the fire. There was no force to the explosions of the .303 as they were not subjected to the compression of a rifle barrel and were consequently more like jumping crackers. The bombs, however, were a different proposition. Large metal fragments scythed their way through the upper branches of the trees, whistling as they went and falling with a thud when their momentum was spent. I felt it was wrong to leave the truck exposed in the clearing, so I ran out and moved it to a safer spot. It was somewhat ironical to be under fire from our own ammunition. The R & R billets were in the woods beyond the fire, so we left the aerodrome and drove along the road to them, only to find that, of course, the place had been evacuated already. Frank Carey, arriving in his Hurricane from Calcutta, thought that the thick black column of smoke visible for miles was due to another Jap raid – but, in fact, the fire did more damage than any enemy attack.

The Japanese were good at timing their raids in order to catch us unawares, so a squadron stood by at readiness on Christmas morning, although there was no action. Enemy fighters were over Maungdaw on 28 December, where the advance divisional HQ was now based, but there was no engagement. I heard the news that evening in the mess at Chittagong, and also received a request to fly General Lloyd down to Maungdaw the next morning. I met him at the plane at first light and warned him that Japanese fighters had been over our destination the previous day. I asked him if he thought it was wise to fly to Maungdaw, and I think General Lloyd misconstrued this as an expressed fear on my own account, as he replied curtly: 'You are to take me to Maungdaw.' I then told him, in as brusque a manner as his own, that I was thinking of him and did not mind about myself. After that, we took off and I climbed as usual to 6,000 feet. When we were halfway there I started to lose height, planning to fly at low level for the rest of the journey.

We were near to Bawli Bazar when I saw two dots in the sky above the Maungdaw area to the south. I peered through the semi-opaque,

discoloured Perspex of the windscreen and confirmed that they were
either aeroplanes or kite birds of prey. After studying their line of flight,
I was satisfied that they were indeed aircraft, and immediately dived the
Lysander, turning at the same time inland towards Bawli Bazar. I decided
to continue on to Maungdaw, so I veered right when I came to the main
road and flew alongside it at or below treetop height until we reached the
road connecting Maungdaw to Buthidaung. The airstrip was north-west
of this point, so I pulled up slightly and turned to the right through 120
degrees, which took me to the end of the strip where I then landed. We
climbed out of the aircraft and I explained to General Lloyd that I had
seen two aircraft. He said: 'That was very good evasive action, but could
you actually see them at that distance?' At that moment I became aware of
an approaching fighter diving on us from the direction in which we had
landed. 'Look out!' I cried, suddenly feeling that my evasive action had not
been very clever after all. I turned to General Lloyd, ready to sweep him
over into the nearby bushes, when I realised he was smiling, and looking again I saw that the fighter was a Hurricane. I learned later from Vir
Singh, who had moved into advance divisional HQ, that they had laid on
fighter cover, and that Wing Commander Smyth – the RAF liaison officer
attached to division – had asked them to jump me as he felt I was getting
careless and needed a lesson! Fortunately the exercise went off well for me.

Chittagong was a pleasant, clean town for that part of the world. There
was an officers' club, which we rarely visited as it was jammed with army
officers. One or two elderly women would be in the bar, the centre of
attention of even the youngest army officers, such was the scarcity value
of females in the Far East. On New Year's Eve, Bingham Wallis, myself and
Hogan, a flight commander from 79 Squadron, attempted to put some life
into the Chittagong club. It was filled as usual with army officers, some
civilians and two old ladies who were taking advantage of the season and
the woman shortage to flirt with the officers. Hogan, with most of his shirt
torn away and a tattered remnant hanging round his neck – the result of
celebrations earlier in the evening – entered into conversation with the
younger of the two women and urged her to 'pickle her bum', a phrase of
which he was fond. Bingham and I, as the remaining representatives of the
air force, gave a tap-dance demonstration on the bar counter. Gradually
the place livened up and by midnight the conduct of the army types was
as reprehensible as our own.

Guy Marsland was keen to repeat his trip in a Lysander, so one morning we set off from the mess in a car that had no brakes, no windscreen wiper and nothing much in the way of headlamps. It was an hour or so before dawn and I had to drive slowly because of the vehicle's lack of essentials. Even so, we were driving along the road by the river that ran parallel to a railway line, when I suddenly realised that we had reached the point where the road did a right-angled turn to the left to cross a bridge, followed by another right-angled turn to the right to leave the railway line after crossing the bridge. The combination of a dirty windscreen, no headlights and no brakes was too much for me, and the car continued straight on over the edge of the riverbank into the muddy depths, with scarcely a jolt. Its nose down in the river, the interior was soon filling with water. We hastily climbed on to the rear seat and from there managed to jump to the bank. Soon a lorry came by and we got to the airfield without bother. However, Guy was wet and shivering and decided to return forthwith to the mess, so that we never did fly together again on operations. When he got back to the mess, he was met by Bingham Wallis, who had heard of the loss of the staff car and assumed that Guy was responsible. They had a stand-up row and Peter ordered Guy out of the place to join the group mess, where he rightly belonged. By the time I returned in the evening to explain my part in the accident, Peter had calmed down and there was no further trouble.

The weather had deteriorated and I received a message from General Lloyd to say he had been standing in a wet paddy field one evening as my Lysander passed overhead on its way back to Chittagong, and he felt envious that I was returning to a comfortable mess while he was stuck at Maungdaw!

The squadron pilots had been taking turns of about a fortnight each in flying the second Lysander, while I had been at Chittagong since October. I had carried out most of the recce and photographic work myself, using both Lysanders for the less-specialised tasks of bombing and ferrying passengers. There was no shortage of bombs at Chittagong, even after the fire, and we used them when we could, feeling that they had probably more actual value than the photographs and information that we brought back. There was a real tendency among many people during the war to avoid positive offensive action, and there was a certain amount of opposition to overcome before we could carry out our bombing attacks. By Christmas I noticed I was losing my enthusiasm for flying and was becoming irritable.

One morning I was in the cockpit of my Lysander at Maungdaw ready to take off. Something had gone wrong and to my surprise I found myself being rude to the mild and pleasant Major Vir Singh, in front of the two mechanics from the squadron. Vir Singh made no attempt to remonstrate but spoke to me later in a very understanding manner, saying that he realised that I had been under a strain but that I should not tick him off in front of the airmen. Considering our relative ranks, this was remarkably forbearing. Irritability and loss of interest in flying was typical after a spell of operational flying and the phrase 'operationally tired' became familiar in the RAF. Another term for the older concept of cowardice was 'lack of moral fibre' or LMF. This was coined by the RAF medical branch, perhaps not wishing to judge their fellow men or understanding that the condition was more complex than was generally appreciated.

On 2 January 1943 I was in Calcutta and delivered a package from Peter Bingham Wallis to his wife. I left my air gunner, Flight Sergeant Murray, in the taxi while I called at her flat. She had a friend with her of the same age and I sat for a while listening to their chatter and feeling a bit dazzled, but then excused myself and rejoined Murray, waiting patiently outside.

I now heard that I was being considered for a decoration, which was unlooked-for but most welcome news. I paid a farewell visit to divisional headquarters, now comfortably settled near Maungdaw. Air Commodore Gray was there in the mess and General Lloyd gave me a glowing introduction to him, but the air commodore was unimpressed.

Bingham Wallis received no thanks for his magnificent job of running the aerodrome and preparing the way for group HQ. He was dispatched to the undeveloped landing ground at Dohazari, which had no comforts and was out in the wilds. On 7 January, I returned to the squadron, which was now based at Charra airfield, some way north of Jamshedpur. I never saw Bingham Wallis again, although I heard that he was in a flying school in north-west India about two years later. I wrote to his home address after the war but got no reply.

November and December marked the end of the Japanese advance on the Arakan, and over the next two years there was a ding-dong battle, where British superiority in men and materials was a decisive factor. However, the main war was to be fought out over the plain of Burma, starting in the Imphal valley to the north.

Chapter 6

Charra – 7 January–11 May 1943

At Charra the camp was still under construction and although the mess had been built, we were sleeping in tents. Work was continuing on the runways, which were some distance from the living quarters and too far away to be reached on foot. Soon after arriving at Charra, I received an invitation to lunch with Major Vir Singh and his wife, who had rented a house in the small town nearby. One or two others were invited, including the little dark-skinned Madrasi, Pilot Officer Rammuny. When he was introduced to Mrs Vir Singh, he bowed humbly, with the palms of his hands pressed together in a prayer-like attitude. They were both likeable people, behaving sociably to each other, but I was left with the impression of two people trying to adopt Western standards, yet with their own caste structure deeply imprinted on their minds. Rammuny seemed to be saying: 'I should not really be here, but I will not presume on the good fortune that has allowed me to greet you in your home.' Mrs Vir Singh appeared to display a similar complimentary attitude in the gracious smile of welcome she bestowed on him. After the main course, when we had used chapatis to scoop up the food, we retired to a corner of the room in turn and a bearer poured water from a jug over our hands. Vir Singh did not stay much longer with the squadron and I lost touch with him.

Changes had occurred in the pilots. The Indians had left to join their own air force squadrons and in their place had come a batch of newly trained colonial pilots, who were a decided improvement. Among those commissioned there was a tall, rather brash, Canadian called Holliday, a quieter fair-haired Canadian with a sandy moustache named Eddie Fockler, a highly strung Englishman, Evers Swindle, and a Scotsman from Edinburgh called John Penman. The NCO pilots included an enormous

Canadian, George Hatch, and a diminutive New Zealander named Sandy McPhail. My first recollection of Sandy was of him sitting astride a chair in the half shade during siesta time, exposing his trunk to the diluted rays of the Indian sun. Everybody else was doing their best to avoid them! George Hatch was always amiable and good-natured. Penman and Fockler shared a tent close to mine and each morning would play Tchaikovsky's 'Nutcracker' suite on their gramophone, so that I still associate that music with Charra.

There was no plumbing in the camp. Each officer had a canvas basin, supported on a collapsible wooden frame, which the bearers kept topped up with water. At sundown the bearers filled canvas baths placed on the ground, with water warmed over a wood fire. I retained a bar of soap in a pocket of my canvas basin, and on two or three occasions I found the soap lying on the ground at a slight distance from the receptacle. One day I discovered that the culprit was a magpie, which I caught in the act of removing an object from my tent.

At Charra, I purchased a wide-mouthed Thermos flask, which was a new design then. I used to fill it with iced lime juice and take it down to the flights for consumption there. It proved very popular with the other pilots and I found there was not much left in the flask by mid-morning when I opened it. Refrigerators were uncommon in India and ice was brought to camp from the nearest small town each day, rather like a milk round.

The sanitation in the officers' quarters was quite inadequate, consisting of a single commode or 'thunderbox' in the mess, which was emptied infrequently. Too often the contents of the bucket reached the level of the seat. Eventually I drew the attention of the medical officer (MO) to this and he improved the arrangements for emptying it. Toilet paper was not the absorbent tissue that we have today, having started off life as a newspaper. We were all aware of the respective merits of different newspapers in this role. We did not have to flush toilets again for the rest of the war, except on those rare occasions when we visited one of the big cities. On arriving at a hotel, we would nostalgically pull the chain!

There was a big change of atmosphere from the life at Chittagong, where we had been engaged in operations. At Charra there was very little flying. Having been airborne once or twice a day at Chittagong, I did not fly at all at Charra for the first fortnight. Fletcher would stay on in the mess drinking well into the night with a small handful of officers, and then fail to appear the next day until the morning's work was nearly done. Once when I was 'duty officer' the phone had rung in the mess around midnight. I was in my tent asleep, but as Fletcher was in the mess with some other officers, one would have thought that someone could have answered the phone. However, Fletcher took the opportunity to wake me up and, in a drunken manner, tick me off for not doing my job as duty officer.

I had been a flight commander now for nearly six months, but still had the rank of flying officer. Even my substantive rank of flight lieutenant was two months overdue. I had seen other officers get steamed up when they had encountered less delay than this in receiving their promotion, and I drew Squadron Leader Fletcher's attention to the matter on a couple of occasions, when he promised that he would get it sorted out.

There was a surprising lack of interest and awareness with regard to the squadron detachment at Chittagong, where Peter Joel now was, and also of the detachment in the Imphal valley, where Peter McMillan was operating a Lysander. One day when we were dining in the mess, John Penman, one of the new pilots, spoke up loud and clear about the lack of operational activity on the squadron. This was a fair reflection of the squadron at Charra, and it was allowed to pass unchallenged by the CO. I appreciated Penman's outspokenness, but it showed how little was known of the detachments.

In the evenings from my tent, I could hear the voice of an airman in the canteen, calling out the numbers for 'housey-housey' as it was then known: sixty-six – clicketty-click; all the nines – ninety-nine, and so on. I became familiar with the phrases as the result of those late evening sessions. I became interested in the President of the Station (or Squadron) Institute (PSI), which was a fund for providing amenities for the airmen. The contractor who ran the canteen paid a fee to the PSI each month, based on the number of airmen using the facility. This money had been given to Fletcher, but there was no record of these amounts or how they had been spent. Fletcher agreed to hand over the PSI to me and I was surprised at the income from the contractor. Football was the main recreation for the airmen, so with the funds available, we subsidised the cost of football boots, leaving the airmen to pay a small part themselves. We also bought sets of football shirts for the teams to wear. Finding there was still money to allocate, I got the building contractor to make a tennis court, and then went off to Calcutta to buy a tennis net and the posts etc. I can't remember what went wrong with this plan, but we carried that net and the posts around with us for a year or two afterwards, without ever putting them to use. I continued with the PSI until I left the squadron and organised several ventures with its funds from then on.

By now the Lysanders were really getting decrepit and 20 Squadron was to be re-equipped with Hurricanes. In January a very unusual character appeared. He was brown-haired with a bucolic face and an RAF moustache. He was a remarkably cheerful person and defied all the accepted rules by flying better drunk than most men did when they were sober. He could well have been the personification of Bacchus. This was Flying Officer Gillies, DFM, an ex-Battle of Britain airman, who had come to convert the pilots of 20 Squadron on to Hurricanes. It staggered me to see Gillies doing accomplished aerobatics after a lunchtime session on beer. My first flight at Charra, after returning from the Arakan, was a check dual instruction with Gillies for 20 minutes in a Harvard, followed by 25 minutes solo. I then went off the next day in a Hurricane IIC, but as I had already flown Tomahawks, this was not difficult. Gillies was eventually shot down in Burma while operating with the Chindits. He was one of the outstanding characters that I recall.

Another unusual individual at that time was an engineer officer called Markham, who had undertaken a flying course and had had some solo experience. While he was with us he flew a Hurricane rather dangerously. At one point his port wing dropped sharply, and he afterwards claimed that he was turning the page of his pilot's notes at the time, having taken them up with him!

The conversion proceeded smoothly, without mishaps, and for a while we had Lysanders, the Harvard and Hurricanes. Some of the Hurricanes were ex-Battle of Britain Mk Is, which we used to gain experience on the type. Others were Mk IICs – probably also not good enough for operations – and then there were the Mk IIDs, which had a 40mm cannon under each mainplane. The Mk IID had been used by 6 Squadron in the desert as a specialist squadron against tanks, and this was to be our role in the Far East. However, that was still some way ahead. In the meantime, I savoured the pleasure of flying behind the Rolls-Royce engine, feeling sure that that was as near as I would ever get to having one. We practised aerobatics, which was something outside the repertoire of the Lysander. One manoeuvre that was quite effective was to dive the Hurricane to near ground level and then pull up into a vertical climb, stall at the top on to one's back, and then roll out into the normal position.

My log book shows that I checked out various pilots in the Harvard during the next few months, including 'dual instruction' to Squadron Leader Fletcher on 2 March. Fletcher then flew off in the Harvard to visit the detachments and succeeded in pranging the aircraft on landing back at Charra. He was a short-legged man and probably did not have adequate rudder control because of this.

We had an air gunner, Pilot Officer Sutton, staying in the mess at that time under open arrest, who was awaiting court martial for some civilian offence. He had a set of records (78rpm) of the Tchaikovsky piano concerto No. 1, which he used to play. This was the first piano concerto with which I became familiar, thanks to Sutton.

Near Charra was a large leper colony run by American missionaries. We were told by Doc Morris that there was practically no chance of catching leprosy unless one was living in intimate contact with a leper. Heartened by this we visited the colony and later invited the missionaries to a concert, which was organised and given by certain members of the squadron. Pilot Officer Evers Swindle was the producer – a rather highly strung individual subject to skin trouble. Even in those days, Doc Morris showed an appreciation of the connection between skin conditions and the psyche by asking me, as Evers Swindle's flight commander, to treat him gently in order to try and help this problem. When the concert took place, some of the jokes were RAF blue and the missionaries were disapproving.

Neville Rowson had acquired a bull terrier bitch called Naomi that used to follow him around devotedly. In February Neville was posted. He was one of the flight commanders and, coinciding with his posting, 20 Squadron was reformed into two flights instead of three. I took over B Flight instead of C, remaining with B Flight until becoming CO. Neville was tour expired and was due to be repatriated. I don't know what happened to Naomi. The third flight commander, Peter Joel, was still away at Chittagong.

During our residence at Charra, Doc Morris was replaced by another MO of the same name, who did not stay long. He in his turn was succeeded by Doc Godber, who remained with us just over a year.

Our adjutant was an Australian flight lieutenant called Sides, who had replaced Bailey while the squadron was still at Jamshedpur. He had been at Rangoon and had had to make his way back through Burma, losing his acting rank of flight lieutenant in the process. I often heard him bemoaning his failure of rank in the mess at Jamshedpur, although it was not long before he regained his 'stripe'. At Charra several of us would go for a walk in the evenings, and once when I grumbled about the long delay in my promotion – then seven months overdue – Sides counselled me not to be impatient! On one of these walks we had a freak storm, with hailstones larger than golfballs. Luckily there were not many of them and no one was hit.

While we were at Charra, Padre Meacham was posted to the squadron. He was a nonconformist, evangelical minister, and he stayed with us for a few weeks only. We did not have another padre for the rest of the war, as there was no establishment for one on a squadron. There was also an Indian squadron at Charra, but they had their own domestic site and we saw very little of them. They, of course, had their own religions, but possibly someone at Delhi saw the total number of bodies at Charra and thought we rated a padre! The Indian squadron had a high rate of accidents to their aircraft, which gave me a poor opinion of their flying ability.

Another innovation at Charra was the arrival of an engineer officer. Until then this job had been undertaken by a warrant officer or a flight sergeant, but from that time a commissioned officer took over, starting with a pilot officer and finishing, by the end of the war, with a flight lieutenant. Our first engineer officer was Pilot Officer Davies, a quiet, pleasant, thin man, who was competent at his job. Our first meeting was outside my flight tent, when Davies approached me rather diffidently and introduced himself. As time went on it became clear how valuable an engineer officer was on a squadron.

Apart from the Pathans, who acted as bearers in the officers' mess, others were attached to the flights and to other sections. They wore khaki-coloured turbans, shirts and shorts, with large army boots and socks. The boots gave them an ungainly appearance, like most Indians in uniform, few of whom had been used to footwear previously. The Indian football teams that had fixtures with the squadron played very competently in bare feet. One stocky and powerful Pathan caught a jackal raiding the chickens at Charra and killed it with his bare hands.

On pay day the enrolled followers from the North-West Frontier Province used to sign a receipt for their pay by making a thumb print. In the past some had claimed that they had not been paid or that someone else had received their pay by impersonating them, so the thumb print acted as an identifiable receipt. The CO stopped the Pathans from taking their rifles with them on leave, as they were liable to pursue vendettas in their native villages. I remember one enrolled follower being overdue on return from leave, who said in excuse that his uncle had been covering the road to the railway station with rifle fire!

One airman was having an affair with an Indian girl at Jamshedpur, which Fletcher was actively discouraging. I never discovered why such positive measures were taken, but he was refused weekend leave to visit his popsie and was warned of dire consequences if he attempted to do so. He did not look well at this time and was suffering from a patchy baldness, which spoilt his appearance. Knowing his activities as a Romeo, I suspected at the time that he might be suffering from syphilis.

On the aviation side of life at Charra, I had been taking pilots up in the Harvard, and one day I arranged to fly with Pilot Officer Penman, both of us in Hurricanes. We were to ascend in formation to 6,000 feet and then carry out a practice dogfight. Usually the two aircraft would do 90-degree turns away from each other, fly for a set number of seconds and then turn to face each other, starting with a head-on attack and trying to get on the tail of one's opponent. However, on this occasion, when I signalled Penman to start turning away, he dived his machine to earth, and the exercise was a washout. This produced an unsatisfactory position for flight discipline, and unfortunately it was never properly resolved.

About this time, news came through that I had been awarded the DFC. Squadron Leader Fletcher's bearer, Mohammed, brought me a piece of DFC ribbon, with a nice message from Fletcher, and I had it sewn on to my bush jacket in time for the celebrations that evening, The next day two officers of air rank called in at the aerodrome, and were met by Fletcher. He informed me later that they had come to offer their congratulations, but that he had been unable to find me. He had also told them that he was not sure whether the DFC had been awarded to me or McMillan. This was probably the first award since the retreat from Burma, which would account for the visit of two high-ranking officers; it would certainly not have aroused this action a year or two later.

Soon after this, Fletcher decided to make his visit to the detachments, and I was left as acting CO. As I was still waiting for my promotion to come through, I took the opportunity to look through the back numbers of the lists containing promotions. As there was one list missing, I borrowed it from the Indian squadron at Charra, and found that my substantive rank had come through at the time when it should have done. My acting rank had also appeared on another list, but I had not been notified. I published the items in the usual way in DROs (daily routine orders). I also had a look at the 'Honours and Awards' file. This was an eye-opener. There was a signal from Delhi asking Fletcher to submit a citation for the award of an immediate DFC for Flying Officer Millar and then a further signal asking why this had not been sent, and finally a brusque communication ordering it to be sent forthwith. Awards for valour were classified as immediate and non-immediate, the former being of higher standing, although it was all the same in the end. In spite of the piffling citation that Fletcher eventually submitted, I was awarded an immediate DFC.

Fletcher was court-martialled and dismissed from the RAF with ignominy after the war for sadistic practices against an airman. He once told me with relish that Wing Commander Yorke had thought I was the man he was looking for, for special promotion, and that he had assured him that I was not really suitable for this.

When Fletcher returned from his visit to the detachments, it was early March and a few days later I went on leave to a fishing village in the Bay of Bengal, well south of Calcutta, called Gopalpur. While at Jamshedpur, we had experienced an earth tremor. We were having tiffin or lunch at the hotel that was the officers' mess when it happened, and it was an alarming experience to feel the whole earth shudder. This was followed at Gopalpur by a tidal wave, which came inland for half a mile. The hotel there was run by an English widow, and consisted of chalets between the main building and the beach. To begin with I was in one of the bedrooms in the main building, but later moved to a chalet that was self-contained. During the first few days I had put my cash – consisting of seven 100-rupee notes – in a drawer under some clothes. When I checked on them there were only six notes remaining. (Each note was worth the equivalent of £7.50 at that time). I reported the loss to the memsahib. I had read that Indians would sometimes take a single note in the hope that it would not be noticed, rather than steal the lot. The lady who owned the hotel felt that this is what had happened, but the bearer who was assigned to me denied that he had pilfered the money. Some weeks after my holiday I received a 100-rupee note from the lady, with a message to say that the bearer had admitted the theft. This must have been as the result of some persistent questioning on her part and I have sometimes wondered if he really took the money or had been brainwashed into confessing.

There were only a few people staying at the hotel: an army major of about thirty, with an MC from his time in the Middle East. He was quiet and neatly dressed, with a thin, dark moustache. We chatted together in the evening or played bridge with a couple more guests. There was an English businessman in his late twenties with a popsie that he had picked up in Calcutta, and one or two other officers. The hotel grounds ran down to the sea, where there was a shelving sandy beach and at times the sea was rough. The Indian villagers were strong swimmers and wore conical bathing caps shaped like a sea-shell. When I decided to go for a swim, two of the men came up to me and offered themselves as escorts for safety purposes, indicating this was the usual practice. I was a strong enough swimmer not to have any worries about my safety, but I agreed to hire them as they looked pleasant and eager to be of service. Another day, as I walked along the beach, I came to the fishing village. All the inhabitants seemed to be on the water's edge, hauling in the nets that the boats had let down at some distance out from the shore. I waited until the nets were dragged up on the sand, to inspect the catch. Apart from a wide variety of ordinary fish, I noticed cuttle fish and sea-horses. The fish were put on the train and sold in Calcutta.

While I was sitting on the verandah of my chalet on one occasion, an Indian 'Mochi' came up and tried to persuade me to buy a pair of shoes, which he was ready to make for me. As the price was very cheap, I agreed to purchase a pair. The Indian then showed me different pieces of leather and I selected some snakeskin. His next move was to spread a newspaper on the ground, getting me to stand on it while he traced an outline of my feet on the sheet. He turned up two days later with a well-made pair of shoes, which lasted me for a long time afterwards.

Another visitor at Gopalpur was a conjuror, who talked me into pay-ing him a small sum to give a performance of his tricks. They were very good although they did not include the Indian rope trick! For a few more rupees he showed me how some of the tricks were done. Towards the end of my holiday, the younger of the two men who had accompanied me on my swims, asked if he could come with me as my bearer. His name was Dataya as far as I could make out, although later I found it was Potty Tatkeia. I decided to engage him as my bearer for the pay of 30 rupees a month, which was the usual rate (there were 13 rupees to the pound). So on my last day, Dataya climbed into the tonga (a two-wheeled horse-drawn carriage) with me and we made our way to the railway station. At

Calcutta, I bought him a white turban, tunic and slacks, which was the standard uniform for a bearer.

As the train neared Charra, I felt very fit and well after my leave. My only worry was Squadron Leader Fletcher, who was becoming increasingly unreasonable and difficult to deal with. At the station I rang up for transport to take me to the camp. I knew the driver and on the journey he told me that Fletcher had been posted and that Peter Joel was the new CO. I felt as though a weight had lifted from me and that life was going to be enjoyable again.

With the change in command, I was now the senior flight commander. Sides, the adjutant, was also posted and the new adjutant was a dapper little chap called Snow. Peter Joel and Snow made a good pair. They were both on the small side, but lively and alert, and both were keen in their new jobs. About this time Mountbatten was posted out as supreme commander in the Far East. There was talk that he had decided to continue fighting throughout the monsoon period, whereas most of the old 'kohais' automatically packed up during that season. Kohai was a corruption of the Urdu for 'Who's there?', which the English called out in their clubs when they wanted a bearer. The term was used for people who had been out East a long time. The Japanese were aware of this attitude of mind and had chosen a Sunday morning to raid Calcutta, while the fighter pilots were having coffee at Firpos in Chowringhee. It was not until some months later that Sunday became a normal working day, and remained so until the end of the war.

Although Major General Lloyd had driven the Japanese out of Maungdaw and Buthidaung, the enemy did not let the situation remain that way for long and were soon staging counter-offensives. For the rest of 1943 the war was fought over this area. Later in the summer General Lloyd was moved to the Middle East. I saw him in Bombay on his way through, and heard later that he had been killed in a car crash while in that region.

A Swedish friend of my father, called Olsen, came out to Asansol to advise the large steel works there about the purchase of plant machinery. The Olsens lived near us in London and I knew his oldest son, Sven, who had trained as a barrister before the war. Mr Olsen sent an invitation to me at Charra to visit him, and I was kindly lent a large American car by the 'works and bricks' contractor for the journey. Asansol was about 100 miles to the north-west. I found Mr Olsen very comfortably ensconced in the suite reserved for VIPs and I was put into the neighbouring suite for the night. I had a very comfortable stay and was shown over the steel works by my father's friend. The heat was beginning to make itself felt after the winter months. I can remember getting my hair cut after the visit to Asansol, and noticing the relief of the cold water on my head, as the barber gave me a shampoo afterwards.

There was a bird at Charra that repeated its call monotonously for hours and even days on end. It was reputed to send men mad by its constant repetition but, fortunately, there were no obvious victims at Charra.

We had the RAF Regiment guarding the aerodrome. There were two men to each gun post. At one of these, one of the men decided to take his tommy gun and leave his post to go into the nearby village, looking for a woman to rape. Having found his victim, her husband courageously went to her rescue, calling on the other villagers for help. They appeared, armed with bamboo-sticks, and, although the airman fired at them with his tommy gun, they were able to disarm him without casualty to themselves. They then beat him with their sticks, leaving him half dead outside the village. Here he was found the next morning and taken to hospital. Peter Joel put me in charge of the Court of Inquiry into the affair. The airman was devotedly nursed back to recovery by a little Anglo-Indian nurse and then invalided back to England. The facts of the case were easily determined. This involved a visit to the village and the house where the woman lived. Her name was Lulu. She was the man's second wife. I learned that the villagers married young and again later, when their first wife was old. The first wife would be kept on to do the cooking. Each man was allowed four wives according to his religion, but it was only economically possible to have two. The mud huts were clean, with shelves made by recesses in the mud walls. The airman could well have been court-martialled for leaving his post. In the following year he put in a claim for an invalid's pension, claiming that he had obtained his injuries in action. We received a letter from the Air Ministry asking for details. Often in wartime there would have been no record by that time of the circumstances, but I was able to supply the details requested.

One day we had a warning that a rabid dog was in our neighbourhood and on the way back to the domestic site from the aerodrome, we passed it on the road, moving in the opposite direction. We were in the flight gharry, a 15cwt truck. The dog looked straight ahead and showed no sign of awareness of us as we passed. It was salivating and looked abnormal. It was later shot on this road and its body lay there uncollected. After twenty-four hours its body became grossly distended by the gases of decomposition. Vultures were the substitute for 'public health' measures in India, but presumably the vultures must have been infected in turn. Stray dogs were known as pie dogs, which was probably a corruption of pariah dog.

With the advent of the Hurricanes, the air gunners were gradually posted away from the squadron. On 9 May we flew the three remaining Lysanders to Asansol, where we dumped them. Flying Officer Ferrier Jones flew in the back of my Lysander. We did a final beat-up of HQ before setting course. I pulled the nose of my Lysander up and did a stall turn down on to the headquarters building, realising with horror that I had not given myself enough height to pull out of the dive. For the next few seconds I concentrated hard and it was an extremely close thing, missing the HQ roof by inches. We were actually climbing as we went over it, reaching the lowest point of the dive in front of the building. Pilot Officer Ratcliffe, our 'codes and cipher' officer, had come out of doors to watch and some months later in Bombay he came up to me and said: 'I can understand how you can judge your height when you are flying in a straight line, but I can't understand how you manage to do it when you are diving down and pulling up again. That day at Charra when the Lizzies were going off, you only just missed the roof and I thought you had hit it. How do you do it?' I don't remember my reply, whether it was facetious or serious.

On 11 May the squadron set off for Bombay. Until now I had been accustomed to flying in India by myself, partly because of the nature of the job and partly because we did not have many aircraft. From this time on we were up to squadron strength of sixteen aircraft, with eight Hurricanes in each flight, although the Hurricanes were still a mixed bunch: there were a few Mk I Battle of Britain Hurricanes, and the rest were Mks IIB, IIC and IID. These were more strongly powered and had heavier fire power. The IIB had twelve machine guns, the IIC had six 20mm cannons and the IID had two 40mm cannons, plus two machine guns. We still flew in threes in V-shaped formation, sometimes with a fourth pilot in line astern of the leader, which was variously known as 'in the box' or 'tail-end Charlie'. A few months later we started to fly in pairs, which became the standard formation for the rest of the war.

On that May day we only got as far as Ranchi, perhaps 130 miles from Charra, I can't remember why we didn't go any further. Perhaps it was to take our leave of the CO of the wing, whose HQ was at Ranchi, or maybe to see our sister squadron, No. 28, who were also stationed there. Possibly we had made a straggly start and waited at Ranchi for the squadron to re-form. Likely we were not in a hurry, for the next day again we did only one leg, from Ranchi to Allahabad, which was 1 hour 45 minutes' flying time or about 270 miles. On 13 May, the first stage was to Cawnpore, a name familiar to me from history lessons as a small boy. From there we flew to Delhi, getting there about midday. Our next stretch was westward across the Sind desert to Jodhpur. The desert contained scrub and was unlike the sandy deserts of North Africa.

Penman was piloting an old Mk I Hurricane on my left. We were flying in wide formation and in those days we did not have radio communication. I was worried by the extent to which he was lagging behind and throttled back to enable him to catch up. The distance to Jodhpur was just within the range of the Hurricanes and we did not have any margin to spend on circling. However, I did a 360-degree turn to see what was happening. By this time Pilot Officer Penman was a long way behind us and when I did another sweep soon after, he was out of sight. We could only continue on our way and report the situation at Jodhpur. Peter Joel was already there and I soon took off in a Hudson, captained by a flight sergeant, to search for Penman. Although we spent 2 hours looking for his aircraft we failed to find it. He turned up at Jodhpur the next day, having hitched a lift in a bullock cart. His aircraft had steadily lost power so that he could not keep up and had finally come down in the desert. We had flown over him without spotting the plane during our search. The next day we completed our squadron move to Bombay, stopping at Ahmedabad before arriving at our destination, Kalyan, a new aerodrome near Bombay.

Chapter 7

Kalyan – 14 May–30 November 1943

Kalyan was another new aerodrome and was not completely finished when we arrived. The flight office smelled of new plaster and cement. On the domestic site each officer had a small cubicle attached to his bedroom, which contained a thunderbox emptied daily by a sweeper, one of the 'untouchable' caste of the Hindu religion. We would have a bath each evening on the verandah of the 'basha' or bungalow where our bedrooms were. The water would be heated by our bearers over a wood fire and poured into our canvas baths. We would then put on bush shirts and slacks and flying boots in lieu of mosquito boots. Peter Joel had a portable gramophone (wound by hand in those days) on which he played records at 'bath time' of tenors singing Edwardian lyrics.

There was a single long runway with a hill on one side, some 2,000 feet high with twin peaks, and just enough gap between them to make a pilot feel that he should try and fly through! In fact, when one got up there, there was too small a margin for safety especially with the possibility of turbulence at the hilltop. Nevertheless, one or two pilots claimed to have performed the feat.

The station was fairly isolated but Bombay was only 40 or so miles away, and we seemed to get in without too much difficulty. It was a cleaner city than Calcutta. The Taj Mahal hotel was a popular rendezvous, with a nice bar looking out over the harbour. Bombay had a racecourse, various clubs like the Hillingdon, named after a former viceroy, and the Yacht Club. They all offered honorary membership to service officers. There were good cinemas and shops and there was a pleasant cafe that served very good coffee, which was not such a common thing in those days. The squadron pilots visited the same cinema in Bombay where I had spent my first afternoon in India. We filled the front row of the balcony to watch the film *Casablanca*, starring Humphrey Bogart.

There was a rocky hill at Bombay where the Parsees placed their dead. As far as I recall, the flesh was eaten by vultures and the bones were bleached in the sun. Although Bombay was then a big city, there were gaps of open country between its outskirts and small villages, through which we passed on the way back to Kalyan. I am told that Bombay has grown enormously now, engulfing these villages as it sprawls outwards.

Our time at Kalyan was spent in developing our tactics with the IIDs. The IIDs had been used by 6 Squadron in the desert against German tanks. In their attacks they had dived down to sand level, let loose their two .303 machine guns – which were loaded with tracer for their psychological effect – and then fired off the 40mm cannon at the correct range. The flying attitude of an aircraft changes with its speed, so that it will fly nose-up at slow speeds and, conversely, nose-down at high speeds. The sights of the IID were harmonised so that the shells would hit the target when the cannons were fired 400 yards from the target at a speed of 240mph. If the speed was greater, the shells would fall below the target, and beyond if the speed was slower. If the cannons were fired more than 400 yards away, the shells would converge and meet before reaching their goal, and then diverge, possibly missing the target on either side. In time we became skilled at flying at the right speed and firing at the right range. The recoil of the cannons momentarily slowed the aircraft by 40mph. If one cannon failed to fire, the aircraft was slewed round by the recoil on one side only. The shells at that time were solid chunks of armour-piercing metal.

At first we used the style of attack that 6 Squadron had developed, honing our skills – but without actually firing – on the ships in Bombay harbour, after first clearing it with the navy. We also had a large square white target placed in the sea off a deserted bit of coast north of Bombay. My log book shows that we practised steadily with the cannons during our stay at Kalyan, experimenting with the number of pairs of shells that one could fire in a single assault. We finally decided that it was better to fire off one pair of shells, or two pairs at the most. We adopted the habit of flying in twos instead of threes. It was only towards the end of our stay at Kalyan that we realised that much greater accuracy could be obtained from the 40mm guns by making steep dive attacks instead of shallow ones. In the desert these tactics would have been suicidal, but in Burma were feasible because the anti-aircraft defences were much less.

Two of the Canadian NCO pilots on the squadron were Blackman and Ashworth. Blackman was stocky, fair-haired and with a straightforward manner. Ashworth was a smooth talker but rarely put forward an opinion of his own or disagreed with one expressed to him. They came to the squadron together but were very different. Within a fortnight of our arrival at Kalyan we were carrying out a 'combined ops' exercise, involving low-flying attacks on ships. For some reason that I can't recall, Blackman had forced-landed on a beach during the exercise and on 1 June I flew over and located his aircraft, subsequently landing at Juhu. Blackman was able to fly his plane off the beach without damage. Juhu was one of two small airfields north of Bombay, the other being Santa Cruz, later to become an international airport. At Juhu I met again Wing Commander Chater and Flight Lieutenant Greenfield, both of whom I had last seen in Assam. I had lunch with them and an odd-looking dark-haired flight lieutenant who had been a fighter pilot in England. Hurricanes were being assembled at Juhu and Chater was the station commander. Juhu was in an attractive location, being separated from the sea by a nice sandy beach.

Sergeant Stone was an Anglo-Indian pilot whose training was inadequate, and I took him up in the squadron Harvard several times to practise 'circuits and landings' – touching down at Santa Cruz – and for dual aerobatics. One day on a formation flight over the aerodrome he flew too close to his leader and his airscrew chewed into the mainplane of the other aircraft, which was flown I think by Les Hill. Fortunately both aircraft were able to land safely. Trevor Stone was a pleasant, plucky chap who subsequently did well on operations. I also took Corporal Hudgell up a few times in the Harvard. He was a very capable fitter and I tried to teach him the rudiments of handling an aircraft, under the guise of air-testing the Harvard!

There was a Link Trainer at Santa Cruz, which I used several times while we were at Kalyan. It was air-conditioned, which was essential in that climate, as one was completely enclosed when in it, but the humid heat on emerging into the open was stifling and oppressive.

Another sergeant pilot was Nutt, who seemed reliable, if of average ability. He had brown hair and a moustache, a bent nose and a London accent. One night when the squadron was practising night flying, a cow wandered on to the runway. Sergeant Nutt had the misfortune to be the next pilot to take off, and collided with the cow on his take-off run. Luckily he was not seriously injured.

The squadron moved up to Poona for a week to take part in another 'combined ops' exercise. The city was about 2,000 feet higher than Kalyan, with a steep rise of ground forming a mountainous area called the Ghats on the way there, which meant that Poona was cooler than Kalyan and we enjoyed our stay there. I met Hugo Gross, who had been a buddy of mine at flying school at Kidlington. He was now a flying officer instructor and while at Poona he took me up in a Harvard to do some instrument flying. My log book records that I did a blind take-off, a stall turn and three loops on instruments.

We heard stories of Indian barbers who could shave you in the morning without waking you, so I tried this out while at Poona, but was disappointed. The men who told the story must have been heavy sleepers.

On the return journey to Kalyan, Peter Joel led one of the flights back. It was cloudy over the Ghats and for most of the way to Kalyan the flight was above the clouds. There were breaks in the cloud near our destination, and Peter, wishing to warn the others that he was going to descend through one of these, called up over the R/T: 'Any moment now, chaps!' This remark tickled the pilots, who were mainly colonial, and for a long time after, if something unusual was about to happen, this phrase would come out with an imitation of Peter's English accent.

An Indian squadron was scheduled to join us at Kalyan. One day a Hurricane landed and a portly Sikh climbed out. He was Squadron Leader Mer Singh, who had come on ahead of his squadron to spy out the land. There was ten-tenths cloud over the aerodrome at the time. He told us that he had flown above cloud, coming down through it at the calculated moment. In view of the mountain and other high ground in the area, this was a risky thing to do, but Mer Singh laughed heartily as he told us what he had done, and he was certainly still alive a year later. He was either lucky or more astute than he made himself out to be.

The squadron crews arrived soon after their leader, and sent an invitation to our CO and the two flight commanders (Peter McMillan and myself), to have drinks at their mess. It was clear that their plan was to ply us with booze. In some squadrons there was a tradition for hard drinking. However, none of us came into that category and after two or three stiff drinks we refused further offers, which disappointed the Indians, several of whom were not imbibing themselves. Mer Singh was a very jovial character but I cannot recall any of the other members of that squadron as individuals.

The air officer commanding at Bombay was Air Commodore Vincent, with the same name as the AOC of 221 Group. An AOC's inspection was held at Kalyan of both 20 Squadron and 6 IAF Squadron. The aircraft and personnel were lined up on the runway for scrutiny, and although it was the only parade we had until the end of the war, the airmen grumbled about it for a long time, saying we would not win the war that way!

On a visit to group headquarters I spotted the pleasant Squadron Leader Friend, who had been with the senior personnel staff officer at Delhi, and was now working as the group personnel staff officer. He looked careworn and his face had lost its smile, while he had gained promotion to wing commander.

For several weeks I had troublesome diarrhoea, and our medical officer Flight Lieutenant Godber arranged for me to be admitted to the military hospital at Bombay for investigation and treatment. Like most cases, no pathogenic organisms were found and the diarrhoea settled down quickly in hospital.

We used to have a substantial lunch at Kalyan and this was followed by a four-course meal at night. This was more food than I wanted, and I developed the habit of going for a walk in the evenings while the rest of the officers were having dinner. On one of these walks I noticed a large tree snake about 8 feet long, and although I understood that they were not poisonous, I was relieved that it was some 20 feet away.

In the mess we had a handsomely bound book with a gold rule across its front cover. This was the 'Line' book, in which was recorded exaggerations made by the pilots, intentional or otherwise. I did not see it again after we left Bombay, and perhaps it was put into storage with the squadron silver.

With Peter Joel's backing, I was able to organise several things at Kalyan. First of all there was the squadron dance. This was held in the Cowasji Jehangir Hall in Bombay, a large building in the centre of the city. Females were scarce in the extreme. I contacted various organisations such as hospitals, women's army units and so on, and managed to produce enough partners for the occasion. Other items to conjure up were booze, food and transport to get the squadron personnel into Bombay and back again. It all went smoothly and was a success.

Another venture was the squadron magazine. There were three issues of this over the next eighteen months. I think Les Hill edited the first number, and Jack Romanes the second, some six months later when we were on the Arakan front. The third and final issue came out while we were at Madras. The magazine was called *The Approach* and had a picture of a Hurricane on the front cover, turning in on its final approach to land.

We decided to start a camp cinema at Kalyan. This involved finding a contractor in Bombay who was prepared to run film shows for us, and discussions with the building contractor on the aerodrome to put up the venue for us. The contractor was a Sikh, similar to Mer Singh, with a plump, burly figure and a jovial laugh masking a shrewd calculating mind. The cinema was erected and I still hold the first ticket sold when it was opened. The building was also used for concerts. Two or three were held, with performers drawn from members of the squadron. Certain turns were popular and tended to be repeated – for example, a corporal called Jock Addie sang a song, 'I Saw a Lady Passing By', the sentiment being that although he never saw her again: 'Change the world and change the sky, yet I'll love her till I die!' This went down very well and was repeated at subsequent concerts. I believe it is a very old song dating back to the sixteenth century. After leaving Kalyan the squadron did not produce any more concerts, but did take part in one that was produced by the wing HQ that we were under eighteen months later. Otherwise we used to get an ENSA (Entertainments National Service Association) concert about every two months and one or two film shows a year. Percentage payments from the cinema contractor and the NAAFI contractor went to the PSI fund.

A number of donkeys were kept near the camp by the villagers, and we grew accustomed to their braying. We noticed that their nostrils were slit open and thought that this custom might be to prevent some condition where the nostrils could become obstructed. I remember having a discussion about the noise made by crickets, who started tuning up in the late afternoon and went on incessantly. Some maintained that you could not hear them after you had been out in India for several years. Certainly one adapted to them and was unconscious of the sound unless one thought about it.

In September 1943, we received a message commemorating the anniversary of the Battle of Britain, which was to be read out at the church service on the appropriate day. We had no padre and Peter Joel was not prepared to take this on, so he delegated the duty to me, and I read the message out to a skeleton representative gathering of the squadron!

Trips to Bombay were made in a variety of transport. Part of the jour-

ney was along the Poona trunk road, which was wide enough for two lines
of traffic, but was disconcerting in that the camber of the road dropped
steeply away, so that it was vital not to leave the central part. On one occasion I was driving a station wagon with a load of pilots on board when a
rear tyre burst. I brought the large machine to rest without much difficulty, but instead of appreciation, I was blamed by the pilots for going too
fast and causing the blow-out! On another occasion I had taken Les Hill
and Jimmy Farquharson into Bombay in a 15cwt truck. Throughout the
journey I had been criticised, especially by Jimmy who did not even hold
an RAF driving licence. In the end, a few miles from home on the return
journey, I handed over the wheel to Les Hill, who managed to overturn
the truck just outside the camp. Jimmy sustained a cut lip, which did not
stop me from laughing my head off!

Another time, while in Bombay, I was standing in one of its main centres, waiting for transport back to Kalyan, when I felt a pricking sensation
in my legs. Looking down, I saw that a number of flies had settled on my
stockings (a long sock worn by men) and were having a nibble at my skin
through them. I suppose they must have been an unusual and unpleasant
variety of fly.

Several times in Bombay I saw a man with an enormous swelling of his
scrotum at least the size of a football. He supported the swelling with a
sling wrapped round his shoulders.

Between Bombay and Poona, the mountainous mass known as the Ghats
caused more than one fatal crash on the squadron during our stay at
Kalyan. Carmichael was one victim. He had flown with me in the latter
part of 1942 on the Arakan front, and had been commissioned at Charra.
He was a quiet man who had lived out in India before the war. At the time
of his death, he was our mess secretary and was unobtrusively a useful
officer. His personal effects were auctioned among ourselves and I bought
his forage cap. It was the only time during the war that I was able to get a
forage cap to fit me. Goodness knows where he managed to find it. I had
not realised that he had the same problem as myself, of needing a size 7½!

Another pilot was McIntaggart, a good Canadian NCO, who was flying
in formation with Peter McMillan when he was killed. Peter had three
aircraft with him, one on either side and McIntaggart in the box, behind
and below him. Flying towards Poona in cloud, McIntaggart did not allow
enough height to clear the Ghats, so that he hit the top of the mountains.

Les Hill and Trevor Stone were flying along the coast one day when they were joined by Evers Swindell. They were flying low and Evers Swindell crashed his aircraft nose first into shallow water, burying the front of his aircraft in the sandy seabed, with only the tail showing above the water.

In November, we took part in a combined ops exercise (the 'in' thing) at Kolhāpur, about 150 miles away on the south side of Bombay. It was of interest to me in that my father had been persuaded (unwisely) to invest some money in Kolhāpur just before the war. We had a rough but serviceable landing strip, and some tents to sleep in, but not much else. We found monkey nuts growing in the earth at our camp site.

One afternoon, Blackman and I arranged to go up together for a practice dogfight. Peter Joel had told me that Blackman was very good and had got on Joel's tail at the very beginning of a dogfight and there was nothing Peter could do to shake him off. We arranged to fly side by side, with set throttle and revs, turn away from each other at a given signal, continue to fly away from each other for 10 seconds and then turn and start the dogfight. My own favourite ploy was to pull my nose up, gaining height and losing speed so that I could veer round in a smaller circle. I did this now but Blackman went into a steep turn, probably winding back the tail trim to tighten his arc. His aircraft was round surprisingly quickly, but at a lower level than mine. Nevertheless, he still had his speed, while mine had dropped off considerably. As he came towards me, he was able to get in a deflection shot, which might well have won the encounter if it had been in earnest. As he went below me, I rolled over in a stall turn and this time I was able to get him in my sights. After a few moments I realised that Blackman was too low and I broke off the engagement and flew off, intending to waggle my wings as a signal that the dogfight was over, so that he could rejoin me. Before I did so, something made me swing round to see what he was doing. Blackman was well below me with the nose of his aircraft pointed up in my direction and, as I looked, I was horrified to see him go into a flat spin, correct it, only to go into a spin in the other direction. The aircraft crashed into the ground and broke up. Blackman was killed outright and we buried him the next day at Kolhāpur. He was a great loss to the squadron, being both a very good pilot, and fearless. I have often blamed myself for my part in the tragedy.

Although our role was low-level flying, we decided we should all have experience of taking the Hurricane up on a height test. The climb to the Hurricane's ceiling in the hot rarified air of Bombay took some time and the exercise was spread over two or three days to enable all the pilots to take part. Normally we did not go above 6,000 feet, and then only on long flights. Kite birds of prey were circling in thermals at 12,000 feet and the earth took on a faraway look when I had climbed to over 20,000 feet. By that time I was using oxygen and the cockpit felt cold – very different from the insulated conditions in a modern airliner. I did not have to use oxygen again until immediately after the war.

For a few weeks at Kalyan, we had a supernumerary flight lieutenant posted to the squadron and attached to my flight. Just arrived from England, James Lacey – known as 'Ginger' – had rather watery blue eyes and a wispy orangy moustache in a plain but pleasant face. He had a DFM and was one of the top-scoring pilots in the Battle of Britain, with a claim of twenty-seven aircraft destroyed as far as I remember. He had brought down a German bomber at Victoria station, which had been trying to bomb Buckingham Palace, although this feat did not receive any recognition in itself, and in fact the DFM seemed a very meagre award for an ace fighter pilot. One could not help wondering whether there was more to the story. Two years later Ginger Lacey and I were squadron commanders under Group Captain Finlay in 909 Wing. Finlay had been Ginger's number one in the Battle of Britain and always called him James, which nobody else did. Ginger was acidly disparaging of Group Captain Finlay, although he never told me why and I never asked him. His expertise was very different from ours and he was posted elsewhere after a few weeks.

In October I took my second lot of leave since arriving in India, choosing to spend a couple of weeks at Ootacamund. I travelled by train from Bombay, finding some other officers onboard who were also going on leave. During the night on the train a spider bit me on the forearm, raising a wheal and blister about 2 inches long, which I was told was called a 'spider lick'. I arrived in Madras at about 10am and found that I had to take a train in the afternoon to Coimbatore, and then another from there to Ootacamund. I learned that there was a swimming pool at the club in Madras and I took a taxi there. I remember the overcast, still October day, with the club empty apart from a solitary bearer, as I had my swim. The train reached Coimbatore in the evening and a meal was served in the station. Restaurant cars did not exist in India. A small boy was lying on the ground outside the dining room with a rope tied to his big toe. He raised his leg up and down, so that the rope – which entered the building just below the eaves –

moved a large fan suspended from the ceiling inside the dining room. He was known as the punkah-wallah. The final stage of the journey was up a steep incline to Ootacamund, which was some 6,000 feet above sea level. The train and rails had a system of ratchets to prevent it from running downhill out of control. At the station were gharries to take us to our destinations. I had arranged to stay at Primrose Cottage. This belonged to a rajah who had lent it as a holiday home for officers. It was very English, with a pleasant garden and tennis court. Wood fires were burning, as the temperatures at that altitude were more like England than India.

A motherly middle-aged Englishwoman was in charge of Primrose Cottage and it proved to be very comfortable. Women were very scarce in India, and soon after we arrived we were visited by a group of young women, who were up in the hills while their husbands worked down on the plains or were away in the services. They were not particularly attractive, but they had rarity value. Each of them selected a partner for a dance that was to be held at the Ooty Club that night. Later in the war even these ladies were not to be seen, as more and more men arrived in the Far Eastern theatre of war. The Ooty Club attracted many of those on leave. There was a pleasant golf course in front of the club. The Indian caddies, who were bare-footed, would walk ahead and sometimes pick up the ball between their toes and carry it some distance before putting it down nearer the hole! Dances were held in the clubhouse, which had a repellent hyena, stuffed but menacing, in one of the rooms.

In Ooty I met a couple who had known my father in London. They had lived in India before the war, and they planned to retire to Australia shortly. Meanwhile, the husband moved down to the plains, leaving his wife up in the hills for a while longer. I had tea with her and she suggested that I should come back in the evening and try her husband's Scotch whisky. She was about forty years of age. I said that I would like to do so, and naïvely asked a naval officer who was on leave at Primrose Cottage to come along for the drink. The lady was annoyed to find two of us on her doorstep, and I realised afterwards that her invitation had had an ulterior motive! She sent us away crossly, without any of her husband's Scotch.

I continued my habit of walking and returned to Kalyan feeling very fit. At Bombay I rang up and asked for transport to collect me. As we approached the camp, there was a horrible smell of putrefaction and in the dusk I could make out the shape of a 15cwt lorry parked about 50 yards from the road, outside the perimeter of the camp. The driver explained to me that a pilot had crashed into the Ghats while I was on leave and they had not found his body immediately. By the time they discovered him, he was covered with a seething mass of maggots, so they had left his body outside the camp to be buried the next day.

Roger Cobley had joined the squadron at Charra and was the next senior officer to myself in B Flight, but my first memories of him are at Kalyan, where he was in the habit of entertaining people in his 'basha' to a cup of afternoon tea, a cultivated English habit that aroused some friendly amusement among the colonials.

At the end of November 1943 the squadron started to move back into Burma.

Chapter 8

Nidania (code name 'George') – 5 December 1943–25 February 1944

We left Kalyan in pairs on 30 November 1943 as our aircraft became available. We were going to fly in a series of hops across India. Our first stop was Aurangabad, where there was a small airfield owned by the local rajah. There was no bowser and the plane had to be refuelled with 4-gallon tins and a funnel with a chamois leather as a filter to prevent water getting into the petrol tanks. Our arrival in pairs prevented too big a pile-up of pilots waiting to refuel and eventually we made our way to the rajah's palace where we had been invited to lunch. We were served curry at a long table, which easily seated the sixteen pilots who made up the air party. However, our appetites had been underestimated and as the dish was passed down the table, it was clear that the supply would not last before we had all been served. Jimmy Farquharson had his leg pulled as the curry ran out soon after he had taken his helping, and it was suggested that he had caused the shortage. We did not see the rajah but felt indebted to him for the pleasant lunch. From Aurangabad we flew on to Nagpur, where we stopped the night. Our first stage the next day was Raipur and then on to a place called Jharsuguda. There was a small airfield on the other side of the town, which I noticed first and alighted there. There was only just enough room for the Hurricane, but I soon realised that none of the others were landing and, taking off again, I saw the proper aerodrome with the other Hurricanes on it. I had made this mistake once before and was to make it once again, with a serious result. When I finally touched down, Peter Joel was annoyed with me, thinking I had deliberately landed at the wrong airfield, and I felt irritated because it had been an accident.

Our final leg for the day was to Kharagpur, where Jimmy Farquharson's plane developed engine trouble during the landing. I don't think he was injured but he was left behind until his plane was repaired.

Peter Joel wanted me to go on with him in advance of the rest of the squadron, so the next day we flew to Dum Dum, one of the aerodromes at Calcutta, and then on to Chittagong, where group headquarters was located. We spent the night at Chittagong and I saw several people in the group mess whom I had met on my previous stay. There was Wing Commander Paul, a solidly built ginger-haired man with a moustache who was an armament officer with pilot's brevet; Lulu Penney, whose twenty-first birthday I had celebrated at Tezpur; and a medical officer whose name I cannot remember, who had a vigorous wrestling match with another officer in the bar after dinner. There was an officer called Wing Commander Hallett – a fluent speaker with a cheerful manner – who appeared to be joking about various non-public funds that he was in charge of. He told me that he had found one that was lying unused, which he had transferred to his own bank account and laughed uproariously at his own story. There was evidently some truth in his remarks as we read in the newspaper a few months later, that he had been arrested for fraud. He had been selling stretches of land in Burma to Indian businessmen, and forging Mountbatten's signature among other things, to make the documents of the sale more convincing. He was flown back to England and I never saw him again.

The next day we flew down to Nidania (or 'George', its code name) for the first time, returning to Chittagong for the night. John Penman was at Ramu, near Nidania. Penman had been sent on as the advance party and had holed up with the men of one of the fighter squadrons, many of whom I had known during my stay on the Arakan the previous year. Penman was surprised to find that I was well known, as Squadron Leader Bletcher's treatment of myself and Peter Joel had been very deprecatory. Joel and I went on to Nidania, where the camp was being finished. An army lieutenant called Don Lowe was in charge of the development of it. He had a party of West African soldiers and local Indian labour. To pay these, he had a large store of silver rupees, which Wing Commander Hallett would have been glad to get his hands on. Don was a friendly chap, quite happy to be left on his own building the airstrip, but friendly and hospitable to Joel and me, sharing his food with us, and his tent until we had sleeping accommodation of our own. On our first night in one of the completed huts, Peter Joel was worried as he had heard a rumour that the Japanese were sailing up the coast and were planning a surprise attack on our camp during the hours of darkness. I did not pay much attention to this, and in fact nothing materialised. One evening in Don Lowe's tent I was bitten on the ankle by a mosquito and it caused more of a reaction than usual. The West African soldiers certainly were a reservoir for the malarial parasite, and it was probably about this time that I got infected too.

One of Don Lowe's problems was a young elephant that would wander on to the site, lean up against one of the bamboo huts and cause it to collapse. However, he managed to complete the camp and the squadron moved in during the second week of December. The site at 'George' was a very pleasant one, alongside a sandy beach with good swimming. In addition we were there at the best time of the year, the days being warm and sunny but not too hot, while the nights were cool. Further inland was the jungle. Sandy paths partially covered with grass led from the mess to our bedrooms. These were in bamboo huts, with four rooms to a hut. Each room had a bamboo worktop to serve as a table. I had brought with me a mirror from a previous station, which Dataya fixed to the wall of my lodging. The rest of the furniture was our own camp beds, camp chairs etc. There was no life outside the camp, and our evenings were mainly taken up with bridge playing, of which the adjutant, Snow, was the expert at that stage, although the rest of us became quite good as time went on.

A few paces away from the mess on some raised ground were the officers' latrines. These consisted of a deep ditch, over which was placed a wooden frame with circular holes cut out at regular intervals. The holes had wooden covers hinged with webbing, with the timber superstructure made to the height of a lavatory seat. The whole contraption was screened by canvas up to shoulder level so that, standing up, one could admire the scenery. Unfortunately, in a short time these facilities proved to be a favourable breeding ground for bluebottles, and there was a multi-engined drone from these as one approached the bogs. When the lid was opened, bluebottles would fly out and buttocks plugging a hole in the superstructure would be tickled by the bluebottles. The answer to this was to pour petrol into the latrine, which killed the bluebottles. For a time this worked well, until some thoughtless individual dropped his cigarette into one of the holes and was blown off his seat by the explosion. An immediate order came down from a top-level officer forbidding the use of petrol. This was a problem affecting the whole command and not just 20 Squadron. The next solution was to use oil and this fortunately coped with the dilemma. For toilet paper we had to rely on newspaper. Luckily the newsprint did not come off so easily in those days!

Between the mess and the flights was a specimen of *Mimosa pudica* or the 'sensitive plant', which folded its leaves up when touched, and was worked overtime until we had got used to it. A consignment of 200 hens arrived for our Christmas dinner. They had to be delivered alive as food did not store for long in that climate. There was a deserted house on stilts adjoining the camp, where Peter decided to keep the hens. Each evening I helped him round up the hens and tuck them up safely inside the house, out of reach of marauding wild animals. It was a relief when Christmas Day arrived and we handed them over to the cooks for the Herculean task of killing, plucking and preparing them. There was a scare when an iguana was sighted in the vicinity of the hens, and we actually caught one at our next station stalking our chickens, which we had started to keep for egg production.

One afternoon, soon after Christmas, I was lying on the beach after a swim when I started to feel ill. I got up and walked back to my room in the bamboo hut. By the time I reached there, I was glad to lie down on my bed. Very soon I began to feel cold but strangely felt too weak to get up to look for a blanket. There was nobody about and I just had to lie there feeling cold. I was now shivering and wishing bitterly that I had a blanket for warmth. Some minutes later my feet started to feel hot! As I lay there, I could feel the warmth creeping up from my feet in a steady tide and with such precision that I could at any one time have marked out the border, below which I was warm and above which I was cold! I realised that the unpleasant, cold feeling would soon be gone. Doc Godber passed by my room at that moment, and I called to him. He placed a blanket over me, but by this time I had a high fever. The next day I felt a lot better, but a couple of days later, the same thing happened again, although in not such a clear-cut and dramatic way. Doc Godber treated me for malaria, after taking me to a mobile pathology lab, where the malaria parasite was demonstrated in my blood on a microscope slide. In this attack I was off work a fortnight, and took the opportunity to grow a beard, which was strictly against regulations. When I refused to take it off, Peter Joel told me I was grounded until I removed it, and this threat succeeded! Doug Stilliard received a DFC at that period for operations at Imphal early in 1943. He came to my room and borrowed my battledress with the DFC ribbon on it as I was confined to bed at the time.

Peter Joel had made contact with the headman of the village at Nidania, who had presented him with a baby female monkey. Peter brought this into the mess and gave it to me to hold on my lap, with the predictable result! John Penman christened it Firkin, a name he had already given to a pie-dog – a half-wild mongrel – that he had left behind at Kalyan, and the name stuck. Firkin remained with the squadron throughout the next two years, mainly in the care of the officers' mess cook, who adopted her.

Jack Romanes, our intelligence officer, used to make a report to group each evening by telephone. The line was very bad and Jack had to shout at the top of his voice to make himself heard. He used the phone in the mess, and as one approached, 'ROMANES – GEORGE' would be heard, shouted repeatedly as Jack tried to contact his opposite number at group. Jack had had an unusually unfortunate experience of flying, having been involved as a passenger in two bad crashes in succession, where he had been almost the sole survivor. As a consequence of this, he had developed a phobia for flying. However, I persuaded him to come up with me in the Harvard on one occasion, when I was careful to do only the most gentle of manoeuvres.

One airman on the squadron move hanged himself. I was in charge of the Court of Inquiry, and it is clear in retrospect that he was suffering from depression. There were no casualties due to swimming, one of our favourite pastimes, but one airman named L.A.C. Dedman was rescued by others when he was nearly drowned. He admitted he had got to the stage where he felt it was quite a peaceful way to die.

The flights shared a long bamboo hut, with their work spaces at opposite ends. The coast ran north–south at 'George', with the flight offices at the north end of the strip, between that and the sea. It was only a few steps from the flight areas to the water. We did not worry about towels, as we dried off fast enough in that climate, and we were accustomed to strip off and swim naked. At that time I was flight commander of B Flight. The NCO in charge of B Flight was Flight Sergeant Hepworth, a small lugubrious individual in a bush hat, with a Geordie accent and a Ronald Colman moustache, who had been on 617 Squadron and who liked to reminisce nostalgically about the crew members. He ran the flight very satisfactorily and I appreciated him. On one occasion we had a bad Hurricane on the flight, which none of the pilots liked to fly. Flight Sergeant Hepworth asked me to take it up and air test it. I can remember it was late afternoon, pleasantly cool and calm, with a game of football going on at the north end of the strip. The Hurricane certainly was heavy on the controls and

tended to wallow in aerobatics. There was always some individual vari-
ation within a squadron of the same aircraft, and occasionally one got a
machine that was noticeably better or worse than the others. This one was
worse, but it was lost on operations a short time afterwards.

We had started to fly in pairs while at Kalyan. My number two was
an Australian sergeant called Roy Bennell. He was a beefy blond-haired
chap who was tough and dependable. He walked with dainty, carefully
picked steps, which was an incongruous feature in relation to his build
and appearance. When he and Anderson, a Canadian pilot, were in Chittagong, they passed an army officer without saluting him. They told me
that their attention had been diverted elsewhere. The officer called them
back and said: 'Aren't we saluting today?' Bennell's imitation of the English
army officer saying this, executed in a mincing manner, was very funny.
Other pairs were Jimmy Farquharson and Sergeant Nutt, John Penman
and Sandy McPhail, and Les Hill and Trevor Stone. Each flight had eight
aircraft, but more pilots than planes, so I shared a Hurricane with Les Hill,
namely HW858.

At the front line, there was still a marked contrast between the two
sides. On the British front, there was obvious movement of troops and
equipment, with clouds of dust that could be seen for miles. On the Japanese side, there was apparently deserted countryside with empty villages
and no sign of life. Our equipment and numbers must have completely
outweighed the Japs, who nevertheless were holding their own against us.
They were capable of living off the land, while we could not. The Americans, who were only present in that theatre in small numbers, required
considerably more supplies per man than the British and were that much
less self-supporting. There had not been much change on the Arakan
front since the Japanese had positioned themselves on the Maungdaw–
Buthidaung line in 1942. They would eventually be displaced by sheer
force of numbers from these two small towns, and then reply by cutting
the lines of communication between them and behind them. Early in 1944
they surrounded a British Army unit in these hills in an area that became
known as the 'Box' and for a time the situation was critical, but eventually the siege was broken. I think the advance divisional headquarters was
inside the 'Box'.

Soon after we arrived at 'George', two of our pilots failed to return from
a sortie. They were Thompson, the tall, saturnine Australian and Sergeant
Pirani, another Australian. They had apparently flown close to the Jap-

anese aerodrome at Akyab island, which was well defended with heavy and light ack-ack, and both had been brought down. We never heard details and they were not recovered from POW camps after the war. Some weeks later I saw a crashed Hurricane on the mainland, south of Akyab island, which could have belonged to one of them. They had gone off in the afternoon and were expected back in under two hours. The Hurricane could stay up for nearly three hours before running out of petrol and as this time approached and was passed, it became obvious that they were not coming back. They were our first casualties of this tour.

Sandy McPhail, flying number two to John Penman, was engaged in attacking river craft, and followed through too closely so that the windscreen of his cockpit was damaged by mud and debris thrown up by the shells. I put up a notice in the flight office, urging pilots to retain their sangfroid during operations. This prompted Les Hill to put up another notice, saying: 'How is your sangfroid today?'

A mile or two down the coast from us was Elephant Point, where there was a leave camp run by the Toc H society. The chap in charge was called Tatum. He had lived in Calcutta before the war and still had a home there. His helper was a striking-looking old man, with a long face and silver hair, called Cervantes. He had been prime minister to the Queen of the Tonga islands before the war. Tatum gave me an excellent dinner at Elephant Point. When his wife paid him a visit, he borrowed my mirror for her, so mirrors must have been in short supply in that area.

On 11 February 1944 I took up a Hurricane for an engine test, which it did not pass, for the engine cut just as I was airborne. Luckily there was enough space left to land on. These episodes were fortunately rare. I experienced engine failure three times during the war, but without any damage. On two of the occasions the engine picked up again, while on the third occasion I was able to glide back to the airfield and land safely without the benefit of an engine.

It was 20 February when Warrant Officer Thompson and I took off on a dawn attack of a Japanese camp east of the Mayu river, not far north of Akyab. Thompson's aircraft was hit in the coolant system and it started to leave a trail of white smoke behind him as it lost height. He was able to cross the river back to the Mayu peninsula but was obviously not going to get over the line of hills that ran from north to south, dividing the peninsula in two. I watched from above as Thompson's plane descended and finally crashed, with its undercarriage up into some paddy fields midway between the river and the mountains, but saw the pilot climb out of his machine. The country was open and suitable for a landing by a small aircraft. I looked around the cockpit for a message bag or some other way of communicating with Thompson. Unfortunately our R/T had not been working, which was not uncommon before the arrival of VHF. I intended to tell him that I hoped to get a small plane for him, but in the end I flew off, hoping that he would still be around when rescue arrived. Thompson and Hill were the two most experienced of the NCO pilots. Thompson was a quiet, likeable man who came from Nairobi where he had worked on a coffee plantation. He was dark-haired with a moustache.

I got back to 'George' and into the crewroom, where Jack Romanes was waiting to debrief us. I told him what had happened and that the site where Tom had crash-landed was suitable for a small aircraft to land and pick him up. CO Peter Joel was called and when he appeared, I told him the set-up. 'Would you be willing to go?' He asked me. 'Yes,' I replied without hesitation. I was glad to go. The army were using L5s, small high-winged monoplanes for spotting for the artillery. One of these would have been acceptable for the task. But, instead, I was informed there was a Tiger Moth kept at 'Hay', a strip a few miles inland. I took a Hurricane and while I was on my way, arrangements were made to alert them to have the Tiger Moth ready. Luckily the pilot who met me at Hay was Flying Officer Ward who had been with me on 231 Squadron in the UK. I was still in my battle-dress tunic as we had taken off before dawn, and this was just as well for the open cockpit of the Tiger Moth. I flew the Tiger to 'George', refuelled, and then took off in an attempt to rescue Tom.

I decided to fly along the coast until I was opposite the point at which Tom had come down, and then turn eastwards over the Mayu range of hills to Foul Point, where the aircraft had crashed. It felt strange to be flying a Tiger Moth into enemy territory, but it was quite an adventure and seemed very worthwhile. On my way southwards, John Penman in a Hurricane caught me up and flew across in front of me with the message, 'Turn back', written on the side of his machine, which I of course ignored. I learned afterwards that group had sent a squadron of fighters to provide cover over the area, but they were so high up that I did not see them. I kept near to ground level throughout the flight, as my best form of protection. When I reached the scene of the crash, the plane itself was burned out, presumably by Tom, as it had not been alight when I had seen it previously, although the engine would have been hotter than normal. There were a couple of Burmese crouching down by the bund of a paddy field, but there was no sign of Tom. I circled around for some time, looking for him and surveying the ground for a suitable landing spot. I had not ascertained the endurance of a Tiger Moth before taking off and, as there was no sign of Tom, I eventually felt I could not risk prolonging the flight any further, so I started back to base. There was a small crowd waiting for the Tiger Moth at 'George', together with the ambulance and the medical section. It was all very disappointing not to have found him and I suddenly felt near to tears as I taxied up to the end of the strip. The flight had lasted 2 hours 15 minutes, so there was probably not much petrol left.

After the war Tom wrote to me to say that he had seen me circling but by that time he had put a fair distance between himself and the crashed aircraft. He was captured by the Japs and released from Rangoon prison camp after the war.

The Japanese had a landing strip at Myohaung, and a damaged enemy bomber was stuck there for a couple of days. We received orders from group to destroy the bomber and Eddie Fockler went off with a Sergeant Sammons on this mission. The Japanese had brought up some ack-ack to defend the bomber and Sammons's Hurricane was damaged. The sortie was broken off and Sammons had to crash-land on an islet on the Mayu river, near to where Tom had come a cropper. His aircraft turned over and Ed Fockler came back to say that there was no sign of life after the accident. Peter Joel decided that the aircraft should be destroyed and Ed Fockler went back and shot it up. In fact, Sammons had escaped from the crash, swum ashore to the west bank of the river, but had then unfortunately been taken prisoner of war. He spent the rest of the hostilities with Tom. Group took a dim view of Peter's decision not to press the attack against the Japanese bomber, which was repaired and escaped from the landing strip.

A few days later I was called to squadron headquarters, where Peter showed me a signal from group to say that a new squadron was being formed and that names should be submitted for its future squadron commander. Peter told me that he had sent a reply, putting me forward as strongly recommended. I felt very grateful and thought it would be a challenging task to form a new squadron, knitting it together as a fighting unit.

One day I was carrying out a sortie at the south end of the Mayu river, with Flight Sergeant Bennell as my number two, when I saw a plane lift off from Akyab aerodrome. It was only a speck at that distance, and although I watched I could not see any others take off. I continued with the sortie and about 10 minutes later we encountered a lone Hurricane flying up the Kaladan river from the direction of Akyab. No. 6 IAF (Indian Air Force) Squadron was based at Cox's Bazar, north of us, and they were carrying out reconnaissance work in Hurricanes, but communications were such that there was no means of checking whether this was one of their aircraft. We passed at a 100-yard distance on that occasion. Subsequently, a single Hurricane appeared over our strip at 'George' two or three times, circling before departing southwards. We suspected that the Japanese had succeeded in patching up a Hurricane that had been brought down in their territory, and as we were unable to check with other units due to the poor communications, we placed a Hurricane at the end of the strip ready to take off and shadow the 'interloper' when it next appeared.

A warning came through one morning that the Japanese air force was planning a massed raid on the Arakan front. Our intelligence was spot-on. We were ordered to evacuate all aircraft from 'George' to an aerodrome well to the north, out of harm's way, which was fair enough as the Hurricane IID was not intended to be a fighter plane. Soon all the aircraft had flown off, including the squadron Harvard. I stayed on at 'George'. True to form the solitary Hurricane appeared over the deserted strip, circling several times before veering off to the south. If now in enemy hands, the aircraft's pilot possibly warned the attacking force that there was no longer a target at 'George' because we did not receive a visit from the Japanese air force, although other airfields were attacked.

A short time later I was standing on the raised ground near the officers' latrines when two fighters appeared from the north flying low down the coast. I was with someone else and we tried to identify the planes, which were unfamiliar. They looked like the newest type of Jap fighter. We had three Bofors guns guarding the strip, placed one at each end and one near the centre. It seemed an odd time to do so, but the operators were engaged in cleaning their guns. The first gun had the magazine off and a single shot up the spout, which they fired off at the leading aircraft. They missed it but knocked a bit off the tail of the second machine. It staggered and then carried on behind its leader. The second Bofors gun was stripped down and could not fire at all. The third gun had time to load and fired off several 40mm shells without hitting anything. However, the explosions were enough to finish off the second machine, which spun into the sea from a height of about 50 feet. I could not see any people, but when the aircraft ditched, a cheer went up from the camp. Later a large patch of oil could be seen on the surface of the sea.

Until that time, the battle in the air had been evenly contested between the two sides. In January 1944 the RAF were supplied with Spitfires, which were decisively better than the Japanese fighters. On this raid the enemy were brought down in large numbers, with very little loss of our own aircraft. Conway, a friend of mine on 136 Squadron, had several 'kills' that day. He later became CO of his squadron. The surviving plane of the two that had passed by 'George' continued down the coast and came to the next strip, called 'Hove', where a petrol bowser had been left out on the sand in full view. The Jap pilot put some bullets into this and sent it up in flames. Following the raid, one could see the wrecks of a number of enemy bombers in the area.

Chapter 9

Madhaibunja (code name 'Hove') – 25 February–25 May 1944

We had been at 'George' from early December 1943 to the end of February 1944, and these were delightful months in that climate. 'George', too, was a place with a natural beauty about it. Towards the close of February, the powers that be decided that 20 Squadron was to move to 'Hove', which was the code name for Madhaibunja, the next strip a few miles down the coast. The runway at 'George' had been made from a series of paddy fields joined together by knocking down the bunds or walls of mud between them. 'Hove' had a natural landing strip, a vast expanse of sandy beach stretching into the distance. This was perfect when the tide was out, but at high tide the sand was covered and no flying could be done. On the whole this caused very little difficulty; once in a while we had to touch down at an inland strip until the tide went out. The coast here again ran north–south. Dispersal for the aircraft was about 70 yards inland at the north end of the strip of beach we used for a runway. It was concealed by trees at the edge of the jungle. At the south end of the strip and 100 yards inland was the domestic site and the headquarters.

The swimming at 'Hove' was even better than at 'George'. Some of the Australian pilots were expert at surf-riding without a board and would come in on a wave with the top half of their bodies projecting forwards, giving an occasional stroke with one arm to adjust their position. With practice the rest of us became fairly proficient also.

One unpleasant feature of the swimming at 'Hove', though, was the presence of stingrays. These would lie in the shallows on the sea bed and if you were unfortunate enough to tread near it, it would lift up its tail as a defensive weapon and impale your foot. Poison in the barb would soon cause the foot to swell painfully. Several people suffered in this way, but it was not common enough to deter us from swimming. Occasionally an Indian villager would be seen fishing with a net, his method being to wade in the shallows and hurl his net at any fish that he saw.

But on the whole we were very lucky to have been at 'George' and 'Hove' with the sea and sandy beaches for our enjoyment, compared with the dusty inland strips where less fortunate squadrons were located. On the Arakan there were Thunderbolts, known as Thunderboxes, and Vultee Vengeances, both used for dive-bombing. They were large, heavy un-attractive-looking aircraft. Also of course there were the fighter squadrons.

On the beach were to be found a species of red crab, capable of moving very quickly, who had burrows in the sand, down which they dived if threatened. I was amused to see the airmen chasing these crabs, two or three trying to bar the escape routes while another was pursuing the crab. The crab always won.

There was a small stream just south of the camp where we found some tree fish, which would dive off overhanging branches of trees lining the waterway, back into the flow, as soon as they became aware of our approach.

The Pathans, who were our enrolled camp followers, brought the body of a small black bear to our mess. They had shot it with a .303 rifle. Pilot Officer Jock Wallace and I went into the jungle with rifles but were only able to find the skull of a water buffalo! We had the bear skinned and the hide hung on the wall of the mess above the bar. There was evidently more skill needed in the process than we possessed, as numerous little flies appeared in the skin and we had to throw it out.

On Sundays a small handful of officers, including myself, used to travel up to the Toc H camp at Elephant Point for a church service. Frank Pegg was one of the other officers, but we were few in number. In contrast, the whole camp turned out to see and hear the 'forces' sweetheart', singer Vera Lynn, when she visited Elephant Point! On one of these trips Doug Stilliard crashed a jeep, to Peter Joel's disgust!

The mess at 'Hove' was a very pleasant place, on slightly raised ground looking out towards the coast. The dining room was situated on one side of a level sandy clearing, while the anteroom and bar was on the other side, both buildings having their long axes running east–west. A few steps inland and then round the corner to the right were the bedrooms, again two long buildings facing each other, this time running parallel to the coast and separated by a level expanse of sandy grass. Once, there was a migratory line of large ants moving for several hours past the side of my bedroom (I was in the end room of one of the huts). Luckily their trek onwards skirted the edge of the camp and did not deviate in.

Our barman was a teetotal airman called Winnifrith, unlike some other barmen who drank away the profits in many mess bars. He stayed with the squadron for a long time and did his job well. Our chef at that time was a young Scottish pastry cook, who adopted Peter Joel's monkey, when others got fed up with it. Our rations while on the Arakan consisted of unrelieved bully beef, and it was greatly to his credit that he was able to devise a thousand and one different ways to serve this up to us, so that it was much less monotonous than it might have been.

At 'George' we had carried out offensive reconnaissance work, attacking river craft, including steamers. Rarely had we found Japanese lorries to attack. Some of the river patrols became routine and were known as the 'milk run'. We did a fair amount of close support for the army. We tried some night sorties, as the enemy moved their transport mainly at night. At first I tried flying as a pair with Farquharson. We had R/T communication between ourselves but no other aids. It was found that we lost all trace of each other as soon as we switched off our navigation lights, and so we operated singly. The night sorties were not very productive and there was a failure to find any worthwhile targets in this way. In January and February I did twenty-five operational flights and this was the average sort of number in the succeeding months.

Three days after we had moved to 'Hove', I went off with five other aircraft to attack a 100-foot boat at Minbya in the Akyab area. Oil was observed in the water after the raid, but two of our aircraft were hit, one of them being piloted by Buddy Date, a Canadian. I heard him call up his number one, Johnny Horrocks, on the R/T and ask in a distressed voice for their exact location. The tide was in at 'Hove' when we returned, and we had to land instead at 'George'.

After lunch, as Buddy Date had not arrived back, I went off to look for his aircraft and found that he had done a belly landing (without his undercarriage) on a strip at Chota Maunghnama. I touched down in my plane and found there was a splattering of blood in the empty cockpit. As I looked at the machine, two army types who were on aerodrome defence duties came up. They said they had helped the pilot out of his aircraft, and although wounded he had been anxious that they should take care of his parachute. Having ensured its safe-keeping, he had been taken off to the

Squadron Leader Andrew Millar, DSO, DFC.
(All images courtesy of Andrew Millar.)

A selection of
photographs from
Andrew Millar's
collection.

A selection of
photographs from
Andrew Millar's
collection.

Number 88865 Rank S/Ldr
(a) Name in full ANDREW PATRICK MILLAR
(b) Date of Birth 27-8-19
(c) Parent Unit
(d) Duty on which Employed G.D.

IDENTITY PASS AIR FORCES IN INDIA.

(1) This pass is not transferable and is to be produced on demand.

(2) In the event of its loss the Commanding Officer is to be notified immediately.

(3) This pass is the property of the Air Forces and is to be returned to the issuing authority when proceeding on leave or on discharge.

Signature and Left Thumb print of holder.

Witnessed   Date 4/10/43

Name MILLAR AP   Pass No. 7462

Height 6 ft 2 ins.
Colour of Hair Dark Brown
Colour of Eyes Green
Visible Distinguishing Marks Scar on little finger of right hand

AIR FORCE (I.) FORM 557-A.

Andrew Millar's identity
card from 1943.

Study of a Westand Lysander, the
'eyes of the army' (via AWM).

ပိုက်ဆွေကြီးခင်များ။

ကျွန်တော်သည် မဟာမိတ်စစ်သည်တော်
ဖြစ်ပါသည်။ ကျွန်ုပ်တော်သည် ဖြစ်စေမြည်ဆုမြည်
သားများ အို ရန်ရှရန်လာ သည့်မဟုတ်။ ကျယ်များ
ကို့ လာ ဖြစ်တမြည်ဖွ ကျက်မြန်ရှ စော်ငြံးဆွက်
ရှ် လာ ပါ အညွ အနိ ဆုံ မဟာ မိတ် စစ် တ လ်အား
ကျွန်တော် အို ပို့ပါ ကျွန်ုပ်တော် အ စ ပို့ရှ ုဆ
ဆ တ်ကျ်ရွ များရွ လာ အ နာ ပါ ဆို့မ္ဆ်။

ကဂရပိုက်လှက်ဆို့တပ်မ္ရွဖြတ်။ ကစ္ဆဖုးစတ်ရှိတ်
ပိုပဆမိဲတ်တ်ဲ့ိ ုင်းကံရ်ို ကစ္ဆမုးကတွက်တ်
လှပြ္ဆပဆ်ကွက်ဲ့ုရန်ကို့ဲ့ဆိ့ုင်းသို့မ်းိ ပို့တ်
ဝ္ုံးလ္ပ္ုဆ်ို့လ်သ်လ် ပေ်ပြက္မ်ဒ္ဂရဲ့ သ္င္ဲ့မ္ုင္က
တိတ္မ္ဖိမ္ပ္ရမ္ပ္ိတ် ကမ္ဲ့မ္ဲ့း္ဝ္သ္ဗ္ု္ိ္င္ိ အို္င္ ကရ္င္ဲ့
ရ္ လှ္တ္ပာ္သ္ုပ္ို္းသ္ဒ္ဆ္းသ္ုဇ္ဝ္ဆ္ မ္းကမ္ဆ္ို္ယ္သ္ဲ့।

ပ္ုးက္ဆ္ို္တ္ဲ့ ဆ္ က္ို္း သ္ုဗ္ဲ့ ဆ္ာ

ယမ္ဲ့ ပ္ုးဒ္ို္ဲ့ဒ္ဲ့မ္ဲ့း သ္ုပ္ိ္တ
လ္းဖ္ို္းဝ္ယ္ဝ္ဲ့ဇ္ဲ့ဏ္းဇ္ န္ဇ္ တ္ က္ဲ့ ယ္ ဝ္ဲ့ဇ္ဲ့း ယဝ္ တ လ္း
ရ္ို္တ္ ပ္ါ ဇ္ဗ္ ရ္ိ္ဲ့ မ္ဇ္ဏ္း ဆ္ ုဗ္ ဲ့ ယမ္ဲ့ဏ္ဲ့ ဆ္ု္တ္ဲ့သ္း က္ို္း
လ္ို္။ ဝ္သ္ားဆ္ုဇ္ ဒ္ို္း မ္ဇ္ဗ္ ဝ္ဇ္ လ္ာ ယ္ တ္ ကို္ တ္ဲ့ဏ္
အ္ဗ္ ပ္ဲ့ဆ္ဲ့ဇ္ ရ္ုဲ့ တ္ က္ား ဝ္သ္ား ရ္ုဇ္ ဒ္ို္း ရ္ုံ ဆ္ုဲ့ ယ္ဇ္ လ္ာ ပ္ုဇ္
အ္ို္း က္ လ္ုဲ့ ရ္ုဲ့ ဆ္ုဲ့ စ္ုဲ့ တ္ဲ့အ္ို္ လ္ာ အ္ဆ္ အ္ဆ္ဲ့ န္ုဲ့
တ္ က္ုဏ္ သ္ုက္ တ္ နဲ့ ဆ္ုဲ့ ဇ္ုလ္ာ ပ္ ရ္ိ္ဲ့ အ္ို္ဲ့ လ္ုဲ့ိ
တ္ို္ ဘ္ုဲ့း။

ဇ္ုဲ့ဆ္ လ္ုဲ့ ဆ္ဲ့ပ္ုဇ္ုဟ္ာ ဇ္ို္ ပ္ုဲ့က္ က္ လ္ုဲ့ သ္ို္တ္ က္ဲ့င္ ဇ္ုဲ့ ရ္ယ္
တ္ုဇ္ဟ္ာ ဇ္ုဲ့ဆ္ု္ ဝ္ စ္ရ္ လ္း ။ က္ ်ာ္ ပ္ို္း ဇ္ ုဇ္ လ္ုဆ္ရ္ လ္ုဆ္ ပ္ုဇ္ ကဂ္
ိ္က္သ္ လ္တ္ဲ့ ။ န္ို္မ္ဲ့ဆ္ုဲ့က္က္ ္ ်ာ္ ဇ္ ဲ့ဆ္တ္မ္ ်ာ္ နဲ့ဆ္
ဗ္ ်ူ ပ္ုဇ္ဟ္ာ ်ူ က္ုဲ့ ်ူာ သ္လ္စ္ုဲ့ ်ူ ်ူာ ်ူ ်ူ ်ူ
ရ္ဲ့ ်ူ ်ူာ ်ူ ်ူ ်ူာ ်ူ ်ူ ်ူ ်ူ ်ူ ်ူ ်ူ

Dear friend,

I am an **Allied** fighter, I did not come here to do any harm to you who are my friends, I only want to do harm to the Japanese and chase them away from your country as quickly as possible. If you will lead me to the nearest Allied Military Post, my Government will give you a good reward.

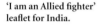
'I am an Allied fighter' leaflet for India.

RAF No. 20 Squadron pilot Andrew Millar DSO, DFC.

The aftermath of Captain Pearce shooting a snake: 'I just folded my hands in front of my undercarriage'. See page 30

Andrew Millar at Charra, 1943.

Andrew Millar and squadron
colleagues in 1943.

No. 20 squadron 1944.

Standing next to a rocket-firing Hurricane of No. 20 Squadron circa 1945 are, from left to right: Flight Lieutenant Peter L. McMillan of Inverleigh, Victoria, Australia; Flying Officer J.D. McPhail of Wanganui, NZ; Squadron Leader Andrew Patrick Millar, DSO, DFC, the commanding officer; Flight Lieutenant Ed Fockler of Vancouver, British Columbia, Canada; Flying Officer Richard W. Parr of Observatory, Johannesburg, South Africa; Flight Lieutenant John Penman of Midlothian, Scotland; Pilot Officer J. Jenkins of Narromine, New South Wales, Australia.

Servicing of a No. 20 Squadron Hurricane IID
at Nidania, code name 'George' (via AWM).

Andrew Millar at the
Heslop's home.

Andrew Millar, Chris,
Rose and Kay Heslop.

Andrew Millar bartering tins
for chickens in Burma, 1945.

From: Air Marshal Sir Keith Park,
       K.C.B.   K.B.E. M.C. D.F.C.

Headquarters
Air Command
South East Asia

24th July 1945

DO/KRP/183.

Dear Millar,

      This note is to convey my
warmest congratulations on the
award of your Distinguished Service
Order. I am delighted that your
gallant record has received this
special recognition.

      Yours sincerely,

K. R. Park

Squadron Leader A.P. Millar, DSO, DFC,
   No. 20 Squadron,
     South East Asia Air Forces.

Air Marshal Keith Park's
congratulatory note to Andrew
Millar on the award of his DSO.

Roy, Rose and Kay Heslop.

Andrew Millar's 20 Squadron colleague Peter McMillan and his rocket firing Hurricane at Monywa in March 1945 (via AWM).

Andrew Millar 'posing by the French Potez in Siam with Ron Ballard and Dai Lewis'.

SINGLE-ENGINE AIRCRAFT				MULTI-ENGINE AIRCRAFT						PASS-ENGER	INSTR/CLOUD FLYING [Incls. in col. (1) to (10)]	
DAY		NIGHT		DAY			NIGHT					
DUAL	PILOT	DUAL	PILOT	DUAL	1ST PILOT	2ND PILOT	DUAL	1ST PILOT	2ND PILOT		DUAL	PILOT
(1)	(2)	(3)	(4)	(5)	(6)	(7)	(8)	(9)	(10)	(11)	(12)	(13)

Summary of Flying.   1939 / 1945.

	1945	TOTAL on type.
Hurricane	180·25	510·45
Spitfire	36·15	39·40
Hombid	56·20	181·25
Sentinel	12·20	12·20
Proctor	8·45	8·45
Tiger Moth	1·20	79·05
Lysander	·45	564·25
Defiant	·50	·50
Oscar	1·30	1·30
Other types		61·40
	298·30	1460·25

Operations : 1945   TOTAL

	1945	TOTAL
Sorties :	89	204
Hours :	150·45	397·15

(1)	(2)	(3)	(4)	(5)	(6)	(7)	(8)	(9)	(10)	(11)	(12)	(13)

YEAR		AIRCRAFT		PILOT, OR	2ND PILOT, PUPIL	DUTY
MONTH	DATE	Type	No.	1ST PILOT	OR PASSENGER	(INCLUDING RESULTS AND REMARKS)
—	—	—	—	—	—	TOTALS BROUGHT FORWARD

Total Flying Hours.

1940	158·05
1941	290·15
1942	288·05
1943	183·10
1944	242·20
1945	298·30
Total —	1460·25

1s.
ROYAL AIR FORCE 1918–1968

GRAND TOTAL [Cols. (1) to (10)]
................Hrs................Mins.

TOTALS CARRIED FORWARD

mobile field hospital. Apart from a bullet wound – which had entered his left side below his heart, passing across to the right and grazing his liver before lodging in his right arm near the elbow – Buddy had also received an injury on landing. The hilt of a large kukri, or Gurkha's knife, worn as part of his escape gear – as many of the pilots did, in case they had to make their way back from a sortie on foot – had forced its way up under his ribs, causing a stab wound. He was faint from loss of blood when he landed and had passed out briefly while he was flying. Peter Joel lent me a jeep the next day and I went off with Doc Godber, the squadron quack, to look for Buddy Date. It was a long roundabout trip to Chota Maunghna-ma overland and from there to the field hospital where we found him, though critically ill. However, he was a strongly built young man, and eventually survived to be posted back to England and then to Canada. Eleven days after his injury, Buddy was transferred to a base hospital, and Doc Godber and I once more sallied forth, this time in a Harvard, to see him for the final time. We traced him to the city of Comilla after calling at Chittagong, Bhatpara and Lalmia. I still remember the last bit of the flight as we returned to 'Hove', swooping over the trees back to our aerodrome. Doc Godber and I had both been to Westminster School, although we were not contemporaries.

Buddy had a dog he called 'Stoopid'. It was looked after for a while by the officers, but became covered with ticks. I forget what ultimately happened to it. One day at 'George', I found a tick on my left shoulder. Various attempts were made to dislodge it, including a lighted cigar, which burned my skin. In the end I pulled it off piecemeal, but the skin healed uneventfully.

We had been at 'Hove' a week, when Peter Joel came to the mess at midday, with a signal from group announcing that I was to take over command of 20 Squadron from him. Peter was disappointed and said that he had hoped to stay with the squadron until the end of the present campaign. It looked as though group were displeased with his failure to press home the attack on the Jap bomber at Myohaung and possibly gratified at my attempt to rescue Warrant Officer Thompson. The next few days were taken up with the formalities of assuming responsibility for the squadron. Peter Joel departed for Delhi. Wing Commander Smyth, whom I had known on the Arakan the previous year, came down to celebrate my promotion and stayed overnight at 'Hove'.

Soon after, we had a 'beer issue'. Officially we were supposed to get three bottles of beer per man per month, but months would go by without any beer arriving, so that it was quite an occasion when some beer actually appeared, and it would all be drunk the same night. We lit a large bonfire outside the squadron headquarters and doled out the beer from the HQ building. There were a few bottles, over and above the official ration, which I paid for myself, giving single bottles to airmen who had been with me at Chittagong a year earlier. During the evening two of the pilots decided to have a friendly wrestle. They were George Hatch, a Canadian who was well over 6-foot tall, and Sandy McPhail, a New Zealander about 5 foot 4 inches in height. Either of them could have taken on any two other members of the squadron, and the fight aroused much interest. The fire was burning strongly and lit up the scene for us. I was aware that we made an excellent target for any night-flying enemy aircraft. Eventually Sandy McPhail managed to pin down George Hatch, but it was a memorable fight.

I found we had an official squadron flag, and arranged for it to be flown from a flagpole outside headquarters. After a month or so the flag was torn to shreds by the weather, so we salvaged what was left and gave up the idea of flying it routinely. As a squadron leader I was entitled to a flag so I had one painted on the side of my aircraft, which I shared with Les Hill, the Hurricane HW858. Les objected to the flag on the grounds that the plane would be picked out for special attention, if we became involved with Japanese aircraft. That flag was also removed!

The two flight commanders were called into my office. One was Roger Cobley, and the other may have been Eddie Fockler. I told them that a flight commander could make a bigger contribution to the war effort than an individual pilot, and that as a squadron commander I was determined to increase my own input, with the greater opportunities that I now had. Over the next two years I found that I was given considerable latitude to carry out operations as I wished.

Peter Joel had planned to recommend Les Hill, Dickie Parr and Eddie Fockler for DFCs and I assured him before he left that I would forward those names as he had intended. It also fell to my lot to write to Warrant Officer Thompson's mother. News had filtered through from 136 Special Force that Tommy had been captured and killed, although his demise was eventually found to be incorrect. His mother was a schoolteacher and her only other child, a daughter, was drowned at sea at that time. At least, so it was said, and I do not know whether that bit of information was also false. It was the first of a number of letters that I had to write to the families of dead pilots, in my capacity as squadron commander. When an aircraft was lost, I also had to sign my signature thirty or forty times in removing the aircraft from my charge. It was in this way that I developed a signature made up of my initials followed by a straight line!

The adjutant then was Flight Lieutenant Snow, who had joined the unit as adjutant when Peter became CO. Our squadron warrant officer was a man named Aitchison, an anglicised Scot. Captain Birchall was our army liaison officer, a tall, dark-haired man with a moustache, and a typical British Army officer. In spite of service rivalries he got on well with the air-crew. One of the pilots was Frank Pegg, whom I had met on leave at Ooty. I had arranged for him to join the squadron, as he was keen to do so and already knew Jimmy Farquharson. He again was a tall, dark-haired chap with a long bony face and a northern accent, who was good company.

Soon after I became CO, a Scotsman called McCullough was posted to the squadron as a flight commander. He was the protégé of the air offi-cer commanding, Air Commodore Gray. However, I wanted one of our own supernumerary flight lieutenants to take over the vacancy of flight commander, and I objected to the posting in of McCullough, although he was harmless enough in himself. He had had some squadron experi-ence before joining us, but he did not seem to me to have a lot of drive or special ability as a pilot. Consequently, when we had a visit from Air Marshal Sir Guy Garrod, accompanied by the AOC, I stuck my neck out and protested at the importation of an outside flight commander. This annoyed the AOC, but in fact we got what we asked for and McCullough was posted away again.

Instructions were sent to squadron commanders that all NCO pilots were to be reviewed each month regarding their suitability for a com-mission. Warrant Officer Les Hill was interviewed, but maintained that he would sooner be top of the NCO tree than the bottom of the officer system. However, after two or three sessions on this subject, he finally agreed to the idea of an upgrade in rank, together with Trevor Stone, who was commissioned at the same time.

We had a Pilot Officer Freeman in charge of the RAF Regiment at 'Hove', who had been unable to interest the two previous squadron com-manders in his scheme for the defence of 'Hove' from a ground attack. Thank goodness we were never put to the test in this respect, but I listened to his plans and gave him verbal encouragement. He was a tall, thin chap, going a bit sparse on top, with a moustache and whinnying laugh, but he was amiable and a pleasant addition to our mess.

George Hatch, who was a good pilot, was keen to get on to a fighter squadron, so I arranged this for him and he left us at 'Hove'. I heard later that he found life on a fighter squadron very boring, lying around at dispersal and not doing as much flying as he'd accomplished on 20 Squadron.

The lone Hurricane that had haunted us at 'George', did not make any appearances at our new location, and we never discovered for certain whether the Japs had used one of our machines or not.

When I took over 20 Squadron I had clocked up 970 flying hours on single-engined aircraft, which was a lot for those days, and I was looking forward to achieving 1,000 hours. This happened at the end of March 1944, on an operational trip.

The squadron Harvard was used for communications and to give the pilots a weekend break in Calcutta. Roger Cobley was fond of fudge, which could be bought in the Army and Navy Stores in Calcutta, and pilots were often asked to carry out small purchases such as this while they were there.

March was spent mainly in sorties devoted to attacking river craft of varying size, although at the beginning of the month I dropped a message on the divisional HQ of the West African troops who were operating in the Kaladan valley at Kyauktaw, and at the end of March I had to make an attack on two Japanese field guns positioned east of Buthidaung.

About this time, Roger Cobley and 'Chota' Hallett were attacking an enemy bomber on the ground, when Roger's aircraft was hit and he had to land in the 'box' held by the West Africans on the Kaladan river. He was flown out the next day back to the squadron by an L5.

On 26 March a raid was planned with five aircraft against a Jap base north-east of Ramree island. As the wind was blowing from the north, we had to taxi down the beach from the dispersal point to the south end for take-off. As I planned to get airborne first, I taxied out last with Jock Wallace immediately in front of me and three others ahead of him. I was doing my cockpit drill as I rolled out and as it was quite a distance to the far end of the beach, I checked out my R/T, which I usually did after taking off.

There was suddenly a loud explosion and my first thought was that we had been 'jumped' by enemy aircraft. I then realised that my 40mm cannons were firing. I feverishly checked the firing controls but could find no cause for the runaway cannons. I was thinking of the four Hurricanes in front of me in the direct line of my cannon fire, imagining a horrible fate for them! I started to swing my nose round so that the guns pointed out to sea. Wallace was in front of me and to my right. As he saw my nose swing round in his direction, he was out of his aircraft at lightning speed. It occurred to me that the R/T had been wired to the firing circuit and I hastily switched off my R/T. There was one pair of shells unfired. The drums for the 40mm cannons carried fifteen shells each, and with one already in the breech, each Hurricane could fire sixteen pairs of shells. The rate of fire was about one pair per second, so the whole episode lasted about a quarter of a minute.

It was lucky for me that I had not switched on the R/T as I became airborne, as the recoil would have stalled the Hurricane and the shells might well have caused damage. As it was, they flew over the other Hurricanes and sent up spouts of water in the sea some miles down the coast, thanks to the nose-up position of the Hurricane on the ground.

That evening I was swimming well out to sea when a jeep drove up to the water's edge and a figure got out and waved to me. It took some time to swim in again and I found the wing armament officer, Flight Lieutenant Udall, waiting to ask me what had happened. Years later we were together as medical students. The sortie as originally planned was carried out the next day, when one of the Hurricanes was hit by light ack-ack.

A Court of Inquiry failed to apportion blame to the culprit for mixing up the wiring, and it was only after the war that I was told that the electrician was deliberately shielded. He was eventually revealed to me at a squadron reunion!

On 29 March, having completed an operational trip in the morning, I flew to an inland strip at Rumkhapalong where a Spitfire squadron was stationed, and enjoyed my first solo in one of these iconic planes, doing aerobatics and low flying for an hour. From my log book, I see that I had a further trip in a Spitfire Vc on 11 April, picking it up at 'George' and later landing it at 'Hove', but I do not recall the circumstances.

One day an army officer called in, who had come to Westminster School shortly before I left. Our paths had never crossed while there, but we recognised each other. I only met him once more, and that was at a dance at the Royal Academy of Music in 1947. On this first occasion, he was sitting beside me in my jeep, as I waited to nose out on to the beach, which was not only the landing strip but also the main communicating road for the camp, connecting the flights to the domestic site. Two aircraft were coming in to land: the first touched down normally but the second failed to level out as it got near the ground, hit the surface, bounced, and finished up with its nose in the sand. It was bad enough to see one of the squadron aircraft crash, but to have a visitor with me as a witness was an additional aggravation! The pilot was Frank Pegg, and I heard later from Snow, the adjutant, that he had astigmatism and blamed the accident on this. I checked him out in the Harvard and was satisfied with his flying, but I think his log book was endorsed on account of the accident.

In April we continued our attacks on river craft, with a few night sorties and occasional targets on land such as lorries or gun positions. One time I flew with Roy Bennell as my number two, with Joe Penman leading Ashworth in the other section. Our target was Akyab. Bennell and I raided a factory, two buildings and a possible barracks in the town, and also beat up a gun post. I realised that Penman was several miles east and was diving on some deserted land well away from the town. I called him on the R/T to join us and received the coarse reply: 'Fuck you, sir.' Ashworth, of course, was quite content to follow Penman's lead and they did not join me.

I reported the incident to the OC, wing, who was a Wing Commander Elsdon. He had a word with Penman, who was a very capable talker and evidently persuaded 'Slug' Elsdon that no action needed to be taken, and so the matter was allowed to drop, very wrongly I think.

Three pilots showed signs of what was called 'lack of moral fibre' at that time. Pilot Officer Ashworth, the Canadian, would call up his leader on a sortie and make some excuse, such as shortage of petrol, for abandoning the mission and returning to base. Before we could take any action, he was posted back to Canada, and the next news we received he had been promoted to squadron leader and was lecturing pilots on operations in Burma!

Another pilot was a Flight Sergeant Davidson, who behaved similarly. When I had reports about him, I took him on a mission as my number two. Either his R/T was not working or he pretended it was unserviceable and he returned to base when we got to the target area. I can't remember what happened about him.

The third was Sergeant Nutt. He openly admitted that he could not face operations and I was asked by the 'higher ups' to submit a report, labelling him as 'LMF'. However, in his case, he had had an accident while night flying that was not his fault and a further incident subsequently, so I felt there was some excuse for his loss of nerve, and wrote the report accordingly.

As Peter Joel had wished, I submitted the citations for DFCs and also recommended Buddy Date for a commendation for flying his aircraft back safely under difficult circumstances. 'Slug' Elsdon thought that this action merited the award of a DFC so, rather against my judgement, I submitted a citation for Buddy Date also (he had already got his commendation). All the awards came through in due course, and I had a letter from Buddy written from England saying that he was very surprised to receive the DFC and had some difficulty in explaining it to his friends!

Non-public funds had to have accounts drawn up annually and passed on to the higher formations for scrutiny and comments. Our officers' mess accounts were very healthy, largely because of our excellent barman, Winnifrith, who looked after the bar stocks scrupulously. As a result we were able to supplement our food supplies out of profits from the bar and at the same time charge less for drinks than any of the other messes. However, Wing Commander Elsdon chose to criticise the mess accounts for making too much profit from the bar. I pointed out that our prices were much lower than those in the wing mess. Elsdon had been in the RAF before the war. He was an affable little man with a DFC, who had done well earlier at Rangoon, but I distrusted his judgement.

'Hove' was a very pleasant place to operate from and we had a number of visits from high-ranking officers. One was Air Marshal Baldwin, AOC-in-C of the 3rd TAF, a colourful swashbuckling character, who arrived with a fighter escort of three wing commanders, including Jimmy or 'Slug' Elsdon.

Baldwin came in for a swim with me and, while we were being buffeted by the powerful waves that gave good surf riding, told me about the enterprise at Broadway, a British airfield behind the Japanese lines. The CO of the fighter squadron at Broadway (I think it was 81 Squadron) was an outstanding chap of twenty-one (possibly Squadron Leader Constantine), who was unfortunately caught by Jap fighters while in his aircraft at the end of the strip.

About this time Doc Godber got his promotion to squadron leader and moved to a job in Calcutta. He was replaced by an inarticulate Irishman called O'Brien, who had not been appreciated at his previous station, but settled down as the squadron MO, staying with us for the rest of the war in Burma.

Peter McMillan had volunteered for the Wingate expedition and I arranged to have him back on the squadron, when he then took over A Flight.

A trip with Flight Sergeant Davidson took place on a Sunday afternoon. We set off for an offensive reconnaissance of Ramree island. Our track took us over the north-western corner of Akyab island. It was a beautiful day, with the sea like a mirror and little rocky outcrops dotted around, reminding me of the scenery I had imagined when I had read books by Henry De Vere Stacpoole, such as *The Blue Lagoon*. There were two men standing on the edge of the wide sweep of sand at that corner of the island, stripped to the waist, which was unlike the Burmese, and puffs of dust were being thrown up at their feet. I was jolted out of my Sunday afternoon reverie by the realisation that they were firing a machine gun at me, with the empty shell cases kicking up the dry sand.

I jerked the Hurricane up 100 feet in the hope of spoiling their aim and turned off to the right, out to sea. I continued on southwards with the island about 500 yards on my left. Relapsing into my daydream, and joking to myself that the Japs had been very uncivilised to behave like that on such a nice Sunday afternoon, I became aware of a splash in front of me and, looking around, I saw numerous black bursts of heavy ack-ack in the sky around me. By this time Davidson, my number two, was a small dot on my starboard side. I called him up but he did not reply. I moved further out to sea and continued on to Ramree. After I had begun to attack a supply dump at Ramree island, Davidson left me and claimed afterwards that as his R/T was not working, he felt he should return to base. I do not recall any action being taken against any of the few pilots whose performance was unsatisfactory on operations.

'Hove' was something in the nature of a holiday resort, which could account for the fact that at one time we had a journalist from *Aeroplane* magazine, one from the *Daily Mirror* and a film crew intent on making a film of the squadron all together there! Doc O'Brien found that he had very little to do, as the squadron members were in good health, so he started doing a daily surgery for the Burmese. This became popular and the villagers used to queue up at the sick quarters building. The film cameraman made shots of this, which eventually formed part of the film of our squadron life.

We were receiving variants of the Hurricane IID at that time. Some had long-range tanks inside the wings, which made the plane heavy to fly but gave a valuable increase in its range and duration. Another Hurricane arrived whose engine was completely armour-plated. The film camera-man decided to have his expensive camera fixed to the wing of this aircraft to get some pictures on an operational flight. The 40mm cannons were fired by pressing a tit like a bellpush on top of the throttle, while the two .303s were discharged by the gun button on the control column. A separate control was rigged up to work the camera.

I took the Hurricane with Jock Wallace as my number two for another assault on Ramree island. We had got a satisfactory column of black smoke rising from what was probably a fuel dump, so I turned in for a dive attack and started the camera. As I pulled out of the dive my feet slid off the rudder bars and, looking down, I saw oil spraying my feet and the floor of the cockpit. The oil pressure, which was usually around 80 lb per square inch, had dropped to 40, so I abandoned the sortie and set course for home.

It was a long haul back to 'Hove' and the land on the way was not very inviting, apart from being held by the Japanese. It consisted of swampy islands, so I headed straight back over the sea. When Akyab came into sight on our starboard side, my oil pressure had dropped to 20 but the oil and engine temperatures remained normal. I kept out to sea from Akyab, and soon noted that my oil pressure had dropped to zero, while there was now a large pool of oil on the cockpit floor. I expected the engine to start running rough at any moment. Wallace kept well out on my right, and we flew on steadily for home, reaching there safely to my surprise.

When I landed I inspected the aircraft and found no sign of bullet holes. I then castigated Flying Officer Bell, the engineer officer (unfairly as it turned out), for sending the machine off on ops in an unsatisfactory condition. When the cowlings were taken off, it appeared at first sight that three bullets had found their way into the engine, but on closer examination the damage had been caused by a single bullet entering the air intake – the only part of the engine that was not protected by armour! The camera-man was greatly relieved to get his camera back and was not willing to risk it again. The bullet had severed the connecting pipe between the oil pressure gauge and the main oil pipe.

In the preceding weeks I had had a bullet in my starboard wing, then one in my port wing and now one dead centre! In those days the odds were in favour of the pilot, at least in the Far East theatre. The anti-aircraft gunner had not only to place his missile in the right spot three-dimensionally, but also in the split second of time when the plane was there. The odds were greatly shortened if the aircraft was making a head-on attack on a gun position, as then the gunner had only to contend with two of the four dimensions.

On one of the occasions that my Hurricane was hit, I had spotted two white-shirted Japanese soldiers sprint up the base of a hill and take cover. I thought it worthwhile to spray the area with machine-gun fire. But they too had a machine gun, and on my return I found a bullet hole in my plane.

We were then using solid armour-piercing shells in the 40mm cannons, and had to rely on the .303 bullets for incendiary effects. To achieve this, the .303s were loaded with incendiary and tracer bullets. Once a lorry's fuel tank had been ruptured by a pair of cannon shells, the .303 bullets could ignite the spilt petrol.

On 10 April I was doing a recce in the Alechaung area, when I noticed a long hut covered by branches. The foliage had withered and not been replaced, so that it attracted my attention. We made dive attacks on the hut and finally set it on fire. As I circled overhead at about 2,000 feet, there was a sudden mushroom growth of smoke from the hut followed by an audible 'woomph', which shook the aircraft. It was a lucky find of an ammunition dump. Les Hill discovered another the following year in central Burma, when I joined him in the attack, and it produced a similar impressive explosion.

When we flew after dark, we put out goose-neck flares along the sand, as a flare path. On one occasion, when night flying was on, I was in a practically deserted mess talking to another officer when McPhail appeared in the doorway with some blood on his face. 'Koochnai height, sahib!' said McPhail ruefully ('No height, sir'!). He was dressed in flying kit and had crashed close to the mess. He had not climbed after taking off but had gradually lost height, finishing up in a sand dune, fortunately without hurting himself. He was extremely lucky. The soft sand had contributed to his escape. Faulty instrument flying had caused his loss of height.

In a game of football on 12 April I managed to go sailing through the air to land with my left arm beneath me as I fell on my back. I felt something crack and when I looked at my forearm, it was no longer in a straight line. It was evident that the bone in my wrist was broken and my arm felt numb and painless. I walked the short distance to the sick quarters, escorted by a couple of solicitous airmen.

Flight Lieutenant O'Brien came quickly and gave me a drink of spirits from the medical comforts stock. I lay back nicely relaxed while the MO went through the routine moves for reducing a Colles' fracture. O'Brien then thought it was necessary for me to go to the nearest mobile hospital and accompanied me there in a jeep.

The hospital was at Cox's Bazar, some miles away. The first part of the journey was along the beach, and then over rough tracks. From the outset, the feeling was returning to my arm and it was becoming very sensitive to the jolting of the jeep. I nursed the broken left wrist in my right hand, trying to cushion the movement as we bounced along. When we got to the field hospital, I was seen by a squadron leader who X-rayed my arm and announced that it needed a little more treatment. He took hold of my arm and as he manipulated it, I had an odd feeling – as when a fast lift accelerates and leaves your tummy behind. The doctor looked at me and asked if I wanted a drink. I brightened up at this, remembering the good effect of the previous drink at sick quarters. I nodded assent. The squadron leader turned to an orderly. 'Get him a drink of water,' he said. After the bone was satisfactorily aligned, he put the arm in plaster, with the wrist dorsiflexed, explaining that in this position one had a better grip. Current opinion regards this position as unfavourable for the fracture, but it gave me good use of my arm during the next few weeks.

I was left to spend the night at the hospital, but the pain stopped me from sleeping and I was given no analgesia. When I was at last dozing off, I was awakened by some drunk flying officer who had just got in, who wanted to sell me a battleship.

In the morning, I recognised some admin officers from wing HQ who were in for varicose veins and other things that did not worry young pilots. The squadron leader did a ward round in the morning and asked me how I was. I was anxious to get back to my squadron and was determined that this injury was not going to incapacitate me any longer than was necessary.

'Is it painful?' he asked. My eyes must have responded to the word, but I replied firmly, 'No.' 'Some people have guts,' he said, and I felt flattered.

I asked that 20 Squadron be contacted so that transport could be sent to collect me. I think the adjutant, Snow, elected to ignore my request. When no lift arrived I got a ride to wing HQ and was collected from there by my own squadron transport. I arrived back at 'Hove' as the officers were having a drink before dinner; Snow appeared, bathed and changed, from the ante-room and I felt tired and annoyed with him for giving me the task of making my own way back to the squadron. That night my arm was again painful, but the pain became less severe as each night went by.

The next day was a Saturday, so I decided to have a weekend in Calcutta and flew off in the squadron Harvard with Ed Fockler in the driving seat. In the city I met Basil Jones who had been with me on 231 Squadron in Ireland. He was now a squadron leader on the PRU Squadron at Dum Dum. We had a drink together at the Porta Rico with some other pilots from 20 Squadron who were in Calcutta on leave.

On the Monday morning we flew back to 'Hove' with me at the controls. On the Wednesday I took up a Hurricane for local flying practice, to test out my broken arm. 'Hove' had a long expanse of sand with no hazards for take-off or landing, so I felt it was safe to try and fly. Wing Commander Elsdon told me later that the squadron leader at the hospital had told him that I was forbidden to fly, but 'Slug' had left the decision to me.

As the Hurricane became airborne, it was necessary for the pilot to change hands on the control column, holding it momentarily with the left hand while the right hand was used to move the lever that retracted the undercarriage. My left hand could no longer do this, so I had to grasp the control column between my knees, while selecting the 'up' position for the 'undercart'. This caused some pitching but not enough to alarm me. The left arm was OK for pushing the throttle open, but pulling it closed hurt a lot. In other words, compressing the fracture was painless but traction or separation of the broken bone ends was agony.

On the Thursday I went off on an operational sortie. On my first pull out of a dive, I was holding the throttle with my left hand, as was customary. The force due to gravity in the pull out was exerted on my unsupported wrist and caused me considerable pain. On the next occasion I placed my hand and forearm on my left knee, so that the wrist was supported evenly while the centrifugal force was exerted, and I found there was no pain on the pull out.

Three days later, on the 22nd, I did another offensive recce (we pronounced the abbreviated form of reconnaissance as 'reckie').

On the 24th I flew to Imphal, where we now had a detachment. On my way from 'Hove' to Imphal, I landed at a place called Kumbhir. The single runway was carved out halfway up the side of a steep mountainous valley. It was spectacular. There was no obvious connection by land with the rest of the world as it was a very hilly area for many miles. All supplies to the base would have been brought in by air. It was a busy staging post and there were obviously no superfluous personnel kept there.

Imphal was a valley in the state of Manipur, about 2,000 feet above sea level and enveloped by mountains. It was also surrounded by Japs at that time. The valley was more or less oblong, with its long sides running north–south. At its south-eastern corner was the road to Kalewa, connecting the valley to the plain of Burma. Another road left at the south-western corner and led to Tiddim. Manipur lay to the north. The valley was flat with small hills, conically shaped, which we called pimples.

The strip at Imphal, which was originally tested by Neville Rowson in a Lysander in 1942, was liable to be shelled by a Jap field gun, located in the mountains on the east side of the valley. It had worked out the range of the airstrip, and discharged if it was used.

Other strips had been built in the valley, and one of these was at Palel in the south-eastern corner. Aircraft bays had been cut into nearby pimples, and both the ground crews and the pilots were sleeping by their machines to repel night attacks, which the Japanese were trying out.

Two or three of our aircraft had been detached to 221 Group at Imphal, as the Japs were using tanks and the Hurricanes with 20mm cannons were unable to make any impression on them. The Jap tanks would go waltzing down the Tiddim road pursued unsuccessfully by the Hurricane IICs, whose pilots would call up over the R/T for a IID. It was the job for which the IID was intended, and the 40mm armour-piercing shells penetrated the Jap armour with no difficulty.

The detachment operated from Palel, but flew out to spend the night at Lanka, north-west of the valley, to save on rations and fuel supplies there, which had all to be supplied by air.

Sergeant Robert Lee was on the detachment, and I asked him to submit his operational hours to me, so that I could consider recommending him for a DFM. On seeing them, I felt that he had not done enough to merit an award, and I think he was very disappointed when no honour materialised. He had probably assumed that it would automatically follow the submission of his operational record. Lee was commissioned soon after, while we were at Chiringa.

During our time at Palel, I flew over to Imphal and visited the AOC, Air Vice Marshal S.F. Vincent at the group headquarters. He gave me the impression of being a friendly, professional man, rather than a regular service officer. He was the only pilot to bring down a German plane in both world wars. I still had my arm in plaster, that first time I met him.

I carried out one recce to Tamu from Palel, landing at Lanka, and returned to the squadron at 'Hove' after five days in the Imphal area. I managed to do fourteen operational sorties in April, in spite of my broken arm.

May continued in much the same pattern. Hurricanes with long-range tanks enabled us to go further afield and pick up targets that had previously been thought out of range of air attack. These were mainly boats from 40- to 70-feet long.

The film of the squadron was made in May, and after the abortive attempt to film a raid on a fuel dump, we decided to do a formation take-off and landing for the cameraman. Take-offs in sections were straightforward and uneventful, but touching down was another story and something we had not practised. Les Hill acted as leader and I flew as his number two for the landing. I found I could not keep close in and stalled on the approach while still some 20 feet in the air. My wing dropped, but the plane recovered with lots of opposite rudder and made a smooth landing. The cameraman thought it was a special stunt for his benefit!

We had one film show at 'Hove', given outdoors near the beach. It was interrupted by one of the airmen's bashas (huts) going up in flames. The noise of the burning bamboo was like rifle fire and the heat was so intense that it was impossible to salvage anything from the blaze.

During the month, the squadron was presented with a Japanese officer's sword by one of the Punjabi regiments, in recognition of our support. They asked us to have it engraved with an inscription to this effect, for which they paid.

At this time we had silver badges made in the form of a spear head, with the squadron crest etched on them. The fighter squadrons started this fashion and we used to wear them pinned to our shirt pockets as a badge. They were in great demand.

The detachment at Imphal continued, with most pilots taking a turn to fly up there. An Indian pilot called Ranjan Dutt joined the squadron at 'Hove'. He was a good pilot and intelligent. After the war he became an air marshal in the Indian Air Force. His father had a flat in Calcutta and hospitality was given to the squadron pilots on leave there. One day Dutt did a 'beat-up' of a small group of us who were standing on the dunes at 'Hove', and brought his machine down so low that we were obliged to duck.

Our life had been very pleasant during the first few months of the year, first at 'George' and then at 'Hove', but the monsoon season was approaching and plans were made to transfer the squadron to a new strip that would be serviceable during the bad weather. This was at Chiringa, north of Cox's Bazar, but no longer on the coast.

Chapter 10

Chiringa – 25 May–24 July 1944

As was often the case, we were to be the first occupants of the camp. When I flew in towards the end of day, only part of the runway was completed. It was being constructed on a new principle, with a metal grid underneath a layer of bitumen, which was put down in rolls. The engineers hoped that this surface would remain serviceable during the bad weather and withstand the weight of heavy transport aircraft. We were all intrigued by the raised paths between the huts, flanked on either side by deep ditches.

Chiringa boasted some high-powered borer bugs, which sent down a steady cascade of sawdust from the bamboo poles in the ceiling to form conical piles on the floor or on the desk in my office. Over the next few days we moved the squadron into Chiringa, which lacked the attractive surroundings of our last two stations.

The first day of June produced a beautiful morning with not a cloud in the sky. I decided we would make the most of it and arranged for a flight of aircraft to carry out a strike near Akyab. Strictly speaking a Met forecast had to be obtained before a sortie, but communications were not good and I did not feel like wasting time waiting for a weather prediction when the weather was so obviously perfect.

We took off and headed south. Roger Cobley, Eddie Fockler and an Australian called Jenkins were among the pilots, but I cannot remember the others. As we flew on, I could see a few cumulus clouds forming ahead of us and as the cloud base was near the ground I decided to hop over them. I started to climb, gradually at first and then more steeply as I found that the cloud tops were piling up and increasing height more quickly than we were. Westwards, out to sea, the sky was still clear, so I turned to starboard and with the seven other Hurricanes continued to climb, hoping to go around the storm that was building up so rapidly over the land.

Within a few more minutes it was clear that we would not only have to abandon the sortie but that we were going to have difficulty in getting down safely. We reduced height to sea level in the pocket of clear sky in which we were flying. To the north the weather had clamped down and there was no chance of getting back to Chiringa. We flew round a storm at sea and then headed towards the coast. We found ourselves near 'Hove' with a curtain of black cloud down to sea level enclosing us in a clear area about a mile across. I switched on my R/T and carefully made my voice sound relaxed so as not to cause any panic among the others. 'Puffball' was our call sign. 'Hello, Puffball formation,' I called. 'Puffball leader calling. I am going to fly north through the cloud, to see what conditions are like further up the coast. Wait here until I let you know.'

I entered cloud at a low height. My climb and descent instrument showed that I was losing height and I pulled back on the control column, just as breaking waves became visible beneath the edge of my mainplane. After that I concentrated hard on keeping the machine straight and level and was relieved to come out from the storm into some relatively clear weather around Cox's Bazar. Quickly I called up the others and told them the situation and then went in to land with a feeling of great relief.

The others came in one by one. The clear patch had already disappeared before the last plane was down. This was flown by Jenkins the Australian, who had recently joined the squadron and was not experienced. However, he brought his aircraft in very steadily in the heavy rain and made a safe landing. Not all the aircraft had arrived. Roger Cobley's Hurricane was missing. We discovered later that he had made a precautionary landing on the sand with his undercarriage up, near 'Hove'. Later, Wing Commander Chater, whose wing we were in at Chiringa, wanted me to bounce Roger for writing off a Hurricane, but there seemed to be ample justification for his action and I refused.

When I landed at Cox's Bazar, the AOC's de Havilland Rapide was picketed down by the runway and the AOC was standing nearby. My heart sank as I was well aware that I had not asked for a route forecast before the sortie, but as I approached him, his first words were to criticise the Met Office who had told him that the weather was going to be perfect, so that he too had been lucky to make it to Cox's Bazar.

With the arrival of the monsoons, the deep ditches at Chiringa filled to the brim overnight. In that rain, ordinary mackintoshes were useless and monsoon capes, which were an issue for the airmen, were the only garments that could keep the wearer dry.

On 6 June I set off on leave for Ooty, flying the squadron Harvard to Dum Dum with Farquharson in the rear cockpit so that he could take it back to Chiringa. I was carrying the Jap sword that had been presented to the squadron by the Punjabi army, intending to leave it at a jeweller's in Calcutta to be engraved. We were met by ground crew at Dum Dum with the news that the second front in Europe had begun, which was a good start to my leave.

We stopped the night at the aircrew hostel in Calcutta, a new venture due to the lack of space in the overcrowded hotels. Later its use was restricted to flight looies and below. We contacted Doc Godber, who came round to see us. He was with another senior medical officer who was obviously anxious to be off elsewhere. I could see that Doc Godber was torn between past loyalties to the squadron and his arrangements for that evening and so I urged him to be off with his friend.

From Dum Dum I hitch-hiked in a Douglas Commando down to Madras via Cuttack and Vizagapatam. At Vizagapatam the weather was bad and the pilot got into cloud on the circuit. We came out of it almost in a stalled position but luckily the pilot recovered and the rest of the trip was uneventful. There was no seating at that time and we just sat on the floor or on baggage with our backs to the sides of the aircraft. I still remember having breakfast at a cafe near the aerodrome at St Thomas's Mount, Madras, before completing the journey to Ooty by train.

At Ooty, I stayed once again at Primrose Cottage and had pre-lunch drinks at the club. At a party I made some critical remarks about the army to an army captain with an MC. He was with the West Africans and had won his decoration in the Kaladan valley. He reacted very abusively and insisted on exchanging blows. I thought over his remarks for a day or two and decided I could not refuse his challenge in view of his insults. I came to the conclusion regretfully, feeling that we should be reserving all our energies to fight the war. I discovered later that he was an aggressive character who became involved in other brawls.

We met behind the Ooty clubhouse. I had an Australian navigator and he an army major as seconds and for a while we slugged away at each other. I had had the plaster of Paris removed from my arm shortly before going on leave. Without its plaster support, at first it had felt as though my arm was made of jelly, but it soon became normal again. Now, in this fight, the arm became very painful and I had to let it hang by my side. Fortunately the army captain had also had enough and I returned to my room with a swollen face. I had landed one good punch on his nose that had momentarily dazed him, but I had lacked the experience to follow it up while he was still stunned. The next day I had to go to the hospital where an X-ray showed that the fracture had come apart and I had to have my arm put back in plaster. As luck would have it, the army major was at the hospital for some reason and learned of my broken arm. The news got back to the captain who must have been impressed. When Bob Lee went to Ooty on leave the captain was still up there and gave him a good time when he heard that he was from 20 Squadron!

On the return journey from Ooty, I again got a lift back to Dum Dum in a Douglas Commando. I called in at the hospital at Calcutta and persuaded the doctor on duty with some difficulty to remove the plaster of Paris from my arm, which was annoying me. I also had a meal with a couple in their home in Calcutta. The wife's family were friends of my parents in London. Her father was a solicitor called Churchill, and he had a bevy of beautiful daughters. During the evening her husband was complaining that his shaving water had been cold that morning and turned to me for support in his contention that this was an essential in life. This tickled me as we had long been accustomed to shaving in cold water. I think he had been in one of the big trading companies in Rangoon and had had to move to Calcutta when Rangoon fell. It was a pleasant change to have dinner with an attractive woman and her husband, but I had to return to Chiringa the next day and never saw them again. At Dum Dum, Doug Stilliard was waiting with the Harvard for the flight back to camp.

The weather was not very good after this, and three out of the five sorties that I flew in the first twelve days of July had to be abandoned.

One day I was walking near the airstrip when I saw a native struggling along with a large branch from a banana tree, loaded with bunches of the fruit. I held out a four-anna piece (worth about 2p today) hoping to be given a banana. He presented me with the whole branch, which I carried to the crew room so that everyone had a share.

About this time the first war medal was issued, later called the 1939–45 star but at that time the 1939–44 star. In the Far East it became known as the Chowringhee medal, as anybody stationed in Calcutta was entitled to wear it. Jock Wallace was disgusted that Indian women clerks in Calcutta were awarded the medal and for a time refused to wear it.

Two Canadians joined us: Warrant Officers Mitchell and Thompson. I told Thompson that we were glad to have him as we had lost two pilots by that name earlier in the year. Thompson had been driver to the First World War ace Billy Bishop, before volunteering as a pilot himself. He was a slightly plump, stockily built chap, dark shaven and cheerful, who called girls 'tomatoes' to rhyme with potatoes, and who was fond of the exclamation, 'Holy Toledo!'

The weather made life rather miserable and the adjutant was feeling low. On some days he failed to turn up for work, and when I went round to his room I was dismayed to see him unshaven and in his underclothes, presenting a very different picture from the dapper little man who had joined the squadron early in 1943. We had a phrase, 'marlish' (which I have spelt phonetically), derived possibly from Urdu. It signified a state of 'couldn't care less' that befell people sooner or later in the Far East, and which seemed to have overtaken Snow now. From that time on, his work was not done as well as had once been the case. I arranged for him to go on leave and tried to get him promotion, hoping that a change of job would benefit us all. He departed to Darjeeling or Shillong where he met a girl called June. She later wrote him a letter saying that she now knew what it was like to have six inches of snow in June.

On 14 July I paid another visit to the detachment at Imphal, but I was only able to get as far as Chittagong when the weather compelled me to return to Chiringa. The following day I reached Imphal via Comilla and the same afternoon joined in a search for Japanese tanks. For the next five days I flew at least once each day in a search for tanks, without success, finding only some lorries on the Tiddim road on one occasion and, on a dawn recce, spotting two Jap soldiers walking along the same highway. This alerted me to look ahead and I could see a Japanese platoon about 100 yards behind the two men. They reacted simultaneously and dived for the ditch at the roadside. By the time my number two arrived, there was nothing to be seen. I had marked the spot where the soldiers had taken cover and attacked the area with my machine guns. We set fire to a lorry on this trip also.

Owing to the shortage of accommodation, three or four of us slept in a small two-roomed native hut, the ceiling being about 5 feet high and the hut swarming with mosquitoes. There was no sanitation and one of the others going into the jungle for a 'rear', came back with a leech attached to his buttocks. In 1942, one of the sergeant air gunners at Chittagong had a leech latch on to his leg above his boot.

In the mess on the aerodrome, I found the mess secretary was a pilot who had been with me at UCH medical school before the war. Michael Veitch had stayed on at the school until he had taken his 2nd MB, and had then joined up as a pilot with John Harries, another friend of mine. I had visited the two of them in London while I was on a squadron in Ireland, and I sometimes wondered whether the sight of myself in uniform had influenced them to abandon their medical studies. Unfortunately Harries was killed at flying school in America when another machine landed on top of him, and Veitch was killed at Imphal a few weeks later in bad weather.

The senior air staff officer (SASO) was Air Commodore Vasse, a very large man known as 'Tiny', who had been on 20 Squadron in peacetime. I had met him while the squadron was at 'Hove' and he gave me the impression that he was fond of good living. While at Imphal we were under Wing Commander Henry Goddard in 906 Wing. He was a very intelligent man who held conferences of his squadron commanders once a week, which he chaired most effectively and which were worth attending. Soon after this, OC wings were upgraded to group captains and a wing commander 'flying' was posted to each wing. The first at Henry Goddard's wing was Patrick Lee, whom I had also met on the Arakan earlier.

There was an ENSA concert while I was at Imphal and I found some space at the back of the hall. There were three or four reserved seats at the front. Pat Lee the wingco 'flying' came in and somehow saw me at the back of the hall. He waved for me to come forward and take the remaining reserved seat. There was a young female impersonator in the show, who may well have been Danny La Rue, but I can't be sure. The impersonator was very good and the stage manager told us that several men refused to believe that he was not a woman. Owing to the shortage of this gender in Burma, female impersonators were not uncommon, but this one was in a class by himself.

Among others at the wing meetings was the Australian, McCormack, who had succeeded Duckenfield as CO of 615 Squadron. During the monsoon period, this squadron was caught in a storm in the mountains around Imphal, with the loss of the complete squadron.

On 20 Squadron, Sandy McPhail, flying as number two to Roger Cobley, had to crash-land near Imphal. As a result, his left arm was paralysed and it was put in an 'aeroplane' splint for a few weeks – that is, with the arm raised horizontally at the shoulder and the elbow flexed. Fortunately Sandy's arm recovered and he returned to fly with the squadron until his time came to be repatriated to New Zealand. When he got back to NZ it was found that he had sustained a fracture dislocation of his neck during the crash and was advised that it would be too risky to try and repair the damage at that stage. In spite of this injury, Sandy captained his rugby side at Wanganui for some years after the war!

On the Arakan front, Frank Pegg was killed in the mountains during bad weather, which was a sad loss.

On 21 July I took off from Imphal and travelled direct to Chiringa. The weather was not ideal, but fortune favoured me in that as I was nearing the end of one valley the clouds would lift, enabling me to fly over the mountains into the next valley. If I had once been forced to fly into cloud, I would have been lost. As I continued from valley to valley, heading in the general direction of Chiringa, the weather improved. It was an extraordinary and memorable flight, with luck definitely on my side.

Soon after this, it was decreed that 20 Squadron should be pulled out of the forward area and back to southern India for a rest. Two Hurricanes were left at Imphal for DDT spraying to control malaria.

In spite of our activities, we were regarded as something of a white elephant on the Arakan front, but fortunately the AOC at Imphal, Stanley Vincent, was quick to see our potential value.

On 24 July the squadron moved off, stopping three nights at Calcutta, another at Vizagapatam and three nights at Madras, finishing up at Trichinopoly on the 31st. We had spent seven months on ops and, as a representative sample, I had carried out eighty-two operational sorties in that time.

By the end of July 1944 on the Arakan, after some hard struggles, the British had recaptured a few miles of some uninviting country from the Japanese.

Chapter 11

Trichinopoly – 31 July–20 September 1944

The airfield at Trichinopoly was called Kajamalai. On 2 August I flew to group headquarters at Bangalore and saw the wing commander in charge of personnel with regard to Flight Lieutenant Snow's promotion. He told me there were many admin flight lieutenants who would like to be promoted, but I put in a strong recommendation on Snow's behalf and convinced the wing commander that Snow was a specially deserving case, so that his posting came through soon after. In fact, I thought it was best for the squadron that Snow was posted as he had lost interest in his work while we were at Chiringa.

The AOC of 225 Group at Bangalore was Air Vice Marshal Mackworth, who lived near us in London and our families were friends. He had been responsible for the editing of the RAF manual of navigation in the pre-war years. I did not meet him out in India. I did, however, come across one of the cipher officers, Pilot Officer Cornish, who had been at Chittagong in 1942, and who was now stationed at 225 Group. We had a pleasant 'reminisce' about those days.

At Trichinopoly, we had left the monsoons behind. The climate was hot and dry. The soil was red-coloured and there were numerous anthills around the camp, built by white ants, with irregular steeples rising 5 or 6 feet high, made of the red earth. Sometimes these anthills were constructed against the inside corner of a building, and on one occasion when I had my blue tunic hanging against the wall of my bedroom, I found that part of it had been eaten away by white ants. Clothes trunks were made of metal to protect them from the depredations of the white ants and the weather.

There was a Spitfire Mk VIII at Kajamalai, and I seized the opportunity of flying it – my third trip in a 'Spit'.

Trichy had a well-equipped club, with two full-sized billiard tables. These attracted the pilots, although nobody was particularly good with a billiard cue. There was a big railway junction at Trichinopoly, and I suppose that some of the civilians were connected with that.

There were two young flying officers at Kajamalai who were ferry pilots, but there was no other activity until 20 Squadron arrived. One of the pilots was a large, self-assured chap called Logan, who was successfully seducing the only young white girl in the place.

Nearly three weeks after we had arrived, I went down with a relapse of malaria, my second bout, preceded by an attack of vertigo one night when I had switched off the light and laid my head back on the pillow. The next morning Logan flew me up to the hospital at Bangalore in a Bisley, which was second cousin to a Blenheim. It was a rather cramped ride and took 1 hour 20 minutes, 15 minutes longer than the journey in a Hurricane. After reaching the hospital I was all right for 24 hours, and then developed another rigor. It was dark and I recall one of the sisters pulling up my mosquito net to take a sample of blood from me. This confirmed the diagnosis and I was then treated for malaria. I remember Ranjan Dutt coming to see me while I was lying in bed, feverish, and I was not sure what he came to see me about!

When I was discharged from the hospital, I went on sick leave to the Nilgiri Hills. I had heard that Coonoor, which was a bit lower than the town of Ooty, had a more relaxed and friendly atmosphere than 'snooty Ooty', so I made my way to the officers' leave hostel at Coonoor, to find that it was bulging at the seams with men. Several beds had been fitted into each bedroom, but space was found for me by setting up another bed. At Coonoor, I played tennis, went for long walks, and undid the good effects of the exercise by drinking at the club each evening. Female company was as rare as gold dust. Even very unattractive women had their swarm of male army officers around them, so that the majority of us would spend the evening drinking.

By the time I was due to rejoin the squadron, it was on the move to Madras.

Chapter 12

St Thomas's Mount, Madras –
21 September–1 December 1944

I reached St Thomas's Mount at the same time as the squadron, who had moved up from Trichinopoly. We were placed in a tented area together with 110 Squadron, who were on Catalina flying boats, based on a lake not far away. The CO of 110 was Wing Commander Thompson, who was a bit 'round the bend' like the rest of us. He was always playing backgammon and was fortunate enough to have a lady friend in Madras. On the tent site, there were some huts as sleeping quarters for the officers, but it was all rather rough.

Soon after we arrived, monsoon weather caught up with us, having presumably swept along in a north-western direction until it had come up against the Himalayas and then travelled south as the 'return monsoon'. One night we had a highly spectacular thunderstorm with non-stop thunder and lightning. During the commotion I became aware of Jack Romanes, moving around hysterically on all fours, as his nerves had already been strained by two serious aircraft crashes.

During my illness, Roger Cobley had acted as CO and had managed this well. The senior medical officer (SMO) at St Thomas's Mount was Squadron Leader Morris, who had been with us on 20 Squadron and who was to have a successful career with the RAF after the war. Fortunately for us, Doc Morris came to our rescue with regard to accommodation. There were some unoccupied barracks on another part of the camp, called the 'Lawrence block', which were very much more comfortable for the airmen, and some bungalows for the officers. With Doc Morris's help, 20 Squadron moved into their new quarters. I had a pleasant pre-war bungalow with its own verandah. Tree rats, like our squirrels, used to run along the branches of nearby trees and come close to where I was sitting.

We used the main mess of the aerodrome, in company with 110 Squadron and the station HQ staff. This was another pre-war building. In the dining room, cane chairs were used around the table, and these harboured bugs that would bite one's skin below the level of our shorts, while we were at table. We soon learned to lift the chair and bang it down on the floor before sitting on it, in the hope of dislodging the bugs. On Sundays, lunch consisted of curry, and one could choose a normal curry or an especially hot Madras curry.

While we were at our new camp, we had a dance for the men of the squadron and another for the officers. The squadron dance was held in a hall in Madras, with contingents from various women's services to provide partners. The armament section held a dinner at the Connemara hotel to which Snow and I were kindly invited. At the end of the meal, I was asked to make a speech. This was completely unexpected and had never happened to me before in my life. I was only able to make the excuse that the squadron motto was 'Deeds not Words' for my lack of ability in this field, and I can say that Snow, who followed me, did not do any better! The third and final issue of the squadron magazine came out at Madras.

On most weekends we went to the Connemara and drank Scotch, watching those lucky enough to have partners to dance with. Sandy McPhail has since reminded me that we had a race down the main street in Madras with rickshaws, having made the rickshaw wallahs climb in, while Sandy and I pulled their machines. Returning to the camp, I would sometimes pretend to be hopelessly drunk, leaving the steering of the station wagon to the pilot next to me, while managing the foot pedals myself. This was for the benefit of any new pilot in the back seat. We never had any crashes but I was obviously well and truly round the twist.

There was a good outdoor swimming pool at the club in Madras, which I had first used on my way to Ootacamund in 1943, and to which we now made regular trips. It was still relatively uncrowded, and we squadron pilots virtually had the facility to ourselves. There was a kite that used to circle about 100 feet above it, and one teatime at the pool's edge, I was lifting a sandwich from my plate to my mouth, when the sandwich was whisked out of my hand by the bird of prey. After that we encouraged it to make its swoop and take food from us, gathering the food up cleanly in its claws.

There was also a bathing beach, which was more popular. An Indian in a canoe about 50 yards out used to stop bathers from venturing too far from the shore, as there was some risk of sharks, but we only visited that beach once or twice.

During our stay, regulations were tightened up with regard to the use of transport for getting into Madras. When we found that we were being stopped at the main exit from the camp, we discovered there was a back way into the city from close to the Lawrence block, where the squadron was billeted. Eventually the station commander cottoned on to this one and that loophole was closed also!

When the weather became too bad at Imphal, the detachment that had stayed on up there to spray the valley with DDT, returned to the unit.

We continued our training at Madras with some air-to-ground target practice, attacks on shipping, dogfights and aerobatics.

At Madras, I discovered we had unsuspected talent in the game of rugby, coming top in the Southern India Rugby League. Two of the stars were New Zealanders: Sandy McPhail and Digger Martin the armourer. We also competed in cricket and obtained a net for practice through the PSI. I recall one game we played on open ground in front of the mess, when I bowled fast but unavailingly for my side against a team led by Jimmy Farquharson.

Soccer was another sport in which we participated and, in contrast to the cricket, I felt so weak in one game that I could not kick the ball effectively. I was a bit under the weather at that time, plagued by minor ills. Prickly heat was a common complaint, causing a red itchy rash on the skin; I had it mainly on my arms and around my neck. My chronic diarrhoea was blood-stained, possibly due to an anal fissure. In addition to this I developed otitis externa (inflammation of the ear canal), which finally drove me round to sick quarters. Doc Morris gave me a sedative that flattened me out for the best part of a day, and when I awoke, I was more relaxed and my ears were surprisingly improved!

I had an argument with Doc Morris as to how long one could blow up a column of mercury, which was part of the medical exam for aircrew. In the end he told me that he would give me 10 rupees for every second that I held the mercury up beyond 90 seconds. At about that point I allowed the column of mercury to dip momentarily, but continued to hold it up for nearly 2 minutes as 10 rupees – or 15 shillings a second – was big money in those days. But the quack excused himself by disqualifying me for allowing the mercury to drop during the test.

In spite of the shortage of women, there was practically no trouble from homosexuals in the RAF. An exception to this was a warrant officer who was posted to us in Madras, and who was an effeminate-looking chubby man. He was hauled up in front of me one morning by Warrant Officer Aitchison, the squadron WO, because he had been persistently importuning two of the young sergeant pilots in the sergeants' mess. I had no experience or knowledge of how to handle this problem, and merely spoke to him severely, warning him that he would be thrown off the squadron if there were any more complaints about him.

One or two of the NCOs had visited the brothels in Madras and got a dose of what Doc O'Brien called 'Cupid's catarrh'.

In a spare moment I got Dingle Bell, our engineer officer, to show me round one of our machines, as I had never understood the engines that I was reliant on in the air. He explained where the carburettor was and so on, but I was still none the wiser at the end of it!

Lord Louis Mountbatten, the 'Supremo', was making a point of visiting all the units in his command – a mammoth task – talking to the men assembled as a group and meeting the officers individually. He visited St Thomas's Mount while 20 Squadron was there. The station HQ staff seemed to object to the presence of squadrons on their station, and I was not informed of the meeting of Mountbatten with unit commanders. However, I met him later when the officers were paraded and I had to introduce him to the officers on the squadron.

While at St Thomas's Mount I also met Air Chief Marshal Sir Leslie Hollinghurst, who had been CO of 20 Squadron before the war; Bruce Belfrage, who had been a radio announcer but was then in the navy; and finally a Battle of Britain fighter pilot who had flown as a pair with RAF ace Mungo-Park and who later became a Fleet Street editor – H.M. Stephen I think his name was.

Neville Rowson reappeared at St Thomas's Mount, having made his way back to India after a short spell in England, which was evidently not to his liking. He was still a flight lieutenant and was now on Dakotas. He was at heart a transport pilot. He had lunch, or tiffin I suppose we called it, with Peter McMillan and myself before returning to his unit. It was the last time we saw him, as he was killed in a flying accident not long after.

Doc Morris enjoyed flying and I sat in the back of the Harvard while he tried his hand at looping and other manoeuvres. Twice we flew to Yelahanka, the aerodrome at Bangalore, with Doc Morris doing most of the flying, but needing a little help with the landing. On the first occasion I took the Harvard back by myself while Ron Morris stayed at Bangalore with friends. On the second occasion, his friends put me up as well for a couple of nights. On one of my visits to Bangalore, I was sitting in the group mess one morning. The only other officer present was seated in an armchair at the other end of the anteroom. He put his hand into his pocket and casually took out a spectral tarsier, which he placed on the floor. It was the first one of these smallest of primates that I had seen. It moved slowly and had disproportionately large eyes. I imagine the officer kept the animal as a talking point or to startle people into thinking they were seeing things!

I had not brought my blue uniform with me, and the evenings at Bangalore proved to be uncomfortably cold, reminding me of a similar occasion in Calcutta two years previously. On the first night we had dined in the group mess and I had had to put up with the slight discomfort, envying the others in their 'blues', but on the next night my hostess kindly found some extra clothing for me.

Ron Morris's friend was a flight lieutenant in his forties, who had been a businessman in the Far East before the war. He and his wife were a very pleasant couple and were on better terms with the AOC than one would have guessed from the difference in rank. On the second day a group captain came to lunch with his lady, who knew my father in London. My father was a GP who had come out of retirement for the duration of the war. The group captain was an ex-film star called John Boles, and was quite an impressive-looking man.

We returned to St Thomas's Mount on 30 November and the next day I left with A Flight for Ranchi, where the flight was to be re-equipped with rocket-firing Hurricane Mk IVs. There were always rumours about getting new exotic aircraft, such as Typhoons or Tempests, which never came true, but the Hurricane was in fact extremely well suited for the operations we had to carry out.

On the evening before our departure, I was driving into town in the station wagon with a number of pilots. We were overtaken and called to a halt by a couple of angry middle-aged officious Englishmen who informed me that I was breaking the speed limit. I don't know what made them feel so aggressive. We were on a wide, deserted road and I was driving at my usual speed, which may have been fast but was safe. I felt glad to be getting away from a backward area and on with the war effort.

At Madras, Snow was posted away – to a squadron leader position at Bombay, I think. We were joined by Flying Officer Dai Lewis, an ex-bomber pilot, ex-schoolmaster and, needless to say, a rugby player. He was pleasant, tactful and good-tempered, and remained with the squadron until the war ended.

Chapter 13

Ranchi – 3–18 December 1944

Our stay at Ranchi was short. I see from my log book that the air party managed to spend two nights in Calcutta on the way from Madras. At Ranchi we traded in the Hurricane IIDs of A Flight in exchange for rocket-carrying Hurricane IVs. These Hurricanes conveyed four rockets under each wing, either 40-lb armour-piercing or 60-lb explosives. They could be fired singly, in pairs, or in a salvo. We were taught to fire them in a shallow dive, allowing for an initial drop when the rockets fell away from the wing. We soon learned the technique, but found on operations that we could achieve greater accuracy by making steep dives with the 40mm cannon. I spent some time on the rocket range watching the trajectory of the rockets from the ground and also the individual performances of the pilots.

One evening I was heading for the mess and leaped over a low wall on the way. Unfortunately there was a brick lying on the ground on the other side, which made me twist my ankle. I felt a snap and an excruciating pain as I fell. Bob Lee was sitting on the verandah of the mess, and he roared with laughter in the way the English traditionally do if they see someone slip on a banana skin. I picked myself up and walked with difficulty to a chair beside him, not caring to show that I had hurt myself. My ankle was painful that night and in the morning was markedly swollen. I went along to the squadron sick quarters but there was no such thing as an X-ray machine among its facilities, so my ankle was put in a crêpe bandage. I continued to fly but it was a bit awkward to use the rudder with a sprained ankle.

The conversion course lasted a fortnight and we then set a course for Imphal, stopping again for two nights in Calcutta on the way. Our aerodrome, Sapam, was in the south-east corner of the Imphal valley, and we were sharing it with 155 Spitfire Squadron.

It was the start of the final campaign. In 1945 the Japanese would be driven out of Burma.

Chapter 14

Sapam – 20 December 1944–16 January 1945

We arrived in Sapam five days before Christmas. The valley was about 2,000 feet above sea level and it was consequently cold. We caught one of our rare glimpses of snow. Once or twice we were given an issue of rum. I remember seeing Sandy McPhail visibly thawing out as he drank his rum ration, sitting outside the officers' mess. For our Christmas dinner, a party of officers went out hunting and brought back a wader bird, which proved to be a failure as far as Christmas dinners were concerned, being tough with a fishy taste.

The women at Imphal wore bright-coloured clothes and appeared in rude good health. They smoked cheroots and joked laughingly to each other as they carried out manual work, perhaps road mending, while their menfolk squatted in the shade.

The mess hut was on raised ground beside the road, which ran north–south on the eastern side of the airstrip, and which separated the runway from the men's quarters. During the Christmas period when there was not much flying, the officers carried out revolver practice on the bank parallel to the road. Luckily there was very little traffic on this route and there were no accidents.

The CO of 155 Squadron was a charming but volatile chap who had not held the position for long, perhaps a few weeks, and who unfortunately had a breakdown while we were at Sapam. No. 155 had Spitfires and I watched them one day as they tried to find out how many consecutive vertical rolls they could do before the aircraft stalled. It was good flying and more rolls than I would have guessed.

Some pilots on the Arakan had flown on operations fully equipped to make their way back to base if they were shot down in the jungle. They wore full-length overalls and carried weapons and emergency rations. I regarded this as a form of insurance, which is something I have never believed in, and chose to fly in shirt and shorts, making myself as comfortable as possible so that my flying performance was at its best. For the advance through Burma, we all had to wear a standard uniform of 'jungle green', consisting of a tunic and long slacks. The medical authorities feared the possibility of an outbreak of scrub typhus when we left the Imphal valley, so we were all inoculated against that and warned to wear boots and gaiters, as the disease was spread by a tick that would wait on some foliage and then transfer itself on to any passerby. I did not like the idea of flying in boots and continued to wear gymshoes until the end of the war. I was once taken to task about this by Group Captain Finlay, but made some excuse that he accepted.

On 29 December we were called on to carry out our first strike with rockets. As the strip was outside our range we were briefed to land and refuel at an airstrip called Yazagyo over the jungle-covered mountains south of the valley. I think Les Hill was my number two on this occasion, and there may have been a third Hurricane. I noticed on take-off what a long run the Hurricane required with a full rocket load weighing 480 lb. On the other hand, I did not open the throttle quickly, as we were taking off in formation and it was customary for the leader to help the other aircraft by holding back a bit so that they could keep up more easily. We climbed gradually and set course over mountainous country that was remarkably devoid of landmarks for pinpointing one's position.

After about the right time I saw a strip in a jungle clearing. There were some aircraft lined up at the side, so I called up the other planes accompanying mine to get into starboard echelon; that is, behind and to my right prior to landing. It seemed a rather small airstrip and as I straightened out into wind, I realised that it was too small for the Hurricane to land in and, even if I did, taking off again would cause problems. At the other end of the strip were pine trees reaching 150 feet into the air. Unloaded, the Hurricane could have cleared them, but with a full load of rockets and my limited experience of taking off under those conditions, I doubted that I could rise above this impediment. If I opened the throttle and attempted to clear the trees and was successful, everything would be fine, but if I failed the crash would be more disastrous than if I crashed undershooting. I decided I was committed to a crash-landing. I was coming in at 105mph on account of my heavy load. If I hit anything at that speed, it would be too bad. Obstacles flashed by a few yards to either side. I tightened my harness and locked it; checked that the rockets were switched to safe; turned off the petrol supply; braced myself with my left arm above the top of the instrument panel and estimated I did not have long to wait for the crash. Each second, however, my speed was falling off and I reckoned my chances were improving proportionately. The Hurricane crashed into a pile of 40-gallon petrol drums placed at the end of the airstrip and tilted up on its nose.

I switched off the ignition and sat there annoyed with myself. Soon some soldiers ran up, asking me if I was hurt or wanted a cigarette or a cup of tea. Smoking would have been a bit foolish in that situation, but I was relieved that the rockets had not gone off. There was a casualty clearing station about 50 yards away, with a bored medical officer who was glad to see me. Les Hill had circled the strip and now set a course back to base. I hoped that the Harvard would be sent to pick me up. Incidentally, the machines I had seen on the runway here were gliders that had been used to land troops at Khampat and then dumped.

While I was having dinner with the MO that night I suffered a rigor and was put to bed with malaria, my third attack. Probably the crash had caused my spleen to contract and expel some malarial parasites into the bloodstream. I told the MO that I wanted to rejoin my squadron as soon as possible, so he loaded me up with quinine to such an extent that the next day I was deaf and unsteady on my feet when I went off to the latrines. He then cut down the dose, but from then on I had tinnitus and a high frequency hearing loss.

On 2 January I hitch-hiked my way from Khampat to Yazagyo along a jungle road that carried a continuous stream of army lorries in both directions. I stopped an army jeep that was travelling in the right direction and got aboard, but after a few hair-raising miles with the Indian soldier at the helm, I moved him out of the driving seat and took the wheel myself.

Yazagyo had a single all-weather runway and looked very long after Khampat's strip. Roy Bennell appeared in a Tiger Moth and we flew to Tamu where the squadron Harvard was waiting and we returned to Sapam in that.

I found that Roger Cobley had been repatriated during the few days that I had been away. Air Vice Marshal Vincent had left a message telling me to come back to the squadron and nothing would be said about the crash! This was a joke, but we were all very accident conscious and aware of the waste that such incidents caused. Each month squadrons submitted an analysis of aircraft lost or damaged, and 20 Squadron had a very good record in this respect. The AOC informed me that he had asked for 20 Squadron to be in his group, as he felt sure we would be of value.

On the Arakan, Air Commodore Alec Gray was replaced by the Earl of Bandon as AOC. Paddy Bandon, or the 'abandoned Earl', was an Irish peer, who remained as air officer commanding 224 Group for the rest of the war.

Our advance through Burma had started, and on 11 January I flew across to group headquarters at Imphal to obtain details of another squadron move, which was imminent. At the airstrip near HQ, Air Commodore Mills, who was number three at group, in charge of admin, showed me the Japanese field gun that had shelled the strip during the siege, and which was now kept as a souvenir.

My ankle was still giving me twinges of pain – hardly surprising after a sprain – and our MO, Flight Lieutenant O'Brien, had arranged for me to have it examined at the mobile field hospital at Imphal. I was given Pentothal intravenously, which was very new at the time, and my ankle was examined while I was under anaesthetic, presumably because there was no X-ray machine available. I came round from the Pentothal feeling that I had just had a drink of Scotch, to find a nursing sister bending over me. Getting my bearings, but still under the influence of the drug, I informed her that Burma was no place for a woman. I had flown over in the Harvard with Jimmy Farquharson in the back, in case I did not feel able to fly the aircraft on the return journey. However, I did pilot it back myself, although modern regulations would never have permitted it.

The squadron was to move into 909 Wing under Group Captain Finlay, whose name was already the subject of several stories as a strict disciplinarian. I flew down to his wing HQ, having shaved carefully beforehand. Our advance party at our new aerodrome at Thazi had already fallen foul of the group captain through being unshaven. There was difficulty in getting razor blades and there was soon to be a rule throughout the group that everyone had to shave at least once a week! Finlay had been an Olympic hurdler before the war and was a fit man in his late thirties at the time. We got on well together and I was careful to be alert and reasonably well turned out on that first occasion, which probably helped.

A new intelligence officer arrived at Sapam, straight from England, called Pilot Officer Crawford. He was a biggish man with a thin, dark moustache, who found our methods very different from what he had been taught. We were given much more latitude on 20 Squadron to decide on our own activities, partly because we were a specialist squadron and partly because we used to go searching for targets such as lorries, rather than attack a pinpoint on a map like the 'Hurribombers'. When I gave Crawford the plan for operations the next day, without reference to group intelligence, he was horrified. Later that evening I was playing bridge in the tent of the OC's R & R party at Sapam when his telephone gave a slight ring. He picked it up and listened for a moment before handing it to me. We had managed to come in on a conversation between our new intelligence officer and his counterpart at group. Crawford was telling the officer how I had picked targets for the next day, and he appealed confidently to the group IO, expecting him to confirm that I should be hauled over the coals for my action. It was very funny to hear the group officer confirming my action as being quite acceptable, and Crawford's incredulity at this state of affairs. He soon adapted to the new conditions and became an accepted figure, although nicknamed the 'Spy'.

I did no further operations until we had moved to Thazi. The army was advancing and targets were getting out of range from Sapam. From the south-east corner of the Imphal valley, the ground fell away through jungle-covered hills to the plains further south. A red earth road had been cut through this country, winding its way down to Kalewa on the Chindwin river. Thazi was over to the east from Kalewa and the squadron moved there on 17 January 1945.

Chapter 15

Thazi – 17 January–12 February 1945

We now began our association with 909 Wing and the legendary Group Captain Finlay, who had his headquarters at Kalemyo.

The wing armaments officer was Flight Lieutenant Vernon Udall, whom I had first met on the Arakan, on the day when I had runaway 40mm cannons. He had now got his eyes unfocused, gazing into the distance, and was 'tour expired'. He was repatriated to the UK from Kalemyo. The next time we met was in October 1946 when we were both starting our 2nd MB course at University College, London.

In spite of our move, targets were still some distance away, either south at Monywa on the Chindwin or to the east on the Irrawaddy, north of Mandalay. There was a ridge of mountains to the east of Thazi and beyond that the ground remained raised.

A logistics problem was that there had been no maps of central Burma, but now that we needed them, the ones we were given were excellent. We were told that they had been compiled and printed in England from aerial photographs by the PRU.

We were carrying out sorties on the day that we moved to Thazi. On the 20th, and again on the 23rd, we attacked Japanese positions at Monywa with rockets. The next day I was returning from a strike of Jap positions on the Irrawaddy when my oil pressure began to fall. This had happened to me twice before; the first time was on a squadron in Ireland, when a bearing had gone, but I returned safely to base before the engine seized up; the second time was on the Arakan when a pipeline was shot away, causing the oil pressure gauge to fail. On this occasion I called my number two and warned him to pinpoint my position if I had to make a forced landing. The oil pressure fell slowly but steadily on the way back to Thazi, reaching zero as we cleared the ridge of hills on the eastern side of the Kalewa valley. Fortunately it was merely a faulty instrument and the engine continued to make the right noises.

By 27 January we were having to refuel at forward areas before returning to Thazi. Soon we were using a forward airstrip at Onbauk for refuelling and then carrying out a standing patrol over our forward troops ready to attack any target to which we were directed. We called this patrol a 'cab rank', with requests coming from a visual control post.

At the end of January, a pilot of a small aircraft, an L5, needed a lift from our airfield to his own at Taukkyan. I forget how he had landed up at Thazi but I took him back to Taukkyan in the squadron Harvard and arranged to fly an L5 a few days later. I was always eager to try new types of aircraft, so I was pleased when he returned as promised with an L5, which I flew for a couple of hours.

The 40mm cannons were so accurate that several times we attacked Jap field guns and succeeded in silencing them. This was with armour-piercing shells. At one stage we ran short of AP ammunition and for a short while had to curtail our activities. There were indignant protests from the pilots, and messages were sent back to England via the journalists who hung around for news and also by more official channels. Next we received some new 40mm ammo in the form of a combined shell. It had an armour-piercing nose, a high-explosive centre and an incendiary rear end. The shell was lighter than the AP one and had a different trajectory, which we had no difficulty in adjusting to, and the destructive power was much greater. Now a single pair of shells fired into a lorry would be enough to set it alight. However, in spite of the shortage of our original shells, Air Commodore Vasse at group would not let us use the new ammunition, on the grounds that it should be held in reserve so that the Japs would not know of its existence, and only be used at a psychologically critical moment. Group finally gave in to our protests after waiting a week for the 'moment critique' to arrive.

On one evening sortie to the east, I noticed that a new pilot, Sergeant Holman, was making low, shallow attacks on the target, which was a gun emplacement. When we returned to Thazi, I cautioned him in front of the other pilots who had taken part in the sortie, pointing out that we made dive attacks, which were not only more accurate but safer for us. He seemed a sulky, withdrawn individual and the next day, making similar long, low attacks, he failed to return from the raid. I have since wondered whether he deliberately looked for trouble, being in a depressed state.

Near the camp was a fast-flowing stream with a basin forming a natural pool. It was within walking distance and we all found it pleasant to swim there in the late afternoon. An Anglo-Indian airman called Beatty was brought to me by the senior warrant officer. Beatty claimed that he had seen a couple of Jap soldiers equipped with a wireless set, as he was returning from the pool. I collected my revolver and asked him to take me to the spot where he had seen the Japs. Eddie Fockler and one or two others followed as we set off down the path. After a short distance Beatty indicated that they had crossed the path at this point and continued through some elephant grass on the other side. He and I followed an opening in it while the others remained on the path. After a few yards, it became impossible to walk through the grass, which was about 10 feet high, and it became clear that the Japs were a figment of Beatty's imagination. He was a good mechanic and a pleasant chap, but on this occasion he must have been dreaming!

Warrant Officer Watson, who was in charge of the armament section and who had been a bookie in civilian life, came into my HQ tent one day, very upset and under the impression that I was dissatisfied with his work. This was completely unfounded, for in fact Watson was a distinct asset to the squadron, but I never discovered how the misunderstanding arose. I was, however, able to reassure him that I held him in esteem. When he was suitably primed, Watson gave an amusing turn of a Hurricane pilot taking off. For this, he would sit astride a chair, go through his imitation of cockpit drill, taxiing out and take-off, finally overbalancing backwards as the 'aircraft' left the ground.

We tried our hand at baseball at Thazi, and I recall feeling weak and lacking in energy while we were playing. This may have been the enervating effect of the valley where Thazi was located, or it may have been partly due to my attack of malaria that had started three weeks earlier.

At Sapam we had had a wooden hut for a mess, but from Thazi onwards our entire camp was tented. There were two or three officers to a tent, while I had a small tent to myself. As CO I tended to become isolated. Dingle Bell, the engineer officer, called me Skipper or 'Skip' and this nickname was also used by the MO, O'Brien. One or two of the senior pilots tentatively called me Andrew, but mostly I was called Sir. The CO of a fighting unit in wartime is in a very powerful position, almost a dictator, but it is a lonely position to be in.

Whenever possible the engineer officer would get a donkey engine going at night, which ran a generator that provided us with electricity. We otherwise had hurricane lamps and I had purchased a tilley pressure lamp in Calcutta, which gave a brilliant light. We also had one of these for the mess.

At night we played bridge, poker and 'liar dice'. One night, a Japanese aircraft found its way into our valley and eventually dropped some bombs on one of the neighbouring airfields. We extinguished our lights and I asked Dingle Bell to get a Hurricane ready for take-off. There was some moonlight and I thought it was worthwhile going after the Jap bomber, whose engines could still be heard. From my previous experience on the Arakan – when we found it impossible to find each other, let alone an enemy aircraft – I should have realised that the venture was ill-advised. However, a signal came through from Vasse at group, whom we had notified of our intended flight, forbidding us to take off.

One evening, as a group of us were standing outside the aircrew tent, Flight Sergeant Goodhew gave us an impromptu display of inverted flying. Usually we stayed inverted for as short a time as possible, so that centrifugal force kept us in our seats and the dust on the floor of the cockpit. Otherwise we would be hanging by our harnesses and bits of debris from the floor would get into our eyes. Goodhew, though, flew across the aerodrome upside down – with only an occasional splutter from the Hurricane – turned and came back again, staying inverted for an appreciable time.

In the latter part of our stay at Thazi, we destroyed several Japanese petrol and ammunition dumps.

Soon we were on the move again, this time to Monywa, a place we had attacked not long before. We were getting accustomed to squadron transfers, which were now done almost entirely by air. Earlier we had had an advance party, air party, ground party and rear party. At Thazi we had still had an advance party, which had included 'laskars', the Pathan camp followers who had dug latrines prior to our arrival. Dingle Bell had been on the ground party moving to Thazi, and had called in at Khampat – where I had crashed the Hurricane – but he was unable to salvage much from this location. Now, with air lifts, we were adapting to a new pattern of squadron move. The whole squadron would be lined up on either side of the airstrip in its various sections, consisting of both personnel and equipment. At the expected time, Dakotas would arrive, take on a load and depart for the new airfield. On this occasion, Warrant Officer Watson, who was an ex-bookie, had a blackboard showing the time that the first Dakota was due to touch down and was taking bets on the minutes before and after this time, as to when the plane would actually land! I provided 'fighter cover' for a C46, which was leaving for Monywa at the same time as I did in a Hurricane IID. I do not think I would have been very effective, but it may have reassured the transport pilot and I would have done my best if the need had arisen.

On the way, we flew over the crater of an extinct volcano, which was impressive from the air.

Chapter 16

Monywa – 12 February–10 April 1945

At Mandalay on the eastern side of the Burma plain, the Irrawaddy turned to flow across the plain to its western side. The Japanese had fallen back on a strong defensive position, on the southern bank of the Irrawaddy, with mountain ranges on both flanks.

At Monywa we were on the plain, above the angle made as the Irrawaddy merged with the Chindwin on its journey south. We were well placed to attack targets all along the front and our stay at our new camp was to be eventful.

I found the air more invigorating here than in the Kalewa valley. At first we drove to the river for a swim in the late afternoon but, although the river was wide at this point, the conditions were unattractive and the squadron pilots took up volleyball as an alternative form of recreation. On the way through Monywa, the sound of temple bells could be heard stirring gently in the breeze. The tide of war had only just receded through the place and its occupants had not yet returned. One of the temples had sculpted and painted wooden figures in its courtyard outside. Of these, there was a macabre carving of a dead man with his intestines spilling out and a bird making a meal of them. I found something gruesomely comic about this figure and took it back to the camp in my jeep. It had a bad effect on the MO, who later attacked it with an axe, after which we got rid of it.

Also at the airfield was the wing headquarters and 60 Squadron. The airstrip ran approximately north to south. To the north-west of the runway was Group Captain Finlay's HQ; 20 Squadron was at the south-east end, and 60 Squadron was east of us. Squadron Leader Humphries had been promoted recently to command 60 Squadron, and had been a sergeant pilot in the Battle of Britain, like Ginger Lacey, but without his outstanding record. He was a talkative man, and seemed to me rather loose-lipped and shifty-eyed. Ginger Lacey commanded the third squadron in the wing, which was 17 Squadron, stationed at a neighbouring airfield.

Since the start of the present tour of operations, A Flight had consisted of eight Hurricane IVs, each capable of carrying eight rocket projectile missiles with either a 60-lb high explosive (HE) or a 40-lb armour-piercing warhead. These were necessary for the German tanks, but the 40mm cannons were quite adequate for the thinner armour of the Jap tanks. The rockets proved to be useful against bunkers, which had a covering of several feet of soil. Three times I blew away the top cover of bunkers with direct hits from 60-lb HE rockets, leaving the excavated bunker exposed. The rockets were much more accurate than the 'Hurribombers' of 60 Squadron, who flew out and dropped their load of bombs on the map reference they had been given at briefing. We would often have to spend time searching the area to make sure we had found the target, which was usually well camouflaged, before releasing our ammunition.

Apart from the newest intake, the A Flight pilots had experience of flying both IIDs and IVs. B Flight consisted of eight Hurricane IIDs firing two 40mm cannons. The B Flight pilots were only experienced on IIDs and were not 'converted' on to rockets, so that the airmen were not readily available for transfer from one flight to the other. However, we had a good reserve of pilots on the squadron, roughly two to each aircraft, so there was no problem in that respect. We also had the squadron Harvard for communication purposes.

All supplies were flown into Burma, as the result of experience gained during the siege of Imphal, thereby overcoming the problem of the absence of overland supply routes. It meant, though, that we were all on half rations throughout our time in Burma. Some contents of the rations were unpopular: 'Victory' cigarettes were of a very poor quality; and tinned herrings were universally rejected when they were included.

I took a supply of these unwanted rations into the nearest village in a jeep. I was soon surrounded by villagers who were cheerful and good-natured. There were men of all ages, but the women were either very elderly or not more than three years old. I only caught a glimpse of two Burmese girls on a single occasion, disappearing up a ladder into one of the stilted huts at my approach. I indicated that I wanted to exchange the rations for eggs and chickens. I flapped my arms and made clucking noises, which caused some delighted laughter from the Burmese. They soon brought out their fowl and eggs, while I showed them my wares. Tinned herring proved to be a best-seller with the Burmese, a tin being exchanged for a chicken. A packet of Victory cigarettes would bring forth a couple of eggs, while a matchbox would get a single egg. I would return to the airfield with chickens flapping around the jeep, partly controlled by the pilot who had accompanied me. The mess cook kept some of the chickens as a source of eggs and cooked the rest. I did several such trips of bartering and enjoyed this contact with the villagers. This was the only fresh meat we had, as our staple diet was bully beef.

In the evenings, before our nightly bath, we played volleyball. We may have caught the craze from wing HQ but it certainly caught on, and was convenient in that no definite number was needed to form a side. Wing HQ evidently studied the game more than we did, and beat us when it came to a match, with some crafty combinations of passes.

We continued to do standing patrols over our own troops, giving support under the direction of a visual control post. These were mainly in the Mandalay area. Although this city was of no significance militarily, its recapture had become a matter of political importance.

On 15 February Sergeant Burkhill was shot down in HW858, the aircraft that Les Hill and I had shared since the beginning of operations on the Arakan front with Hurricane IIDs. Burkhill had been a dancing instructor before joining up, and wore side whiskers – which were not common then – and a 'Ronald Colman' moustache. Later, I had letters from two girls, each of whom thought she was his fiancée.

Our own troops were preparing to cross the Irrawaddy. We were sent on patrols, looking for enemy tanks that were being deployed over their defensive position. These were very carefully camouflaged during the day, but after three days of searching, two pilots found a couple of tanks, which they destroyed. This was early in the morning of 19 February, and the pilots were Farquharson and Ballard, both of B Flight. Jimmy Farquharson did not think there were any more tanks around, but I sent out another section to rescan the area, and it soon became evident that there were plenty more. The machines were hidden in dried-up gulleys, well covered with branches and foliage, so they could only be confirmed as tanks when they had caught fire and the camouflage had burned. Some of these armoured vehicles were kept under trees and some between the huts of a nearby village, but all were well hidden.

As each section returned with news of more tanks set on fire, it appeared that we had destroyed some twenty of them. However, a careful analysis by our intelligence officers – with the aid of a large-scale map of the area – narrowed our claims down to thirteen enemy tanks destroyed. This event is recorded in the official war history of the RAF. It was a significant event and as Jimmy Farquharson had started it all, I put his name forward for the award of immediate DFC. This was approved by the higher authorities and was announced soon after.

That evening, we had a record number of newspaper reporters at the mess, seeking details of the day's happenings. Ginger Lacey joined us and told me how he had shot down a Jap fighter that day with a short burst of gunfire from his Spitfire, using about six shells in all. He had hit the pilot in the head as he made his single attack and then continued his dive to ground level. If he had hung around, he said, he could have been bounced in his turn. I suppose that is how he had lasted so long. His number two did not know much about it, but the Jap plane was found and the claim confirmed.

The Japanese must have been busy overnight, bringing anti-aircraft guns into the area. The next morning our planes went off in sections looking for more tanks, but not only did we not find any, but every aircraft except mine was damaged to some degree by ack-ack fire. Farquharson had a bullet through the side of his cockpit, which luckily missed him, and I can remember a young sergeant pilot, Farrer, posing for a newspaper photographer with his head looking through a large hole in his rudder. I was worried by the amount of damage to the squadron aircraft and unfairly tore Farrer off a strip for getting hit by ack-ack!

On the following day, 21 February, the OC 60 Squadron and I were invited to have lunch with the general commanding the area, at the small town of Allagappa. All I recall is that the general looked carefully at Humphries and me, and then said to Humphries: 'You must be the CO of 20 Squadron'!

In the last few days of the month, I did an offensive recce of a Jap airstrip, finding only a steamroller; a dawn recce from Mandalay to Maymyo, which was sited in the hills to the east; and two night 'Rhubarb' raids. In the first of these, I was able to locate an enemy field gun by its flash and silence it; in the second I attacked some railway trucks.

While on the Arakan front, road transport was only an occasional target, but here it became our staple diet. The nature of the country meant that there were a limited number of routes available to the Japanese for bringing up supplies. We would study the maps and pick out what would have to be the Jap lines of communication. If there were any aircraft not needed for demands from the war room at group, these were sent off to look for enemy lorries and destroy them.

The Japs nearly always travelled by night and as one flew along in daytime, it was no use looking at the roads as these would be empty. Instead, we learned to study the land on either side of the highways, which were lined with trees for shade, looking for a foliage-covered shape large enough to be a lorry. A pair of shells fired into a suspect shape, could blow off some of the foliage and reveal part of such a vehicle. One or two more pairs would then set it alight.

The beginning of March saw us attacking dumps in the Mandalay area. I scored hits on a Jap bomber on the ground at an aerodrome that we were to occupy later and did a dawn recce of Heho airstrip, where I was met with medium ack-ack. The tracer shells in the early light sped past my aircraft, very different from the tired effect of .303 ammo, which described a parabola as it lost velocity. That was on 5 March, a year since I took command of the squadron.

A few days later I dropped leaflets in the Kyaukpadaung area. The British leaflets compared badly with their Jap counterparts, which were much more graphic.

On 11 March we found a concentration of M/T (military transport) as well as more dumps. Petrol and ammunition stores continued to be our targets, together with bunkers.

We carried out an evening strike on a railway junction on the outskirts of Mandalay on 13 March. I think Jimmy Farquharson was given the opportunity of flying a Hurricane IV and that Mandalay fell the following day – not that these two events were causally related!

By mid-March we were once again looking for tanks. On the 17th I led four Hurricane IVs in a rocket attack on a railway train with fifteen trucks, on which we scored two direct hits. The same day, Group Captain Finlay allowed me to take up his Spitfire VIII for local flying and aerobatics. The Spitfire had the letters 'DOF' on its side. Usually the first two letters identified the squadron and the last letter the individual aircraft, A Flight having the letters A to H, and B Flight the next eight letters. In this case there was a bit of individualism. Later Finlay said it would have been all right if I had taken it to the forward area to look for targets, but I was not told that until afterwards.

On 22 March I took six Hurricane IVs on a strike south of Letse, when the VCP reported: 'Hit HQ.' We were finding more Jap transport, which we only claimed as destroyed when we set them on fire.

Goodhew and I wrecked six lorries on the 23rd, four of them travelling out of Kume fully loaded, as our army moved in from the north. Kume was sited behind some hills, which cut off our reception of the other VHF users on our channel and, I assumed, obstructed our communications from them. Goodhew and I, in separate aircraft, had excited conversations about the Japanese transport and soldiers who were sheltering in a ditch. When I got back to Monywa, Ron Ballard told me that our transmissions had been clearly audible, blocking the channel for other users, who together with Flying Control had made many rude requests for us to shut up!

I took six aircraft to attack a target near Yenangyaung. On a squadron of sixteen planes, one soon learned the individual differences between the aircraft. Although most of them ranged around an average performance for the type, an occasional one would be much better or much worse than the rest. It could be 10 or 20mph faster or slower, heavier or lighter on the controls or, in the case of the Hurricane I flew on this occasion, heavier on petrol. It was for this reason, as leader of the formation, that I was given this plane to pilot. If I had enough fuel to return to base safely, everybody else would know they had!

We took off for Yenangyaung. I set a course and flew on it as exactly as I could. There was a slight wind from the west and I added on 2 or 3 degrees to my compass course to allow for drift. There was a temptation for the pilots to head down the river and turn right at the bottom instead of flying a direct course for this city. It was simpler to do but added several minutes to the flying time. I was gratified to find that we came out dead on target. We carried out our attack, and by that time I had used up both my main fuel tanks. I switched to my reserve tank, containing 25 gallons, called the others to re-form, and set a course back to base, working out the reciprocal of the outward course and knocking off about 4 degrees for the wind. I was certain of my route and knew that I would have just enough petrol to get back. After some 5 minutes of the return journey, one of the pilots (Sergeant Farrer, I think) called up to say he was having to switch

over to his reserve tank. I reassured him that I had already done so. On
nearing the aerodrome, I told Farrer to land immediately after me and we
all got safely down. I heard Goodhew afterwards talking to the 'chiefy' –
the NCO in charge of the flight – criticising me, saying that we only had
just enough to land and would have had no reserve if we had encountered
enemy fighters. 'So what?' replied the chiefy, 'you got back safely, didn't
you?' It would be called a calculated risk today.

On the 28th we were sent off on a rocket strike, but on arriving at the
target, found this to be a small lake. I thought at first that this was a mistake by the war room, but in fact the Japs had flooded the area.

Three young pilot officers joined us at Monywa: Hunter, a gaunt but
pleasant Aberdonian; Hinstridge, a black-haired, stocky man; and Gerry
Astley, a quiet, shy young man, rather like a budding Roger Cobley. He
was interested in photography and was unfortunately killed in a flying
accident after the war.

On 30 March we did an early morning strike on a Jap position. Later in
the morning I was just going off to the mess for lunch when a command
came through for a sortie to Yenangyaung. Nobody else was available, so I
arranged to go, taking with me one of the new intake, Pilot Officer Astley,
on his first operational flight. Once airborne we headed for Yenangyaung,
which was an oil town defended by the Japs with heavy ack-ack. As we
neared it, I began to feel queasy, and soon after cramp-like pains developed in my tummy and spread to my arms and legs. My aircraft started
to lose height and turn to port, and I found that I could not overcome the
cramp sufficiently to hold the machine straight and level. I was still alert
mentally and, as I wandered off course, I wondered what Astley would
think was happening on his first 'op'. Soon I was getting uncomfortably
near to the ground, and with both arms around the control column I was
exerting all my available power to keep the aircraft's nose up. I had to tell
myself to use whatever reserves of strength I had, if I wished to survive.
If I had had the energy, I could have used the tail trim to help me keep
the nose up, but if I had taken one of my arms from the control column,
I would have lost charge of the machine. Gradually the cramp wore off
and my body began to behave normally again. I decided to abandon the
sortie and return to base. On the way, again I thought that Astley would
be mystified by my performance.

I felt it would be unwise to report to the MO in case I was grounded, but it was worrying as I did not understand what had happened. In retrospect, the attack was probably caused by a combination of missing my lunch and a loss of salt due to the heavy sweating that occurred in that climate. Soon after this we received salt tablets to supplement our diet, but these acted as an emetic so they were never taken.

On the evening of that day I was feeling better and took part in a rocket strike with five aircraft on Singu. I think at that time there was a shortage of experienced pilots. On the trip I felt I was giving myself an 'air test' and was relieved to find I had no repetition of the earlier trouble.

In the period from 4 to 30 March I carried out thirty-seven operational sorties with a total of 60 hours 55 minutes' flying time. My only non-operational flight had been in the group captain's Spitfire, making a total of 62 hours 10 minutes.

Some pilots had remarkable escapes. Sandy McPhail's night-flying accident has already been mentioned. Another New Zealander, Geoff Sharp, who had flown Brewster Buffaloes at Rangoon, flew into the trees in the jungle during a monsoon storm, and came to rest unharmed in the branches. Douglas, a flight commander on 60 Squadron at Monywa, suddenly peeled away from the planes that he was leading and crashed into a dried-up sandy riverbed. He could not recall any details as he was concussed and had a loss of memory for the whole event. However, he recovered and returned to the squadron. The story I heard was that Humphries was drinking a lot and Douglas had been taking on a heavy share of leading the squadron on operations. Douglas was one of the rare married pilots and his wife lived up in the hills in India. He told me that once when he arrived home on leave, his son greeted him with 'Hello uncle', which was a title widely used by children in India for any male visitor.

Flight Lieutenant MacVicar was on 28 Squadron for a long spell before he was shot down in the jungle. He then performed the unusual feat of successfully making his way back. At one point he was given food in a Burmese village but, while he was eating, the villagers summoned the Japanese. Enemy soldiers appeared at the other end of the village clearing and MacVicar promptly took off in the opposite direction. The Japs fired their rifles but failed to hit him. When he returned, he was taken off operational flying and given the job of touring around, telling other aircrew how to walk back to base if you had to.

One evening, Thompson the Canadian was standing smoking his pipe

and watching the setting sun, dressed only in his peak cap and his socks
and boots. A Women's Voluntary Services (WVS) van drove by and there
was a shriek from the driver as she did so. She was a middle-aged woman
who had just arrived in the area and had come to stay in the wing mess,
where competition for her favours became fierce.

At the end of March we had a dance for the officers. There must have
been some nurses in the vicinity and of course the WVS lady who lived at
the wing HQ. I cannot remember what other women attended. We had
a large tarpaulin for the dance floor, sprinkled with 'prickly heat powder'
to give it the right surface. A wooden fence was erected to screen off a loo
for the ladies. Most of the officers took on some job for the occasion. I
do not remember much about that night. The squadron leader who had
set my arm on the Arakan in 1944 was there with the nurses. The night of
merrymaking ended with my being given a tumbler of Scotch to drink. A
minute or two later, this turned out to be my nemesis and I set course for
my tent with all possible speed. I undressed as quickly as I could, struggling to retain my senses, and succeeded in falling into bed before losing
consciousness. I surfaced about noon, feeling ill and weak. For some reason Doc O'Brien was not on the camp and by the evening I sent for the
wing MO, who was understandably unsympathetic and told me it was my
own fault. Fortunately, by the next morning I had recovered.

A few days after the dance, we were playing volleyball in the evening
when someone noticed a small black cloud over the mountains to the
west, which separated us from the Arakan coast and the Bay of Bengal.
It looked like a cloud of dust – which indeed it proved to be – and it was
growing rapidly larger. Very soon the dust and wind were upon us. With
some others I ran to the mess tent, which was being shaken by strong
gusts. Although I held one of the upright poles of the tent with both
hands, it was jerked forcibly out of my grasp, and I had to find my way
out of the canvas that had collapsed about me. I was then picked up by
the wind and carried along with my feet touching the ground only every
few yards. Each time, I tried to brake my forward momentum but without
success. A large metal cauldron from the mess went sailing past me in
mid-air, followed by a stream of letters that had been left in the mess for
censoring. Ahead of me I could see the wooden fence erected as a screen
for the ladies' loo and which, remarkably, was still standing. As I was being
propelled past this, it coincided with my feet touching the ground and I
gave a huge lunge over to my left into the lee of this screen, lying flat on

the ground behind it.

Next came heavy rain, which soon caused pools of water to form. At the height of the storm, I could just make out the incredible sight of a Hurricane coming in to land. Visibility was about 50 yards and it disappeared again within seconds. The pilot was Les Hill, and the ground crew picketed the Hurricane down where it came to rest at the end of the landing run. The next day one of the junior pilots was sent off to taxi it back to the flight dispersal point. Carelessly he put the machine up on its nose in the wet ground. I had a green endorsement placed in Les Hill's log book for saving the aircraft and a red endorsement placed in the sergeant pilot's log book for crashing it. We learned later that the storm had swept across the east side of India, over the Bay of Bengal and across the Arakan, causing damage on aerodromes along its route. That evening the light lasted long enough for a few tents to be re-erected and we were able to get a scratch meal.

Squadrons had been instructed to keep a diary of the events taking place, and the junior officers took turns at recording these. The objective was to provide material for a history after the war. The 20 Squadron diary was eventually lost at sea when a ship transporting our equipment to Bangkok sank in the Gulf of Siam immediately after the war. All our literary efforts had been in vain.

I received a policy letter addressed to all squadron commanders, saying that in the European theatre of war, squadrons were being divided into two components: flying personnel would form the squadron, while ground crew would become a servicing echelon. If they had to move, only the aircraft and pilots would relocate, the idea being that the ground crew were interchangeable, and this would lead to greater mobility. The plan would obviously cause loss of morale in the ground crews, who identified themselves with their own squadron. The servicing echelons would retain the squadron number with an additional two figures in front, so that 20 Squadron ground crew became 7020 servicing echelon, under command of Dingle Bell, the engineer officer, who was promoted to flight lieutenant and transferred to the wing mess. This meant less work for me, which I appreciated at that time, although I did not approve of the scheme from a wider angle. Group Captain Finlay, however, implemented the scheme enthusiastically. As we were a specialist squadron and each flight had a set of armaments unique in the Far East, it was very unlikely that the two parts of the squadron would ever split up.

Don Finlay had been an Olympic hurdler before the war. Dingle Bell told me he had been a boy entrant at RAF Halton, and had later trained as a pilot. He married a barmaid and, according to Dingle, when he was commissioned he felt he had made an unsuitable marriage and separated from his wife. He had the ability to arouse great antipathy towards himself. In the Battle of Britain he was a flight commander and Ginger Lacey was his number two. Ginger obviously bore the group captain a grudge and referred to him scornfully as 'a certain former Olympic athlete'. Both Ginger Lacey and Alan Deare in their autobiographies are critical of Finlay, Alan Deare implying that Finlay had used the excuse of a sprained ankle to avoid operations during the Battle of Britain. Once, Air Vice Marshal Vincent said to me in Finlay's presence that Finlay would like his job. It was said gently, and with a smile, but he gave me the impression that it was a mild reproof.

In March 1945 D.O. Finlay was a man of thirty-eight, with regular features, graying at the temples, good physique and a soft, sibilant voice. Our relationship was friendly but it was not the case with the other airmen of the squadron. Although it was generally agreed that shaving once a week in Burma was acceptable, Finlay was keen on men being clean-shaven. He told one of the cooks in the airmen's mess that he must shave. The cook replied that he didn't have any razor blades, and after an argument Finlay sent one to the cook from his own supply, saying that he would have no excuse in future. We used to make blades last a long time in Burma by carefully stropping them on our hands, and a stock of three or four lasted me through the campaign.

I once watched a football match in which the group captain took part. He was involved in a scuffle with one of the other players, and ordered him to come to his office the following morning. A more serious episode occurred when we had a beer issue at Monywa. Officially there was supposed to be an allocation of three bottles per man per month. With the difficulties of supplies by air, in practice this was about the only beer issue we had during our advance through Burma. We were fully prepared to accept a little drunken singing on the night we consumed it, but apparently Finlay objected and sent over the Special Police. The next occurrence was that the airmen were singing the 'Red Flag' and preparing to march over to the wing site. Events settled down, but it was the nearest thing to a mutiny that I knew.

Periodically the three squadron commanders would meet Finlay at his mess to discuss various matters. After one of these meetings I returned with Humphries to the 60 Squadron mess, where he offered me a drink and insisted on mixing it himself when another officer offered to do it. He finally gave me a tipple that obviously contained gin. I apologised and said that I never drank gin. Humphries looked annoyed and gestured to the airman who had offered earlier, to fix me another drink. In the meantime more officers had entered the mess and Humphries handed the original drink to Douglas, the senior flight commander. When I finally rose to go, Douglas still had half his drink left and Humphries told him to drink up. Douglas replied that there was enough gin in the drink to float the *Queen Mary*. I felt that I had had a lucky escape as I would probably not have noticed the alcohol content of the drink I was given, and would have been properly smashed. Normally, whenever a 20 Squadron pilot went to Calcutta, a stone jar of rum would be brought back, as rum and orange was a favourite drink in our mess during an evening.

In accordance with the policy laid down, each month I reviewed all the NCO pilots with regard to their suitability for a commission. I received a 'demi-official' letter from the air commodore commanding 'Records' at Bombay, to say that he was a friend of the father of Warrant Officer Birch, one of the squadron pilots, and asking me to put him up for a commission. I replied that I did not think he was quite ready for the promotion. An official letter then came through telling me to do as the air commodore had suggested. I took the letter to Group Captain Finlay, who agreed that I should reply, refusing, and pointing out that we were busily engaged on operations!

Mepacrine had been developed as an anti-malarial agent. US commanders in the South Pacific were being held responsible for the failure of their troops to take proper precautions against malaria, according to a directive we received. Those who took their mepacrine regularly could be distinguished by the yellow colour of their skin. The wing adjutant was the only yellow man at Monywa! Mepacrine caused indigestion, which put us off it.

Guy Marsland visited us at Monywa. He had been driving a jeep while nursing a tommy gun in his lap. The tommy gun had gone off, firing a bullet through his penis. However, he had made a good recovery and became a proud father soon after the war. He had been supposed to join 909 Wing as the wing commander 'flying', but had elected to move from the Arakan to the Burma plain on foot, over the mountains. This had taken a long time and in the event he did not accept the job when he finally appeared. Marsland and Finlay would not have mixed.

Some of the pilots from the 'colonies' had shorter overseas tours of duty than the British, and were now due for repatriation. Dickie Parr left for Rhodesia, Peter McMillan for Australia and Sandy McPhail for New Zealand. I saw Sandy off in a DC3 from Monywa. He had been a loyal friend and as the Dakota trundled away down the airstrip, I felt a sense of loss. Roy Bennell, who for a time had been my number two, was getting bad dreams and came off the squadron for a rest. I found during the war that all men had their breaking point sooner or later. The toughest and most phlegmatic of men would become 'operationally tired' eventually. I noticed, too, that as a result of having to suppress one's instinct of self-preservation, we took unnecessary risks with our lives when there was no need to do so, and I had to guard against this.

We were all a bit jaded by this time and I felt I was going well and truly round the bend. Finlay intercepted me one day and said that the war was entering its final critical phase and that we needed one last all-out effort for victory. I had been considering that it would be in the interests of my sanity if I asked for a rest from operations, but in response to Finlay's appeal I decided to carry on. The policy of dividing the squadron into flying and servicing components had reduced my workload and made it easier for me to do so.

The Japs had been using a 20mm cannon for ack-ack at one of the points we were attacking, and I gave the bad advice in the mess that it was worth attacking this cannon if it could be located. I can't imagine what put this idea into my head and Peter McMillan frankly disagreed with me at the time. Keith Bailey, a nice chap who had been training as a solicitor, was shot down soon after and his plane was never found. I have sometimes had tortured thoughts that he might have been following my advice.

I had had a girlfriend before leaving the UK and letters to and from her had helped my morale since arriving in India. Now I received a 'Mespot', so called because airmen serving in Mesopotamia had sooner or later received a letter saying: 'Dear Joe, I love another. …' Most of the squadron received one! My girlfriend had given me a Bible when I left England and while in India and Burma, I had made a habit of perusing a bit each night, and reading my way right through the Bible during my tour overseas. My

Christian beliefs at the time helped me to face dangers and gave me courage in critical conditions. The Japanese Kamikaze pilots firmly believed they were taking a short cut to paradise when they flew their planes into enemy ships, which was an extreme example of the same principle.

I finally decided to put in an adverse report on John Penman. Peter Joel had warned me of him when I took over the squadron, saying that he too had been warned by Fletcher. I had already lost confidence in his performance as a pilot and now I felt, rightly or wrongly, that he was a disruptive influence on the squadron and should go. I called him into my office and showed him the report before passing it on to Group Captain Finlay. Penman was a plausible talker and managed to persuade Air Commodore Vasse that the charges against him were groundless. He was attached to 60 Squadron for a fortnight. Their ops were of a simple nature of bombing on a map reference, and Penman was reported by Humphries as being perfectly satisfactory. John Penman was then promoted to squadron leader and moved back to Bombay.

At Monywa we had a visit from a member of the Air Council, Air Chief Marshal Sir Christopher Courtenay. I was told that he was studying routes to the Far East for use after the war. Burma never did become part of the international air route, so from that angle his mission was fruitless. He was accompanied by a young Jewish group captain without wings and two wing commanders who were both pilots. One of them asked me what I felt about using more modern aircraft for the job we were doing, as apparently the Hurricane was no longer being made. I replied that the Hurricane was very manoeuvrable and stable, while newer aircraft would be faster, which would make it difficult to do low-level reconnaissance work, spotting small camouflaged targets and pinpointing them on the map. The wing commander was unable to follow my remarks and called the other wingco over, admitting disarmingly that he wasn't very quick at catching on! Probably at that time my speech was a bit jungly, with RAF slang larded with phrases from Indian dialects!

I took the ACM to the crew room and introduced him to the pilots. He asked Anderson the Canadian about the situation on our part of the front. Anderson started to reply and made some slight error. I began to correct him, but the ACM stopped me and said he wanted to hear Anderson. Anderson then talked fluently (like many Canadians) and gave a good account of our activities.

For entertainment, we had two ENSA concerts in the town of Monywa. In one of them, the star was Patricia Burke, the daughter of Marie Burke, while the other production was a Ralph Reader Gang Show. This was an all-male performance. One number consisted of a line of chorus girls. We were getting used to female impersonators, but this was burlesque and, when they broke into a dance, their short skirts revealed that they were well endowed with male characteristics!

We had a film show in a blast-proof pen at Monywa. These were three-sided bays with high earth walls to protect aircraft from air attack. The first feature proved to be the one made of 20 Squadron while we were on the Arakan. We did not know that it was on the programme and, of course, it was enjoyable. The next movie was *Champagne Charlie* starring Tommy Trinder. It was not all that wonderful but during it I was surprised to see someone get up and move along to the left, followed by another figure, and soon others in the same row. There was now a group of people over to the side of the seats and, going over to them, I could see they were surrounding a large yellow Russell's viper. I found a stick and killed this highly poisonous snake, after which we returned to the film, but we had all rather lost interest.

An army captain stayed in our mess at Monywa for a week or so. During his visit he joined the poker school that operated in the evening and managed to lose a considerable sum. I had not realised that such high stakes were being played for and felt it was an abuse of our hospitality for the pilots involved to fleece a guest in this way. I did something to redress the situation, limiting the stakes for the future, but I can't remember whether the army officer recovered any of his money.

Our air liaison officer (ALO) at Sapam had been a Captain Magan, a balding sandy-haired officer. He had been replaced by Bob Adams, a cheerful dark-haired captain with a moustache, who was well liked by the aircrew. He had gone on ahead to our next port of call, an airfield east of Meiktila called Thedaw. The Japanese were still surrounding the area and our advance party was besieged on the airstrip. Bob Adams was standing on a lorry directing return fire, when he was hit and killed. Generally speaking, the ALO had a safe job and we all felt sorry for Bob, who was a married man with a family. On our way back from the flights in the evening, we passed the sergeants' quarters, and I was told to look out for a certain sergeant who was said to have an unusual penis. I drove by in the back of a lorry with several other pilots, and sure enough the sergeant was standing stripped, having his evening wash. His penis was over a foot long and most spectacular. I found myself laughing helplessly with all the others once we were out of sight.

My minor ailments continued, although fortunately did not incapacitate. There was a pleasant dentist at wing HQ, whom I consulted as I was getting toothache. The pain seemed to be coming from an empty socket. The dentist had a drill that he worked with his foot by a treadle. He drilled the gum gently, presumably to placate me! Fortunately the toothache settled down in due course.

I also found the light was hurting my eyes. This was eased by the tinted Crookes lenses of the flying goggles but not by the sunglasses that I wore on the ground. The Canadians had Polaroid lenses but we were only able to get smoked glass, which did not relieve my discomfort.

We were visited at Monywa by Freeman, who had been in charge of the RAF Regiment at 'Hove'. A year in that climate had aged him a bit, and he probably noticed some changes in us too.

What with the party and the storm I did not fly again until 4 April. I had two unusual flights on the 9th. The first one involved a dawn take-off for an attack on Yenangyaung, where Japanese tanks were reported to be massing. I had two other Hurricane IIDs with me, flown by Les Hill and Sergeant Tuffield, both excellent pilots from B Flight. As we approached the town, the Japanese fired a single shell of heavy ack-ack, which burst with a cloud of black smoke about a mile ahead of us. It was obviously intended to warn us off, but had the opposite effect of annoying me. Did they hope to scare us away with just a warning shot?

I told the others to get into a long line astern and the next time the gun fired I was able to locate its position. I dived down to a low level, limited by the numerous hillocks or 'pimples' in that area, and also by the oil rigs. As I approached the gun, I again saw the flash of its explosion; I dropped a little lower to my right and then continued towards the weapon, counting as I went. When I had reached the number eight, I heard an explosion behind me and then I fired off two pairs of shells. Les Hill and Tuffield were able to attack before the gun was reloaded. We made two or three more strikes, which followed the same pattern. Tuffield claimed he had hit the officer standing on the revetment around the gun with his machine guns.

I called off the attack, remembering that this was not our target. As we looked round the area, having climbed to about 2,000 feet, I suddenly thought of the gun and looked over in its direction. An anti-aircraft shell exploded about 50 yards short of me, between me and the gun. I pulled the nose of my machine up and a moment later felt the turbulence of the explosion pass beneath me, and possibly fragments of shell. It must have looked like a 'hit' to the gunners and I embarked on some clowning, allowing the plane to fall away to its right until I was down to ground level, when I straightened out.

Fortunately there was only the one heavy ack-ack gun in Yenangyaung by that stage. We were unable to find any tanks and so really the mission was unsuccessful, but very stimulating all the same. Instead, there were other targets to focus on, such as attacking a working factory, causing the escape of much black smoke and steam. We also set a lorry on fire and blew the bonnet off another.

Later in the morning, two ALOs from group came over to our mess to find out more about our brush with the heavy anti-aircraft fire. They told us that 8 seconds was the minimum time that the fuse of the Japanese ack-ack shell could be reduced to, and that the gun would have been firing at us over open sights.

The second flight was in the afternoon. We had a call from the army to attack some tanks in a village south-east of Thazi, which was east of Meiktila. Several Hurricane IVs took off, first of all under Johnny Horrocks, and I arranged to follow up with some Hurricane IIDs. Johnny was still over the target when B Flight aircraft arrived but they had not made any strike as no tanks had been spotted and Johnny had not found any tank tracks leading to any of the buildings. A Flight returned home with their rockets unfired, and the army came through on the R/T to say that the tanks were hidden in the village in a large building with a red roof. There were certainly no signs of tank tracks, but as the army wanted the building demolished, we did this and found that we had started some impressive fires. These were accompanied by appreciative noises from the VCP over the R/T. Some weeks later, when we were down at Toungoo, an army officer visited to tell us that we had indeed destroyed several tanks and he had called to thank us.

Group decided that the situation at Meiktila now permitted a forward move and on 11 April 20 Squadron transferred to Thedaw, an aerodrome with a proper tarmacadam runway, a few miles east of Meiktila.

Chapter 17

Thedaw, Meiktila – 11–28 April 1945

We flew over to Thedaw in the late afternoon of 11 April. I took the opportunity of looking round the aerodrome from the air, getting the lie of the land more quickly in this way. Our intelligence officer, Pilot Officer Crawford, otherwise known as the 'Spy', had arrived earlier with the advance party, and was obviously not feeling well. However, he gamely carried on, refusing to give in to his nausea. The tents had not arrived, so we made our camp beds up in a blast-proof pen and, as darkness had fallen, we had an early night. The Japanese were still retreating through the aerodrome, and we had strict orders not to move around in the dark. The RAF Regiment also had instructions to shoot at anybody doing so. It rained during the night and there was a pool of water on top of my camp bed (which fortunately was waterproof) when I woke in the morning,

Thedaw was an aerodrome that I had attacked from the air a short time previously, although the only target had been a steamroller at the end of the runway. There were one or two abandoned Jap fighters beside the airstrip, which we inspected with interest. None of them were serviceable.

Our tents arrived the next day and I had mine put up in a neighbouring, blast-proof pen with another tent belonging to Major Piercy, who had replaced Bob Adams. We had cheese for supper and during the night I was wakened by a rustling noise outside my tent. I listened as the rustling noise recurred and I had visions of a Jap lurking around, with evil intent. Finally I got out of bed with my revolver and ventured outside, only to find that the wind was causing movement in the branches of a palm tree and that this was the noise I had heard. Possibly the cheese had contributed to my having an uneasy dream of a Jap intruder!

I had developed the habit of killing snakes whenever I saw them, and one evening on the runway I saw a small snake, intending to crush it with my flying boots. As I advanced it reared and opened up its hood behind its head, showing itself to be a small cobra. This was the only time that a snake showed any inclination to fight back. I stamped my foot on the runway as it approached me, and it quickly slithered off into the undergrowth.

Another time, after an evening visit to the wing mess, I was returning to the squadron quarters by jeep when I saw two large snakes gliding across the road in the moonlight. I accelerated and managed to run over them, but somehow this had no effect and they continued on, sliding into the vegetation by the roadside.

Major Piercy had worked with the Americans as a liaison officer and had got on well with them. He had a large station wagon, loaded with useful equipment, which he took with him on his moves. Our own equipment, on the other hand, was getting more and more sparse as we ventured further into Burma, and we were rapidly getting down to the bare essentials. The major soon settled in with the squadron, although at first he was not used to the lack of formality in the RAF.

Somebody found a booby trap in our new camp, in the form of a wire stretched across a path and connected to a grenade. We took this to Major Piercy, who very knowledgeably said that the trouble with Jap grenades was that they blew into such small fragments that they did not do any serious damage. We studied the bomb and noted that it had a pin that could be pulled out, but also a percussion cap, unlike a Mills bomb. It looked as though one had to pull the pin and then strike the percussion cap in order to fire the bomb. We decided to experiment by fastening the bomb in the ground and tying a string to the pin. We then placed a large stone over the bomb, supporting the stone with a stick, to which we fastened another string. Major Piercy then retired to a trench about 8 feet away, leading the strings off to his trench. I pulled back a distance of some 30 feet and lay on the ground, while a few other observers went to a more discreet distance.

Major Piercy pulled the string attached to the pin and we waited for a while for something to happen. Nothing did, so he pulled the second string, which caused the stone to fall on the bomb. I started to count. I had got to eight when Major Piercy scrambled out of his trench and said, 'It's a dud!' Simultaneously there was an enormous explosion and earth and rocks were thrown high into the air. These started to fall around the spot where I was lying and I began to wish that I had moved further away.

As I sprung up, Major Piercy was running towards me, bent forward with blood streaming from him. His first words were: 'What did I tell you? Not one bit big enough to kill a man!' He was peppered with tiny bits of metal, with one or two bits in his eyes. These had to be extracted at the nearest field hospital, but the other bits gradually worked their way out of his body. As we all worked stripped to the waist, we were able to watch his progress with interest over the next few weeks!

We had no furniture in the mess, so we went on a scavenging expedition into Meiktila. The main requirement was a table for our meals. I took two or three officers with me in the jeep and I was soon called to look at a Jap brothel, which one of them had found. Upstairs there were several beds in each room, made of simple bamboo matting. On the floor were many discarded condoms, a high-heeled shoe and what looked like red face-powder. The ladies probably never got near to the front line and would have been moved out of the area in good time. This was the only evidence I saw of a brothel in Burma.

At one road fork, there was a strong smell of decomposition, which we traced to a small bunker or foxhole. This had been destroyed by a direct hit, and probably contained one or two dead Japanese.

In the main street of Meiktila, we came across a bank with tall doors. We detached one of these and found it was just the length for the mess dining table. The next time we went into Meiktila, we were stopped by the Special Police, who said they were instructed to prevent looting, but by that time there was not much left to take.

There were two lakes in Meiktila, which were soon being used as swimming pools. One day I was driving in with about eight pilots loaded into the jeep. There were metalled roads in that part, in contrast to much of the countryside that we had seen. They had been left untended during the Japanese occupation, and now with heavy use they were beginning to crumble. I was driving along at my customary high speed when I met a lorry coming in the opposite direction, with an Indian at the wheel. He was in the middle of the road and the lorry seemed to have taken over control of the driver, who was going at the same speed as I was. I had to leave the road to avoid a collision, then immediately ahead was a large pit, so I had to swerve quickly back on the road again. I felt that I had dealt with these two hazards very creditably. In swerving, an Australian pilot called Jenkins fell out of the jeep, but fortunately he was not hurt and was able to pick himself up and run after us. I stopped and waited for him to climb back in. At that point Jimmy Farquharson got out of the jeep, condemned my driving and called on the others to disembark too. Luckily he got no support. Jimmy was probably round the bend by that time, as most of us were. I thought it was wrong to attempt to undermine my authority in this way, but I said no more about it.

Our offensive reconnaissances continued, finding M/T as our main target, many of them on the move. This contrasted with the earlier part of the war, when we were fighting an unseen enemy. We also found and destroyed a number of dumps. On 16 April, flying with Pilot Officer Astley as my number two, we discovered a large dump area, which I reported later. At the end of the sortie I also spotted a sizeable camouflaged object under some trees near a house. It looked to me as though it could be a tank, and I started to attack it. We were unable to get a fire going in spite of several strikes, and we had used what remained of our 40mm shells without causing a blaze. I made a last run with my .303 bullets, which included tracers, and there must have been petrol on the ground by then as I saw a sudden burst of flame as the bullets hit the target.

But now we had very little fuel left and I set course for home without delay. After we had been flying for some minutes I realised that I had not seen any familiar landmarks, whereas we should have reached our aerodrome by that time. I had to do some quick thinking. There were no landmarks that could be pinpointed on the map. In the end I decided that we must be too far west. If we had been too far east, there would have been some distinctive features. I turned on to a course of about 100 degrees and was relieved to see Meiktila and Thedaw appear a few minutes later, so it was with relief that we got back safely.

The next time I flew back to the place where we had started the fire, I found that the camouflaged object was in fact two lorries, now burned out, and not a tank at all.

Wing HQ moved in across the road, and 17 Squadron used their airstrip, while 60 Squadron joined us on the main aerodrome.

We were short of pilots at that time, as several colonial airmen were repatriated. I borrowed a flight lieutenant from 17 Squadron who flew as my number two on 21 April to a place called Salin, to the west of Meiktila and north-west of Yenangyaung. As we flew over a road lined with trees, I spotted two jeeps driving down the road, with the white star on their bonnets that acted as a recognition signal for the Allies. However, these vehicles pulled into the side of the road as I passed overhead, and I could see that the occupants were Jap soldiers, obviously having managed to capture the jeeps. I called up the flight lieutenant and told him that we were going to attack. One of them allowed a fairly easy approach and, although I did not set it on fire, I was satisfied that I had put it out of action. The other jeep was difficult to attack because of the trees, whose branches were in the way of the shell trajectories and screened it from my view during my approach to the target.

When we returned to the aerodrome and were being debriefed by Major Piercy, I was interested to hear the flight lieutenant say that he had not seen anything of the vehicles and did not know what he was supposed to be shooting at! This was not surprising as it took practice to spot camouflaged transport or small targets like jeeps hidden by trees. Jimmy Farquharson flew over the area the next day and reported that there was only one jeep there and that it had plainly been there a long time – implying that I had dreamed the whole episode. I did not trouble to check to see whether the second jeep had got away. I could see that Major Piercy was very perplexed by the situation, not knowing what to make of it all.

No. 20 Squadron was given a very free hand to choose their own targets, with occasional requests from the war room for offensive reconnaissances in certain areas and general guidance as to where we should concentrate our efforts. In one case, I carried out a recce in an area that had already been surrounded by our own troops, without my realising it. I discovered a Jap dump near the roadside, which I attacked, causing a fire and explosions. Some 2 miles further along the road I found our own troops advancing in the direction of the dump, which they would have captured intact. Nobody seemed to mind, but my leg was pulled when I reported all this to the intelligence officer.

On 23 April we were asked to give a demonstration to the army in conjunction with 60 Squadron. The targets were two enemy bunkers situated about 2 miles south of Thedaw. The ALO for 60 Squadron was with the army observers and 20 Squadron had to open the batting, so to speak. First of all I identified the group who were watching. They were about 600 to 800 yards from the bunkers. I had two other pilots with me and we were flying Hurricane IVs with rockets. We made four dive attacks, each aircraft firing a pair of rockets on each dive. My second pair hit one of the bunkers, destroying it, but we did not manage to score direct hits on the second. We were in R/T communication with ALO and I said that it would leave 60 Squadron something to aim at. Apparently 60 Squadron over-dropped their bombs on their first run, none of them within 100 yards of the target, and then left. This illustrated clearly the different standards of the two squadrons and the ALO for 60 Squadron was surprised and critical of his airmen's performance in the mess that evening.

One late afternoon towards the end of April, a message came through that a Jap corps headquarters was beating a retreat from an occupied position and had not waited for the cover of darkness. It sounded a straightforward job and I asked Johnny Horrocks to lead the formation on the sortie. It proved to be an exhilarating mission, with the largest enemy column of transport on the move that we had yet encountered. The pilots came back very thrilled, and in view of its significance I put Johnny Horrocks up for the award of an immediate DFC. He was eventually given a non-immediate DFC.

On the morning of 28 April, we moved to Tennant, near Toungoo. The airlift was carried out by US transport. The first American pilot complained to me that his coffee had been cold at breakfast that morning, but coffee was something that we had not seen for a long time and my heart did not bleed for him. He asked me to stop my jeep as we passed one of the Jap fighters by the runway. He got out a screwdriver and started dismantling bits for souvenirs. He said they were quite valuable and would also show that he had been 'there'.

On this occasion we were going to keep the main part of the squadron at Thedaw, operating from Tennant with the minimal amount of crews and equipment. Pilots were to take only what they could store in their Hurricanes, which was not much. Major Piercy did the journey by road in his station wagon and was thereby the best-equipped man at Tennant.

Chapter 18

Tennant, Toungoo – 28 April–11 May 1945

We were now entering the final phase of the war in Burma. The Japanese retreat was becoming a rout. Only a short time ago, the enemy had been retreating through our aerodrome at Thedaw by night, and already we were within striking distance of Rangoon, on an aerodrome some 150 miles further south.

At Thedaw we had used the door of a bank as a dining table for our mess. At Tennant we had no mess tent, let alone a table. Meals were served in the open, and we had to borrow from airmen who had been provided with their own plate, knife, fork and mug. There were no washing-up facilities that I recall, and the utensils were handed over to the next man to use as soon as the plate was empty.

At Tennant, I met an Air Commodore Chacksfield. I think he told me he was connected with the engineering branch, although it was odd to find a high-ranking officer on his own, as he was. We queued up together for meals, borrowing plates and utensils from those who had finished their food. I remembered how I had had to queue up for meals at Uxbridge at the beginning of the war, and found it amusing to be doing the same thing now as a squadron commander in company with an air commodore. After the war, I met Chacksfield at a reunion in 1947, when he told me that he had steadily lost his acting rank. Subsequently he became an air marshal with a knighthood and later became Chief Scout in England.

The airfield was on the bank of a wide river, the Sittang, but we were unable to make use of the water as the Japanese were on the opposite side and were sniping at anybody who showed himself. Accordingly, the army had dug us a large well on our site, which supplied us with adequate amounts of very muddy liquid. Understandably all water had to be boiled before drinking. It was very hot and humid at Tennant and we would all have been glad of some clear, cold water. It was not possible to tell from its appearance whether one was drinking 'char' or plain water. One of the officers had taken an empty stone rum jar, knocked out the bottom, inverted it, filled it with earth and then filtered water through it, collecting a glassful of clear water each day.

We had taken with us only what we could fit into our Hurricanes. There was a single large tent for the pilots to sleep in, but when I saw that Major Piercy had arrived with a 180-lb tent, I moved in with him.

On the first night we sat out in the open and watched moths impinge themselves on our Hurricane lamp. As they fell to the ground, stunned, they were pounced on by ants who pinned them down before they could recover and fly away. The ants then took them below ground to their nests.

Piercy was already in bed when I decided to turn in. I took my flying boots off, which I wore as protection from mosquito bites, and as I put my foot to the ground a snake slithered away from underneath; by the light of the moon, I could see that it had hidden under my flying boot. I woke Piercy and asked him if he had a kukri knife, guessing that he was so well equipped that the answer would be yes! With the knife in my right hand, I lifted up the flying boot with my other and sliced the reptile in two. The other pilots had heard the commotion and now gathered round to identify the snake. We diagnosed a banded krait, but subsequently I found that they would have been much larger. However, at the time, it appeared to have been a poisonous snake and I asked Major Piercy what he would have done if it had bitten me. He said he would have used the kukri to excise the bite, so I felt I had had a lucky escape!

Not far from our tent was an enemy grave, consisting of a painted white board placed upright in the ground, with Japanese lettering on it that ran vertically. The grave was in a small enclosure with a path leading to it. The Jap had evidently been of some consequence during life.

Beside the airstrip was an underground bunker, covered with earth to a height of about 8 feet above ground level. This had been destroyed shortly before we arrived, and continued to smoke throughout our stay.

By night the army was shelling the Japs on the other side of the river and, as I reclined in bed, there would be an explosion near the strip as the gun was fired, followed by a noise like a London tube train passing through a station, as the shell passed overhead, and then finally the explosion as it arrived at its destination. At least we were not at the receiving end.

On the Arakan in 1942, the Japanese were like a ghost army, with no sign of life or equipment on their side of the front. In subsequent years, I saw a single Jap lorry in motion on a handful of occasions. More commonly we found them camouflaged and hidden off the roadside. As we penetrated into Burma, more targets came our way, culminating on 30 April with a line of 200 to 300 enemy M/Ts of all varieties. The bottleneck was at the Mokpalin ferry, which would have transported them across to Moulmein if it could have operated.

I felt it was important to destroy them that day, to prevent them from getting away under cover of darkness. The squadron set fire to forty-six M/T and damaged many more. I flew on to Moulmein and found railway carriages in a siding with red crosses on the roofs of the carriages, the only ones I saw during the war.

There were no reserve pilots at Tennant. Each one of us had his own aircraft, and as the planes were needed throughout the day, we were flying more than usual. That night we were all very tired and were glad to flop down on our beds. I was awakened an hour or two later by the noise of machine-gun fire, with bullets whistling over our tents. I felt I should get up and investigate, but I was so tired that I rolled over and soon went back to sleep. In the morning I found the rest of the aircrew had reacted in the same way! Some Japanese had crossed the river during the night and attempted to reach the aircraft. The RAF Regiment had dealt successfully with the raid, killing three of the intruders within 50 yards of our tents.

We continued our offensive recces on 1 and 2 May, but then the weather started to deteriorate. I did a further reconnaissance of the Prome road to the west on 5 May. Although I did not realise it at the time, this was my last operational flight of the war. The monsoon arrived much earlier than in India and flying was greatly restricted. However, by now there were only pockets of resistance to be mopped up, and the main campaign had been brought to a successful conclusion.

Rangoon had been evacuated by the Japs and we only became aware of it when Beaufighters saw the information written on the roof of the POW camp there by the inmates. Victory in Europe occurred at this time. We probably heard by wireless rather than via the daily paper of the South East Asia Command (SEAC), started by Mountbatten for the services, with Frank Owen as editor. It would not have reached us at Tennant. On VE night, supplies of alcohol were unearthed and there were sounds of merry-making throughout the camp. My main worry was that the Japs would seize the chance to raid us from across the river, but fortunately this did not happen.

We managed to get some plates and cutlery from our mess at Thedaw, and were returning from a meal, when an unfortunate snake broke cover and crossed the path in front of us. Looking around, I could see no stick handy to strike it, so I threw the plate that I was carrying, This landed on the rear half of the reptile and was sufficient to hold it in the soft mud until I found a branch with which to kill it.

On 6 May I flew back to Thedaw for some stores, taking the Harvard. Before I left I told Jimmy Farquharson that the ground was too soft after all the rain for the Hurricanes to fly. Apparently I had no sooner taken off than Farquharson turned to the pilots and said: 'Right chaps! The CO's away! Let's fly!' He authorised a section to go off on a sortie, but both aircraft went up on their noses while taxiing out for take-off. I came back with a 180-lb tent and other items in the back of the Harvard. It was so heavily loaded that the stalling speed was appreciably higher than usual and I had to bring her in at well above the normal speed.

It seemed to me there was no excuse for Farquharson's act in sending off two aircraft in direct defiance of my orders. The two damaged planes were the direct result of his action. It certainly merited punishment. On the other hand, Jimmy was an excellent pilot and I did not want to do anything that reduced the squadron's potential as a war weapon. In the end I had him in my office with Dai Lewis, the adjutant, present, and gave him an unofficial reprimand, pointing out that it was a disloyal, stupid act and that it was only consideration for the squadron's efficiency that stopped me from having him properly disciplined.

I watched two Spitfires take off from Tennant. The port wheel of the second aircraft detached itself on take-off and disappeared into the undergrowth to the left. The Spit continued on its flight, probably unaware of its loss, retracting what was left of the undercarriage in the usual way. I contacted the ops room and reported the loss, but I never learned what happened. I suppose the pilot did a belly landing on his return to his own airstrip.

As flying was restricted, I did a foraging trip with a couple of pilots in my jeep towards Toungoo. On our way we found a case of artillery shells by the roadside, probably for a Jap field gun. A bit further on, we could hear gunfire, with the sound of shells exploding ahead of us. When we reached Toungoo, we were surprised to find a NAAFI shop in the main street, but in view of the recent shelling, the shop was closed and the staff had not yet returned from their place of shelter.

On another trip we passed a village with a green, very reminiscent of England. There was an English-style church that had been fortified by the Japs, which rather horrified me at the time.

Also in this area, we came across the Temple of a Thousand Buddhas. Outside the walled perimeter was a clay model of a life-sized elephant, complete with figures of men riding in a howdah, and with attendants alongside. On entering the monastery we were received in friendly fashion and given tea. One of the monks spoke English and told us that the tea set had been buried during the Japanese occupation. He enlightened us about the temple and showed us round. There were shelves containing countless small images of Buddha, with an occasional bigger model among them. At the focal point of the temple was a very large statue of Buddha. I enjoyed the gentle courtesy of the monks, and regret that I do not recall more of their lifestyle.

The rains continued to fall, and we could do no flying. Group Captain Finlay was at Tennant and joined us one evening as we sat in the main tent, chatting, before we turned in for the night. Finlay wore a dressing gown, which hung loosely open at the front, and I reflected on the different standards of dress in the jungle, compared with the UK. Finlay was still a strict disciplinarian, but by now 20 Squadron stood high in his estimation, and he was prepared to relax with us. I think he was planning to give me the job of wing commander 'flying' on 909 Wing, but that night I told him that I wished to stay with the squadron until I left the RAF. The job would have been great if I had been physically and mentally fit, but by that time I was just not up to it. However, I was never officially offered the position.

Altogether, we were at Tennant for thirteen days before returning to our base at Thedaw.

Chapter 19

Thedaw Again – 11–31 May 1945

Once we were back at Thedaw, there was very little chance to get airborne and no operations. Rain and cloud conditions made flying difficult.

Diarrhoea was always a problem in the Far East. At that time, Thompson, the Canadian, and I both had a severe attack of the 'squitters', so that we could not have flown anyway. As I made my way to the latrines, I would meet Thompson coming away, and as I returned wearily to my tent, Tom would pass me on his way back to the latrine. We would chuckle as we met. Within a day of this, we had worn tracks between our tents and the latrine. Eventually Thompson collapsed and had to be flown to hospital. Fortunately my attack settled down to the usual, less-severe chronic diarrhoea, which many of us experienced.

Maymyo was not far distant from Meiktila and had been the hill station for the Burmese government before the war. I flew up there with Major Piercy in a Sentinel, landing on the racecourse. I was a bit wary of this, as the air was thinner at the height of Maymyo, and I was afraid that it would give less lift to the aircraft, especially on take-off. However, all went well. I returned next day with Pilot Officer Hinstridge, who had driven Major Piercy's station wagon up to Maymyo.

This scenic town was in the hills to the east of Mandalay, where there was a tableland of beautiful country very similar to the English countryside, and very different from the scorched scenery of the Burma plain. Here was a meeting point for the states to the east of Burma. The market at Maymyo was very colourful, in both people and produce. The women wore make-up, which seemed strange to our eyes – a kind of clay smeared unnaturally over their faces, but was probably regarded as terribly sexy by the local men. There were strawberries for sale and we brought some of these back to camp, as we were planning another dance at Thedaw on

22 May. Again, I visited the field hospital and booked up all the nurses. We sent invitations to the air officer commanding and various others. I had been given two sabres captured from enemy NCOs and sent to me by General Leese. These were laid out on a table in the mess tent beside the Jap officer's sword that had been presented to the squadron in the Arakan.

The evening was most enjoyable. The AOC turned up accompanied by the queen bee of the nurses, with whom he was friendly. One of the nursing sisters was quite young and attractive and agreed to come with me for a visit to Maymyo. I weaved off and found Group Captain Finlay and asked his permission for a couple of days' leave at this town, which he cheerfully gave. I thought it was a good time, tactically, to ask him, but unfortunately the next day he remembered nothing of it, and when I returned from Maymyo he gave me a rocket for going off without asking him!

Two young army officers came to the dance but got very drunk and made nuisances of themselves. They refused to go back to their quarters near the aerodrome, so in the end a Canadian pilot from 60 Squadron and myself put them in the jeep and drove them back. On the way one of them was very noisy, so I told the Canadian to knock him out. He gave him a hearty punch on the jaw, which had no observable effect. The next morning, I was awakened very early by one of the army officers, who had come back to apologise for his behaviour. When I got up, I found that one of the Jap sabres had been stolen. This turned out eventually to have been taken by Dingle Bell, the engineer officer who, like everybody else, was well and truly round the twist.

I drew out the pay that had accumulated over the last few months in Burma, intending to buy savings certificates. Unfortunately the savings officer had run out of certificates, and I was left for the time being with the money in my wallet. This amounted to some 1,500 rupees, or about £115.

Within a day or so of the dance, I was off to Maymyo, with the nursing sister, in the squadron Harvard, while two of the pilots took the jeep by road. At Maymyo, the officers were billeted in the house used at one time by the governor, while there was a separate residence for female officers a short distance away. The governor's house was in good repair and there was a number of pre-war servants to look after the officers who were on leave there. My bulky wallet was a nuisance and I tried hiding it in my bed, but an honest bearer brought it to me, thinking I had left it there unintentionally. After that I decided I would have to carry it around with me in my hip pocket. During the afternoon, the two pilots, myself and the nursing sister went for a ride in the jeep. After we had got out and walked up a hill, at the top I realised that I no longer had my wallet. I retraced my steps carefully but, in spite of a thorough search, the wallet was never found. It was annoying, as £115 was quite a sum in those days. However, there was nothing to be gained by mourning its loss.

Maymyo had a cinema (not working), a swimming pool (which we used), and a racecourse (which I used as a landing ground). The signposts to the swimming pool were reminiscent of some of our rural English ones, stating the distance to the pool as, say, ½ mile, and then after a considerable walk, the next sign would again indicate ½ mile!

The nursing sister was a Roman Catholic who had recently broken off her engagement on religious grounds. Standards were stricter in those days, and while she was game for a little 'necking', we got no further, and I was by no means skilled in the art of seduction. After two very pleasant days at Maymyo, we flew back to Meiktila.

Group Captain Finlay set up an evening at the wing headquarters, when three or four 20 Squadron pilots talked in turn to an audience of airmen, describing our operational activities. Anderson was one of the pilots and I rounded off the proceedings – not very excitingly, as I was a poor speaker.

An order came through that all camp followers were to be evacuated because of the difficulty of flying in supplies. This included my bearer, Dataya, who had been with me since the days at Charra. As I had lost the large amount of money at Maymyo, I was unable to give him the present that he should have had. Many years later, I traced him to his native village, only to find that he had died a few months earlier of alcoholism. I forwarded some funds to his widow instead.

Group Captain Finlay sent over a message that he wished to see my log book, which meant that I was being considered for a decoration. I felt the time had come to put in commendations for the other pilots also, as the campaign had come to an end. I accordingly got several pilots to submit a list of their operational flights and their log books. I put forward Jimmy Farquharson for a bar to his DFC, Chota Hallet for a DFC, and several others. I took these along to Finlay, as recommendations at the end of a period of operations, known as non-immediate awards. Unexpectedly I met opposition from Don Finlay, who said he was not prepared to forward on non-immediate awards unless the pilots had done 200 hours of 'ops'. He suggested at one point that I should convert them all to 'immediate' awards, but this seemed to me to be wrong, as they were obviously not in that category. In the end I abandoned the attempt to push them through, and have since regretted that I did not make a greater effort, possibly appealing to the air officer commanding over Finlay's head. It was a serious failure on my part.

We were next informed that the AOC wished to honour the squadron and was coming to take the salute at a formal 'march past'. No other squadron was given this honour. There had not been a display like this since we were at Bombay and the airmen had grumbled for weeks after! However, they appreciated the nature of this occasion. The squadron was all paraded for about 20 minutes before the AOC appeared, accompanied by Finlay. We had worked out the order of marching, but Air Vice Marshal Vincent said that he would like me to join him on the saluting base. I hurriedly asked Jimmy Farquharson to lead the squadron in the march past, while I moved off with the AVM and the group captain to a spot some distance away.

The squadron approached, with Jimmy leading and Dingle Bell a few paces behind him, followed by one of the flights, with the officers behind their flight, and so on. As they drew near the saluting base, I heard Dingle Bell whisper hoarsely: 'Go on, Jimmy, go up and join 'em!' Jimmy, like an automaton, wheeled to the right away from the squadron and stood to the side of the three of us. Dingle Bell was then left at the head of the squadron and gave the command, 'Eyes right.' We were a motley collection with our ill-fitting 'jungle greens' and wasted appearances, and yet with our results we could justly claim to be an outstanding fighting unit, more relevant to war perhaps, than the extravaganza seen now at the annual Trooping the Colour. For me, the march past was the crowning moment of 20 Squadron's war effort, and in spite of the rather comic shambles, it was a proud event.

About this time, I decided that Jimmy and I were incompatible and asked the senior air staff officer (SASO) to find him a job at group, giving him a first-class reference and using as a reason for his transfer that he had completed his tour of operational flying.

At Thedaw, we made a list of targets attacked and destroyed by the squadron from January to May 1945, which was entitled '20 Squadron Game Bag 1945'. This included 213 M/T destroyed and 141 damaged; 24 tanks destroyed and 1 damaged; 3 railway trains destroyed and 1 damaged; 70 ammunition and stores dumps destroyed and a similar number damaged; 34 bunkers destroyed and 53 damaged; 11 gun positions destroyed and 17 damaged. Various other targets were also listed.

Life at Thedaw was tedious, with rain and mud and no flying. There were rumours of another squadron move and I would enquire of the wingco 'org' – Wing Commander Vernon – whenever I saw him, if there was news of this. On one occasion, probably because he did not like to disappoint me, he gave an equivocal answer, which I construed as authority for the relocation. I formed an air party and told them to fly to Calcutta and wait there for further orders. It soon became clear that this had been wishful thinking on my part and that I had jumped the gun. I was called to meet Air Commodore Vasse at Meiktila airstrip and was asked what the squadron was doing at Calcutta. Henry Larsen was there, previously CO of 28 Squadron and now a wing commander at group, looking very svelte in a tailor-made bush jacket and trousers of 'jungle green'. Apparently the CO of Alipore had complained of the presence of the squadron aircraft picketed down on his aerodrome. I explained my version of events to Vasse, who told me to carry on with the aircraft to Madras. My recollection of this time is a bit confused, probably reflecting my mental state. He may well have said that I was to get them away from Alipore and nothing more specific as to their destination. I reported to D.O. Finlay that the squadron was off to Madras and that I understood that the CO at Alipore was annoyed that the aircraft had been parked on his aerodrome for several days. Finlay very kindly gave me a letter to the group captain at Alipore, who was a friend of his, which worked like a charm, as I was given VIP treatment when I presented it, having made the journey in the squadron Harvard.

We then flew on to Madras.

Chapter 20

All Over the Place – 1 June–25 August 1945

I had not realised how completely exhausted were my reserves of strength. I arrived in Madras in the squadron Harvard and booked into the Connemara hotel. For the first time in months I ordered a glass of beer and was promptly sick. In fact, I flaked out before I could finish my first glass and had to be carted off by ambulance on a stretcher.

My chronic state of diarrhoea improved quickly in hospital. Others with amoebic dysentery returned to the ward with hair-raising stories of their experiences of being sigmoidoscoped, and I was greatly relieved not to have to undergo this ordeal. One day a bevy of doctors did a ward round and one tall, slim, dark-haired man with spectacles detached himself from the retinue to come over to my bed. 'Are you always as thin as that?' he asked. Certainly my ribs were very prominent and I weighed just under 10 stones, instead of my usual 12½ stones. The main interest, however, is that I recognised the doctor again at UCH after the war. His name was Exton Smith and he became professor of geriatrics.

When I came out of hospital, the aircrew were settled at St Thomas's Mount but there was no news of the rest of the squadron. On my first night out, I went to the Connemara hotel to spend the evening with some of the pilots. At the next table was an American soldier with an Anglo-Indian girl. I stood up and invited her to dance. The soldier objected to this, quite understandably as there was an extreme shortage of female partners and he did not want anyone butting in on his territory. He got to his feet and he was a powerfully built man. 'Siddown!' he said. I felt he had had some aggravation before in this respect, but also knew I was not going to accept orders from him. I realised, though, that I was still extremely weak. I told him that I was sorry that I had annoyed him but that I was not going to sit down. For a critical moment we stood confronting each other and then the American recovered his temper and sat down.

Also at the Connemara I met a chap called Frank Fales Richardson, who had been captain of cricket at school when I was in the Colts team. He was now a businessman in India, somehow avoiding war service. He was a very personable chap, leading an active social life.

My first flight after reaching Madras was not until 30 June, when I took up a Bolton Paul Defiant that was standing unused on the aerodrome. It wallowed around in the air, too heavy and sluggish for an operational aircraft. I did not get airborne again until 25 July when I flew to Bangalore for the day with Squadron Leader Morris in the Harvard. On the 28th I decided to fly to Rangoon to find out what was happening to the squadron. The round trip took 20 hours 50 minutes' flying time in the Hurricane IID, made up of sixteen hops over a period of five days. I wrote down a record of the trip soon afterwards in note form. Reading it since I noticed that I had become unreasonably intolerant of delay and inefficiency, and that the RAF organisation just then was in 'status shambolicus'. The notes, unaltered, read:

28th July 1945. Wakened by Harry the bearer. Still dark & the bearer had brought a lamp. 'All right sahib?' he asked. 'Yeah, all right,' I said & looked at my watch. 5 am. I was taking off at dawn for Rangoon. Had packed the night before & as I finished dressing, the lorry drove up in front of the billet with ground crews aboard. I asked them to drive as far as the mess and wait there while I had a quick breakfast. Waited 10 minutes for a fried egg, after which Harry the bearer took his leave.

Harry served in the Madras flying club in peacetime when he had known Neville Rowson, Flight commander on 20 Sqdn 1942/43.

Out to the aircraft. Dropped kit by plane – Highland Queen. Proceeded to control tower – mass of documents: flight plan etc – finally cleared & back to plane. Flying control sent lorry out to say no refuelling facilities at Vizatapatam. Another trip to control tower, but decided to carry on in spite of signal. Plane refused to start. Ack run down. Sgt O'Reilly sent for starter ack. Called him over & asked him how he thought I was going to start it at other stops. Swore at him a bit & changed over to N for nuts, which served without trouble throughout the trip. Smiles to & from O'Reilly.

Finally took off at 8 o'clock – one hour late. Nearly an hour's flight over the sea to Gannavaram at 6000'. Cloud 7/10 with towering white cumulus. The wind was from the SW on the complete trip & gave me a ground speed of over 200mph. Not bad for the old Hurricane.

Slight rainstorms around Gannavaram – strip wet. Refuelled & off again. Uneventful journey to Vizag. Slightly off course towards end of journey. Landed after two T'Bolts had taken off. Another had left the runway at one end [RAF euphemism for a crash – probably an overshoot]. Three more taxied up & waited in position while I landed. Directed to far corner of the aerodrome, where I waited hopefully for petrol. Provided with 90 Octane by a team worthy of the music hall in view of their inefficiency. Finally got away & set course for Cuttack to the NE flying at 6000'. Watched the scenery & felt cool at that height although now midday. Climbed to 6500', the height of Coonoor above sea level. Wondered what Ron Ballard was doing. Flew through some towering white cumulus for several minutes. Slightly bumpy but no sign of the monsoon which I had been expecting as I made my way north.

Refuelled at Cuttack & started off on final leg for that day to Calcutta. Sun on head unpleasant & had difficulty in keeping awake – 5 hours flying. No R/T used on journey. Attempted to obtain R/D/F call signs on several occasions when weather seemed bad en route, but never succeeded. Weather again uneventful. Cloud about 7/10ths.

Remembered call sign for Alipore was scrummage & called up in circuit without response. Gave it up & made nice landing. Dakota coming in behind, given a red although he could have made it. Told ground crews that I was taking off at 8 o'clock the following morning & rang up H.Q. Burma to find out where the Squadron was. Told they were leaving Thedaw for Hathazari en route for Amarda Road. This seemed to settle the main point of my trip. Secondary mission was to collect mail for the men. Undecided whether to proceed or return to Madras. In the meantime offered bed for the night by O'Shea F.C.O. at Alipore whom I had previously met at Ranchi. Very comfortable mess. Found the other occupant of my room an old acquaintance – Beaumont ex M.T.O. 909 Wing. Seemed happy enough in new job – probably glad to have been sent away from 909.

Excellent food & pleasant lounge. Went for walk along streets after dinner. Warm & sticky in Calcutta – some glamour in spite of it.

Early bed & up early. To aerodrome with O'Shea in F.C.O.'s bus.

Ground crews reported oil leak in N for nuts, now repaired. Further orgy of briefing by Navigation, meteorological & flying control experts. Took off & flew for one hour at 6000' – an easy journey with one rainstorm at the end of it. Brought the aircraft close to control tower at Hathazari which was manned by Americans. They said they had all been posted to China three weeks ago but were still waiting to go. Asked the usual question as to whether my R/T was working. 177 Beau Squadron refuelled my aircraft. I rang them up & a S/Ldr Gibbs replied. I asked if he had seen anything of 20 Sqdn. … Told me to hang on & he would ring back. Wet weather & began to feel cheesed & unproductive. Wandered out to aircraft, but not yet refuelled owing to rain. Saw 3 airmen approaching & decided to ask them if they had seen anything of 20 Sqdn. Recognised the centre airman as F/Sgt Thaxton. Tried to remember quickly whether he was still on the Squadron. Hailed him by name to gain time & asked him how he was doing. Told me he was with 177 Sqdn. Told me also where 20 Sqdn were. S/Ldr Gibbs arrived simultaneously with transport & I recognised him as an old acquaintance. Things were beginning to happen. Drove down to 20 Sqdn billets. F/Lt Bell emerged from a basha hut, looking well & cheerful. We exchanged news & views. Bell was the vanguard of the Squadron move & had arrived at Hathazari the previous evening with two Dakota loads of men & equipment. Told him I was going on to Rangoon to make arrangements for the move from Hathazari to Amarda Road. Nodded to some familiar faces & returned with Gibbs to the aircraft. He told me that 177 had disbanded. He was posted & the C.O. was the last pilot left. Gibbs had got his half stripe about three months before. First met him at Jamshedpur in 1942.

Airman walked up to the aircraft as I got in. Seemed to think I should know him. Pretended to do so. Asked me some questions as to the future movements of 20 Sqdn. Took off for Akyab. Had to make detour at one point with clouds on hills. Flew down Mayu river at 0'.

New atmosphere about the Arakan. Villagers again working in the fields. No sign of bombholes at spot where we attacked river-steamers in November 1942.

Runway at Akyab land subsided badly in many places but surface O.K. with metal covering. Rang up Flying Control & tried to get R/DF call sign for Meiktila in case weather was bad on the journey. No clues at all at the tower & gave it up. Took off & climbed through 10/10ths

on course. Broke cloud after 10 minutes & passed close to Dakota
going in opposite direction. Passed two more at intervals, so guessed
I was on track. Weather improved & was quite fine over Meiktila.
Circled Thedaw. Saw figure beside officers' tents & the two Jap fighter
aircraft still in position. Beat the place up once & came in to land.
Taxied up to our old dispersal, now overgrowing with grass. Climbed
out & decided to p. Noticed solitary figure starting to walk from
Mess site. As I finished, heard motorbike coming up to aircraft and
expected to find D.R. Instead Les Hill. Climbed up behind him & set
off for Domestic Site. Time 1340 hrs. Arrived at airmen's cookhouse,
where, after a few minutes, was presented with several slabs of fresh
meat, fried potatoes (canned American) & peas. While waiting, Les
Hill said 'Congratulations.' 'Mm?' I asked, 'on what?' Les smiled & said
on my D.S.O. It had appeared in SEAC the previous day. One or two
airmen also congratulated me & I began to believe it. We went back
to our tent & I had a look at the newspaper. It was two months since
we had stopped operating & I felt no immediate thrill at the news. Les
then told me that Neville Rowson had been killed. Kite caught fire
shortly after take off from Hathazari. Neville in SEAC previous day,
having flown an iron lung down to Rangoon. 2nd Pilot off colour,
not on board for fatal trip. Les had several bottles of beer in water &
we drank one. I salvaged a stretcher for a bed & slept while he went
off to supervise the airlift. Six months previously he had been the
officer in the Advance Party into Burma. Now he was the last officer
to leave. Several of the original airmen were there too. In the evening
I had my bath & walked off down the road we had formed originally
to the dispersals. The sun was sinking and it appeared one of the
most beautiful sunsets I had seen with beautiful clear colouring in the
west & to the east where we had been operating over the mountains,
dark heavy grape-blue clouds. All around was most peaceful – it
was Sunday evening – a contrast to our first disturbed arrival, with
Japanese troops in the area.

Another beer in the tent & off to an ENSA concert at the old Wing
H.Q. – now an army site. After the concert, more beer in the M/T
drivers' tent & Spam sandwiches. Finally to bed. Awoke on 30th at
6.30 am. Wakened Les Hill. Washed & shaved – said 'au revoir' & went
off to my aircraft, driven by a new M/T driver who had come straight
from my old station in N. Ireland – Newtonards.

Taxied out along the familiar runway – 152 Sqdn of Spits at the
other end of the strip had refuelled my aircraft. Cutting – test pilot
of the R.S.U. & now a F/Ltn had asked them to do so, at my request.
Checked over the cockpit before take off – everything as it should
be – wondered what the chances of sabotage were now. Looked at
the trees at the end of the runway & decided to use +8lbs for take
off. Pushed the throttle up to the gate, & trundled forward. Soon
travelling faster & let the nose come down. Past the watch office &
travelling quickly now. Soon be airborne. Off now and wheels up –
passing 152 (Sqdn dispersal) & some men watch as the Hurricane goes
by. Climbing now, practically on course already. Check a landmark
after 10 minutes & then no more landmarks. Note time of take off
& have calculated length of flight and time when I should reach
Rangoon. Am now flying in and over clouds with only occasional
sight of jungle-covered hills. No landmarks. Check approximate
length of time that I should be flying over hills. Weather seems
healthy enough in spite of cloud. Gradually horizon disappears &
becomes dark. I keep watching carefully & after a time realise I will
have no alternative plan but to make Rangoon, owing to the distance
& the endurance of the Hurricane. Luckily the weather holds & ten
minutes short of ETA I fly down through a gap in the clouds & find
myself slightly east, to the left of my track. Reach Mingaladon & come
in, doing a perfect three pointer. Taxi back & stop near the Watch
Tower. The Group H.Q. is about 10 miles away in town & apparently
takes transport ½ an hour to come out to the strip and half an hour
back. Spent thirty minutes in Air Transit Rest Room, drank tea and
a tinned fish sandwich, got bored waiting for the transport to arrive,
worried Flying Control & finally decided to go away without paying
my visit to Group. Delayed again as aircraft had not been refuelled.
Driver of transport eventually approached me to say that Jeep was
waiting – tried to find out cause for delay without satisfactory
answer – it was now 11.30 am & the greater part of the day would be
lost for travel by the time I had returned from Group. Decided to
spend the night at Meiktila, & set off for Rangoon along a good road
with residential houses on either side – little bomb damage evident.
Arrived at Group 1200 hrs, ordered Jeep to be ready at 1230 hrs. Went
upstairs, visited 'Organisation' & enquired about the Squadron move
from Hathazari onwards – 'Org' mildly interested to know that

a Beaufighter Squadron were still at Dohazari after 7 weeks.
Gave me names of people of other formations who might be
of assistance & passed me on to SPSO, where I enquired about
Horrock's D.F.C. Vincent had changed this to a Non-Immediate
award, hence the delay. My D.S.O. had come through the previous
day, one day after being announced in SEAC. SPSO told me that the
A.O.C. had sent me a congratulatory telegram. Went downstairs &
found F/Lt Farquharson, lately a flight commander on the Squadron,
now officer i/c accidents. He congratulated me on my gong, told me
he had written to me about it. F'son looked much thinner & had had
no leave. We exchanged news & I commented on his accidents job,
boasting that we had had no accidents for three months as we had
done little flying. F'son said that we had had one now & lost one of
our best pilots. I wondered what gen he had & he gave me a signal
announcing that W/O Tuffield had flown into a ship during practice
attacks, killing himself & wounding several Squadron personnel
who were watching on board. This was bad news on top of Neville
Rowson's death. Les Hill & Tuff good friends.

   F'son pressed me to stay for lunch. Went round to M/T & ordered
Jeep for 1 o'clock. Group Mess, a large house. Numerous familiar faces
– Major Shields, Vernon – the V3! etc. F'son complained that this
did not compare with Squadron life & that he lacked company. After
lunch, found my driver waiting. He explained that he had been on
duty all night, had not been expecting this call but that the F/Sgt
had seen him. Consequently he was in shorts & had to change into
slacks for any trip out of camp. Did I mind if we stopped at his
billet while he changed? He added 'Must have identification card,
driving licence as the M.P.s always pull you up the time you haven't
got them!' Did a quick change & on our way. Talkative. Prices high
in Rangoon. Quick, sharp individual with specs, reminded me of
our old M/T driver Phillips. More interested when we arrived and
he found that I had my own Hurricane – nothing to tell me from
an 'Admin' type these days, when I am not wearing wings! Old and
grey! Stopped to watch me start up – Fortunately! Finger trouble –
had left IFF on & battery flat. Driver did excellent work – drove off
in Jeep & returned dragging starter battery. Called out that he was a
fitter himself when I suggested that he should get somebody to help
him plug starter battery in. N for nuts started right away & I taxied

out waving thanks to a helpful M/T driver. Set course over clouds with one pinpoint after ten minutes flying. Continued on this course for nearly an hour. Weather gradually improved towards Meiktila. Flew over Thedaw – saw all the tents were down & circled Meiktila. Came in on a green. Taxied back near the control tower. Met by fair haired Flight Lieutenant with moustache. 'Are you a replacement sir?' he enquired. Proved to be 28 Sqdn. Taken to their mess & very hospitably received. Good mess, well organised. All pilots F/Lts except one F/O, sweating on his second ring. Given tent & bed prepared by an old enrolled follower who had been on the Squadron several years, & knew Hammerbeck when I mentioned his name. Very pleasant evening, talked mainly with F/Lt Hicks who had received me. They were operating with one flight at Meiktila, the other at Mingaladon, Rangoon. Only one Hurricane aircraft left at Meiktila & Flight Commander had sent through a strong signal to Group saying they would all go off on leave if replacements did not arrive. Result, F/Commander at Rangoon that day seeing A.O.C. – personal interview – raspberry. Eventual result, several Spitfire XI given to the Squadron. This I learnt over a month later from the F/O now F/Lt Hind. Dawn, the following day, one hour earlier than at Madras. Up at 5.30 am, early breakfast, found F/Lt Hicks ready to drive me to my aircraft & unwilling to accept payment for Mess bill. Finally took off after delay due to non-refuelling of aircraft the previous night. Gave F/Looie salute from aircraft as I taxied away, in thanks for hospitality. Usual cloudy weather presenting no great difficulty to Akyab. Refuelled & took off for Hathazari, weather not looking too good. Cloud flying had been successful so far, so climbed to safe height of 6000' & flew on instruments. This leg was up the Arakan coast which I knew intimately. If necessary, I could come down through cloud over the sea, by flying due west for several minutes. After flying for half an hour, clouds increased in bumpiness & became darker. Instruments working well, so continued, finally finishing up in monsoon cloud. Turbulence frightening. Head banged against top left corner of cockpit – used left arm to steady myself in seat, although tightly strapped in. Artificial horizon toppled & Direction Indicator showed change of course. Unable to help myself. Stick forward & speed going up & yet altimeter recording rapid rate of climb. Struggled through in very split arse manner, reckoning that I had at last met weather which was more than 'interesting'. Came out in clear pocket, surrounded by dark cloud in all directions. Unable to decide my attitude relative to the earth & realised I must get down below cloud somehow, although I could not attempt to descend through cloud without my artificial horizon. Heavy rain coming into cockpit. Praying as usual. Realised only a few seconds & I would have to go into cloud again. After another few seconds, hectic, saw break down to ground level. Made the coast & flew up at nought feet, visibility bad and rain widespread.

Hathazari, still low cloud, & rain but able to land.

Picked up by Dingle Bell in lorry & taken to camp. Delivered & collected various messages. Met by the quack, now S/Ldr O'Brien, who was posted to Ceylon. Camp at top of muddy hill – Bell slipped on way down. Took off for Calcutta hoping to have no more shaky experiences. Low clouds in parts but otherwise 'interesting' weather only.

Lunch at Alipore Mess & in to town. First visited H.Q. Burma at Belvedere. Saw Org. staff & promised by them that train would be arranged to collect Squadron from Hathazari within 8 days. Bought D.S.O. ribbon at Tailor's in Grand Hotel block. Reserved seat for 'Three Caballeros' Walt Disney film, collected Gold Squadron badge for Johnny Horrocks. Disappointed in film. Unable to get taxi after show & forced to walk most of the way back to Alipore – finishing journey in rickshaw.

1st August. Took off 9 o'clock for Cuttack. Usual F.C.O. at Control Tower. Asked him if he were on duty all the time. Cuttack–Vizag. Met Sikh at Vizag who wanted a posting to the Squadron. Flying Control tried to stop me from taking off.

Vizag–Gannavaram. Flying Control Officer at Gannavaram tells me FCO at Vizag has rung through to hold Hurricane KW 789 as St Thomas' Mount is not to be landed on this afternoon. I tell him I wish to land there urgently & FCO rings St Thomas' Mt. Airman at desk smoking Gallaghers. I compliment him on his taste. Airman is Irish & insists on my taking the packet although I tell him that I do not smoke much. St Thomas' Mt tell me it is O.K. to fly to Madras. FCO starts talking about 906 Wing & G/Capt Goddard – he says he remembers us when we were at Sapam – Imphal valley. Obliging type & shouts out to bowser to speed up refuelling Hurricane. Ring up adjutant & ask whether any mail has been delivered to Gannavaram

for 20 Sqdn. Reply no, but asks where the Squadron is located as new
M.O. replacing O'Brien is in his office looking for the Squadron!
Leave Gannavaram & fly over the sea on the last leg to Madras
– finish of a trip which has proved useful, interesting & at times
exciting. No sign of work being carried out on aerodrome. Circle
billets, watch 15cwt come out to dispersal; land. Smedley, the driver,
groans when I say there is no mail.

On my second visit to Hathazari, described above, Dingle Bell asked me
to do a beat-up of the aerodrome to cheer up some of the squadron, but
for once I refused the request, feeling that I had been too close to death a
few minutes earlier in the monsoon storm.

The CO of a Beaufighter squadron was put up for a DSO at the same
time as myself. He was a pleasant man with a good reputation. He had
a double-barrelled name that I have forgotten. He stayed a night with
20 Squadron while we were at Monywa. Unfortunately he was killed before
his decoration came through, so that it was never awarded.

At this time in Madras, I had a restful interlude. I had a cousin in India
whom I had never met. She came from New Zealand and was a missionary, married to a missionary. They were in an isolated part of southern
India but, looking at the map, I saw there was a small airfield at Hindupur
where they lived. My cousin Chris had spoken Tamil before she married,
but had to learn a new dialect, Telugu, when she joined her husband at
Hindupur. The Indians told her that she spoke Telugu with a Tamil accent.
There was a small civilian machine called a Proctor in the hangar at
St Thomas's Mount, which was not on the books and did not belong to
anybody. I got the ground crews to service it, contacted Chris and Roy
Heslop, and on 3 August flew with Johnny Horrocks to Hindupur in the
Proctor. Horrocks took the machine back to Madras.

Chris and Roy were very kind to me, putting me in their bedroom while
they made a shift elsewhere. At that time their elder daughter was about
two, while they had a younger daughter, Kay, aged only a few months.
The homely atmosphere was something that I am sure we all missed in
the jungle, with the absence of feminine influence. I had become very
irritable and impatient, liable to blow my top too easily, and my week at
Hindupur was very relaxing, although not long enough to make any real
change in my mental state.

The Heslops ran a mission school for boys. There was only one other white couple in Hindupur, so that a knowledge of the local dialect was really essential. In the main street of the small town, there was a busy market. I noticed large monkeys in the tall palm trees, who sometimes came down and walked unmolested in the street. Roy told me that they were regarded as sacred, and if they took something out of a woman's shopping basket, she would not try to recover the article.

We were eating an Indian diet, mainly of cereals, as European food was difficult to obtain. Chris had a large ulcer on her shin, known as a tropical sore, which may have been partly due to her diet. On one occasion I accompanied her to the medical clinic. An Indian woman doctor was running it and she ignored Chris until she spotted that she was accompanied by a white stranger, when she became more attentive.

One evening Roy took me out to a temple, a few miles from the town. Outside the temple was a giant paw mark imprinted in a rock. Roy told me the story of the white monkey who had his base in Ceylon and was regarded as a good god. The paw mark was made on the occasion when he leaped from the ground at this spot to intercept the baddie of the piece. Later in Siam, I found that the same legend and characters were commemorated in a temple in Bangkok.

I went for walks at Hindupur, and on one of these saw a mongoose in its natural surroundings, having only seen them previously in captivity, and used by Indians in the streets of Madras as an entertainment, when one would be set to fight against a cobra.

On 11 August Mike Deasy turned up in the Proctor as arranged. I took Chris and Roy with one of their boys up for a flip. The Proctor had a long take-off run and I was getting uncomfortably near the end of the runway, with the load of passengers making the take-off longer than ever. I reached for the flap lever and with the aid of a few degrees of flap got her into the air. After a 20 minute flight, I took three more boys up at Roy's request and got Mike Deasy to do one more trip. Mike and I then flew on to Bangalore, refuelled, and returned to St Thomas's Mount.

Previously at Bangalore I had bought myself a new peaked cap, as my original one had called forth comments from all and sundry, being oil-stained through being tucked away in aircraft during flights. It had lost its stiffener, a circle of thin cane, which was removed from the cap by other pilots when I first joined a squadron in the UK and I had assiduously tried to mould it into the shape of a German officer's cap ever since. It was very comfortable to wear and I did not like my new cap nearly so much!

We had understood that Mountbatten had plans for an invasion in the Singapore area, in which we would have taken part, but the atom bomb was dropped and a few days later Japan capitulated. On the last day of the war, Wing Commander Nicholson, who had won the Victoria Cross in the Battle of Britain, was killed off Akyab.

At Madras, a tailor asked me if he could have the contract to make clothes for the squadron. He offered to make me a pair of pyjamas as a sample of his work. I agreed to this but found that he had made the pyjamas to fit me like a suit, which did not please me. When I tried to pay him, he refused and evidently regarded the pyjamas as the bribe for the contract. Usually, any contractor paid a fee into the PSI funds according to the number of airmen involved. I do not recall what happened to this tailor.

On 20 August Ballard, Horrocks, Sergeant O'Reilly and I climbed into the Proctor and headed for Coimbatore at the foot of the Nilgiri Hills. Coimbatore was a naval air station and we parked on the perimeter furthest away from the watch tower, hoping that no one would notice us! We then climbed on a bus that took us up to Coonoor via some alarming hairpin bends. That evening in the Coonoor club I met a naval captain with his girlfriend. I told him I was just there for the weekend and had flown to Coimbatore. It was as well that I mentioned it as he had wanted to know who had left their machine on his station without booking in. We returned to Madras on 23 August without Johnny Horrocks, who was going to make his own way back.

A week later we set off for Amarda Road, where we were to re-equip with Spitfires. It was a misty morning and I was leading three other aircraft. One of them was flown by a Flight Sergeant Wilkinson, who had not been long on the squadron, but who was a good, reliable individual. As usual our R/T was faulty. On leaving Madras we flew over the sea for some distance and encountered layers of cloud. I signalled to the others to get into close formation, which they did except for Wilkinson who continued at a wide distance. We soon lost visual contact with him, and although the weather improved, we did not see him again. Apparently he had bought an expensive camera in Madras, because in reply to my letter of condolence to his next of kin, I received anxious enquiries about the camera, and I had to explain that it was with him in the aircraft when he was lost over the sea. It was the last death of a pilot during my time on the squadron, although Gerry Astley was killed in a flying accident after I left.

Chapter 21

Amarda Road – 27 August–29 September 1945

Amarda Road was an RAF station that ran fighter instruction courses. It was under the control of Wing Commander Paul Louis, who had trained with me at Kidlington in 1940, and who later became a flight commander on 615 Squadron at Chittagong. Also on the station was Flight Lieutenant Artie Lee, a plump Irishman who had been my flight commander on 231 Squadron in Northern Ireland. He was still a flight lieutenant, and this was not altogether surprising as he was not a good pilot and had made no secret that he intended to avoid operations if possible! He had originally been an army officer, who had transferred with others to the RAF in 1940.

At last the war had ended and we were all looking forward to our liberation from the services. My release group was twenty-six, which was calculated on several factors, including my age and length of service. Although it was a fairly early release group, it was not going to get me out of the RAF in time for the start of the university year, which was early October. This meant that I would not be able to pick up my medical studies until October 1946. Consequently, in my case there was no tearing hurry to leave the RAF. On the other hand I was now so 'puggled' that I felt I should not stay out in the Far East longer than I had to. I was no longer capable of sustained concentration on administrative details and flew into rages when I encountered any obstacles, instead of tackling them rationally.

Les Hill was tour-expired and due for repatriation. He asked me if there was any point in his extending his tour and I advised him against it. After the war, he pointed out that he was one of the most experienced pilots on the squadron at that time, and might have been considered for the post of flight commander. This was true, but somehow the possibility had not occurred to me; perhaps because Les did not push himself forward as a candidate. I had got into the habit of taking him for granted.

Dingle Bell was also repatriated from Amarda Road, probably for release, as he was a bit older than the rest of us. He had a garage business to return to. Before he left Dingle produced the Jap sabre that he had taken at Thedaw, but one was enough for me and I do not recall what happened to this other one.

My state of mind was not helped by a severe tinea cruris or 'dhobi's itch' as it was called. This was a fungal infection of the skin in the groin area, supposedly introduced when the clothes were being washed by the dhobi. My skin became raw and weeping and stuck to my underpants, so that removing them made the skin bleed. I finally went to the medical officer who of course was able to cure the trouble. We had a replacement MO for O'Brien who had problems with alcohol and depression and who was only with us for two or three weeks. At that time, the officer in the next room to me had a gramophone, and a record of some South American music, which I found curiously comforting. I would borrow his machine and play the record frequently.

A rajah had placed his bungalow on the coast at the disposal of aircrew stationed at Amarda Road, and the squadron made a trip down one week-end, having a pleasant break, and getting in a swim or two.

Fletcher, now a wing commander, visited us at Amarda Road. During the evening he became quite sozzled, so two of us took him back to his part of the camp by M/T and saw him to his room, calling in at the HQ mess en route. Paul Louis told me later that the next day, Fletcher accused us of fixing his drinks. Fletcher paid us a further visit a couple of nights later, accompanied by another officer and asked some strange questions. He seemed to be thinking that I had designs to remain on as a peacetime CO of 20 Squadron. It all seemed pointless but I assured him that I was going back to my medical studies as soon as I could.

We embarked on a 'conversion course'. For me this consisted of ten flights in Spitfire Mk VIIIs, when I did aerobatics, some formation leading and one lot of dogfights. On my fourth trip, I was flying inverted above cloud when my engine developed an airlock. I remembered how a pilot had had to force-land in Jap territory on Elephant Point on the Arakan in 1944 because of this. I was unable to remove the airlock and so called up Flying Control and warned them to clear the runway, telling them what had happened. When I came down through cloud, I was a few miles to the side and upwind of the airfield, but with enough height to get me there without difficulty. I decided on a downwind landing, having to side-slip off a little height on the approach. As I finished my landing run, Control called up and kindly asked if I was all right. Unreasoning rage bubbled up inside me. What a b. silly question to ask! He can see the engine is dead! 'I'm all right,' I said with a tone of sarcasm, 'except that I have no engine.' 'I can see that,' answered Control. Of course my sarcasm was not justified. Two engineer officers from the station came buzzing down the strip in a jeep and after a minute's chat, whistled up a starter battery. They kept turning over the engine until it started. My hands were shaking in reaction to the forced landing. It was considered advisable in these circumstances to fly again immediately and not brood over one's narrow escape, so I climbed back in the Spitfire and continued my flight. In the evening, Paul Louis said he heard that I had had some excitement and added that it was fortunate it had happened to me and not to one of my other pilots. Certainly just then we were not very impressive, but with time the pilots would develop skill. Most of the experienced airmen had been repatriated, as the tour for colonials was shorter than for British pilots, and we had a bunch of new aviators who were not highly accomplished. Ron Ballard and Johnny Horrocks were flight commanders and Goodhew, who was a good pilot, was still with the squadron.

Word came through that 20 Squadron was to transfer to Siam as part of the occupying force. Once again we were on the move. For me, it was to be my last stint with the squadron.

Chapter 22

Don Muang, Siam –
30 September–3 December 1945

We were routed to fly to Bangkok via Baigachi, Akyab and Hmawbi. The first leg to Baigachi was a short one. Here we found a group captain in charge, trying to develop the place into a regular staging post. He was a caricature of an RAF officer, with a typical RAF moustache and all the more refined RAF slang. He had four ground-type officers with him and he was encouraging them to ply the squadron pilots with soft drinks and generally cosset them. The A & SD officers looked sheepish and exchanged glances behind the OC's back. As we had only been flying for 45 minutes that day, we were also taken a bit by surprise, but appreciated the un-accustomed concern that was being lavished upon us. I remembered that Akyab was in a pretty bad condition when I last touched down there and was not too happy about some of the pilots landing there in Spits. I voiced my doubts to the group captain during our briefing but he overruled me, saying that he had had a vast amount of experience on Spitfires. At Akyab, our next stop, two of the Spitfires were damaged by water on the runway, and had to be left behind for repair. We were held up at Akyab for two days by the weather, before we could complete our journey.

Hmawbi was near Rangoon. From there we flew across towards Moulmein and then we had to fly high to be sure of clearing the mountains, which rose to about 5,000 feet on the way to Bangkok. For a time we had to stay above the cloud and use oxygen, which was unusual for us, as our job had always been low-level work. There were no landmarks to assist our navigation, and I relied on my watch to tell me how far we had travelled. I was therefore disconcerted to find that my watch had stopped, when I consulted it above the clouds. I had to make an estimate of the time we had been airborne. Luckily the sky above Bangkok was clear and, after nearly two hours of compass flying, I was very pleased to see the city ahead of us in the distance.

The war had taken us steadily further east to more and more jungly places. This final step made me wonder how primitive Siam would be. Because the Siamese had cooperated with the Japanese during the war, the Allies had decreed that they would not be allowed to use the name Thailand – which meant the 'land of free men' – and Thailand was known as Siam during my stay there, and for some time after.

D.O. Finlay proved to be in charge of AHQ Siam and 20 Squadron was the only fighting unit in the command at that time. The currency unit was a tical or tikal, so we converted our rupees and made a beeline for the capital. Bangkok was a beautiful, modern city. The streets were clean and wide, with Western-style buildings in the main streets. The shops had glass windows and one store had dinner jackets for sale, which were something from another world! The Siamese girls wore Western clothes and were obviously emancipated, whereas in Burma we had never caught a glimpse of the womenfolk.

On the aerodrome at Don Muang, it was the custom of the Siamese Air Force to open their mess for free drinks at midday to all-comers. I never made use of this offer, but it soon became known to various thirsty types, and not long after we arrived, this arrangement was discontinued! Whenever I landed at a Siamese airfield, I would be met by an air force officer, escorted by a servant carrying a tray with Siamese whisky (made from rice) and soda. Evidently the Siamese Air Force did not try to separate drinking and flying!

We gave a lunch to this air force, at which the Siamese heavily out-ranked us. I think the lowest rank among them was a group captain. The lunch went off very well and Don Finlay decided to give a party for the civilian internees. We had a mess meeting to discuss the project and Finlay gave considerable attention to my opinion, which was reassuring as I thought I had blotted my copybook by moving the squadron prematurely from Thedaw, and also because I thought I was obviously bonkers at that stage. This party, too, went well. Various French and Dutch who had been interned throughout the war, came to the gathering and I met the French consul and the French military attaché for the first time, together with their wives.

On 8 and 12 October we flew over Bangkok in squadron formation, which was probably quite impressive. The internees hailed us as the representatives of the victorious powers.

We had a number of Japanese POWs attached to the aerodrome, and each day they would come along and ask what work they should do. It was easy at first; we would ask them to build a road from our sleeping quarters to the existing road, but they would build it in record time – making a really good job of it – and be back too quickly asking for another task! The dental officer told me that if a Jap needed a tooth extraction, he had only to put the pliers on the tooth and the Jap would practically do his work for him by waggling his head, helping to loosen the tooth. On one occasion, I was driving along a road and noticed two Japanese soldiers a little distance ahead. They turned round, saw my jeep, and instead of just standing at the edge of the road, as I expected, they threw themselves to the side of the road.

As my watch was unreliable, I found a watch-maker's shop in Bangkok and had a look at his stock. Most of the stock was second-hand and I had an uneasy feeling that they might have come from European POWs. However, I picked out a good watch and asked the price. After some mental arithmetic, I calculated the shopkeeper was asking £19, which was a high price at that time. I told him that he was demanding too much and gave him £15, walking out of the shop with the watch. Over the next few days, I thought it over and decided I had been too high-handed in my action, so I returned to the shop with the balance of the sum that the shopkeeper had asked. He told me that he had not been worried. He knew that I would return because of the honour of an Englishman! There cannot be much of that sentiment left around the world, unfortunately.

There was a Lysander on the aerodrome that needed air-testing, so I gladly accepted the chance to do this. I took two ex-POWs up with me – an Australian flight lieutenant and a naval lieutenant commander. They had both been captured early on in the war, at a time when I was a flying officer, so that by now they could have made much headway in rank – or, alternatively, be dead. The Lysander was very much more powerful than the Mk IIs that we had used in Burma. I thought they were possibly Mk IIIs modified with an auxiliary fuel tank and a constant-speed airscrew unit. It may have been called a Mk IV.

In the mess we had large quantities of Siamese beer made from rice. We had taken over the output of a brewery in Bangkok, and this happy state of affairs continued until the army reached Siam, when they assumed control and rationed our supplies!

On the way into Bangkok, we had passed one or two temples. At the corners of the roofs were spikes curving upwards, which we were told were in honour of the rain god. Along the telegraph wires were thick clouds of spiders' webs, with residents whose bodies were the size of oranges. One of these arachnids found its way into our sleeping quarters, carrying a bag containing its young. The young spiders were the size of a large one in the UK.

We visited the temple of the emerald Buddha, the idol being carved out of a single giant emerald. We were told that it had a long history, had been captured by the Burmese and recaptured by Siam. The priests dressed it in gold leaf clothes appropriate to the season. Being near the equator, I got the impression that the climate did not vary greatly, being hot and humid most of the time, with the sun setting a little before six in the winter and a little after six in the summer. On the floor of the temple, incongruously, was a grandfather clock given to the King of Siam by Queen Victoria. In the cloisters nearby was a sequence of pictures around the walls, telling the story of the white monkey who had his base in Ceylon. The pictures were very old and were overpainted periodically to renew them.

Some of the RAF officers took the opportunity to fly to Saigon and from there to visit another temple, the Angkor Vat.

A directive came through saying that as the war was now over, we must economise on the use of fuel, and make considerable reductions on the amount of flying that was carried out. Life in the peacetime RAF was already showing signs of change. I was invited to move into the HQ mess, as I was a senior officer, but preferred to remain with the squadron.

I took a small L5 aircraft and visited a prisoner of war camp. All the ill POWs had already been flown out, and there were very few inmates left. They told me that each had had to catch a daily quota of flies for the Japanese. I do not remember much more about it. The Japanese general who had been in command in Siam, committed hara-kiri soon after we moved in, leaving a note saying that he had lost at chess and there were no flowers in his garden. The internees said that he had spent some time in America before the war and had behaved civilly towards them. They used to see him riding his horse, when he would acknowledge their greetings with a salute.

In the evenings, we would meet the internees at parties in Bangkok. The Dutch had held the Dutch East Indies until the war, and a large number of them had been taken prisoner. Some of them were musical and occasionally provided music for dances, with an accordion and other instruments.

There had been a French consulate in Bangkok, and the staff had been interned for the duration of the war. The consul was a small, pleasant man, and his wife seemed to me to be typically French: she was small also and not particularly pretty, but she was carefully groomed and had a good manner. I liked the military attaché, Colonel Albert de Fauque de Jonquières. He was a good bit older than the rest of us and was later promoted to general. He and his young wife had a baby only a few months old when we arrived in Bangkok. His spouse was a good-looking, charming woman.

One couple I was destined to remain in touch with over the years was a Dane and his French wife. At that time they had two infant daughters, the younger one again just a few months old. Wife Jackie could only have been about twenty-one at that time. Aage, her husband, was in his late twenties. I was never quite sure how to pronounce his name. It was something like the English word 'ogre'. Jackie and Aage Mork had a bar in their house where we would sometimes foregather. The only alcohol the internees had tasted during the war was made from anise and they had got very tired of it. We brought them supplies from the mess, and I remember how appreciative they were when I offered up a bottle of Sandeman's port. Ron Ballard and I would often begin or end the evening at their house, and pass a pleasant time with them or other French families. We met one or two Siamese princes and princesses, who seemed to be fairly numerous, and Ron became very friendly with a princess whom we called Puck, as we could not pronounce her proper name.

Meanwhile, some of the squadron were taking up with prostitutes and there was worry about the amount of venereal disease throughout the area, which had until recently been under Japanese occupation. A meeting was called by D.O. Finlay when he, the padre and the MO addressed the station on the subject of sex, as seen from their individual viewpoints. Two of our officers were casualties.

We were told of a theatre in Bangkok where the girls danced with something like a postcard tied round their waists with string, to conceal their pubic region. If coins were thrown on the stage, they gyrated more vigorously so that the card flapped up and down, giving momentary glimpses of the 'goodies' beneath. I went to this show once; the girls were very young, probably in their early teens. Apart from the anatomical revelation, there was one good dancer who performed in a grass skirt, but there was nothing else memorable.

One of our air liaison officers, Peter Daw, bought a Siamese wife for £5 from her parents. He said there was no liability and they would take her back when he left the country. She was apparently very good and obedient and he used her as a photographic model, showing us some of the pictures that he took, of the 'tasteful nude' variety.

The senior ALO was a little major called Sutcliffe, who had lived in Paris before the war. Both he and Ron Ballard, whose mother was French, could speak this language fluently and got on very well with the French internees. On one occasion in the French consulate, I noticed that everyone in the room was speaking English, although I was the only British person there. When I commented on this to the two people I was talking to, they said this was being done on my account. It was a crowded room and an impressive display!

Bananas were plentiful and we were given them at almost every meal in the mess. In the UK, by contrast, they were exceedingly scarce. By the time I returned to England I felt I never wanted to see another banana, while the people in England would have welcomed the chance to eat one.

Outside the billets at Don Muang were large reservoirs of water, which we called tanks. One of them was used for swimming, while I noticed an airman casting a fishing line from his bedroom window into another. Unrelated to this, I had wondered whether I would see any Siamese cats during my stay, and in fact spotted them lurking in back alleys in Bangkok just as their English counterparts might do.

The airmen made three trips down to a seaside resort on the eastern side of the Gulf of Siam. On one of these, a non-flying officer called Mike Kelly, who was slightly more crazy than the rest of us, dived into an apparently inviting harbour from the jetty, but discovered the water was only a foot deep. Luckily he was not seriously injured. On another excursion the party consisted of Aage and Jackie, Peter Daw and myself. We had to cross the Mekong river by ferry with our jeep. On the return journey in the evening, it was noticed that we were being carried downstream and not making progress. It became clear that the man in charge of the ferry was drunk and incapable. We relieved him of his command, brought the ferry close in to the bank where the current was less, and gradually made our way back upstream. When we were again at the starting point, the boat was headed out into the river, with its nose pointing enough upstream to allow for the current, and made the journey safely to the other side. Peter Daw was cross with the drunk for endangering our lives and ordered him into the jeep, having drawn his pistol. After we had travelled a mile, we set him down, reckoning that the walk back would sober him up.

The aerodrome at Don Muang was far removed from the war, and had only one raid carried out on it, surprisingly by fighters. These were long-range Mustangs of the USAAF who strafed the buildings without causing any great damage. We found a First World War French Potez on the airfield, which had been taken over by the Japs and used by them during the Second World War. The French roundels had been painted over with the Japanese rising sun. It was an interesting machine with large, solid wheels and an exhaust pipe that went vertically upwards like a chimney stack. Ron Ballard, Dai Lewis and I posed in front of it while Gerry Astley took a photograph. Dai Lewis wore a false moustache for the photo, and we made some adjustments to our clothes to impart a period flavour.

One day a junior officer turned up in the mess, who did not appear to be attached to any unit. He was snooping around for radar tubes, which he believed to be stored on the airfield, and which he hoped to sell elsewhere as television tubes.

Green silk parachutes were used during the war for dropping supplies to the special force in Siam, and the salvaged 'chutes were sold more legitimately in Bangkok for £50 each. I was given one later by the special force, and passed it on to Jackie Mork and the wife of the military attaché, who made linings for their children's coats with it, while Madame de Jonquières made me an embroidered handkerchief, which I still have.

One of our camp followers applied to me for leave on the grounds that his wife had reached the age of puberty and he wished to consummate his marriage. It was a gem of a letter, and I should have preserved it.

On 18 October, Group Captain Finlay went on a week's leave to Bo Fai, on the western side of the Gulf of Siam. I offered him the use of the squadron Harvard and said I would be glad to come down with him and fly the Harvard back. As he had considerably more rank than I did, for once I flew as second pilot. Don was already sitting in the Harvard when I appeared. When he saw me he nearly had a fit, as I was wearing shorts. The regulations were that one should wear long trousers while airborne as these would afford some protection in the event of fire. There was some sense in this on operational flying, although I had only worn slacks since the beginning of 1945. In peacetime it seemed pointless. However, to avoid his attack of apoplexy, I hurried to my billets and changed into a pair of casual trousers before setting off to Bo Fai. There was an airstrip not far from the attractive sandy beach on which the hotel was sited, and Finlay settled in, while I returned in the Harvard to Don Muang.

I did not fly again until a week later when I went to pick him up. In the meantime, I had visited a convent near Bangkok where they made silk. I bought some Thai silk to take back to England as a present for one of my sisters. By chance, the mother superior of the convent wanted to visit Bo Fai, and so I arranged to take her with me. Strictly speaking I should have got her to sign a chit absolving the RAF of any liability in the event of a crash, but I felt this would only worry the old soul, and I deemed myself capable of bringing her down safely whatever happened. However, Finlay discovered that I had not got her to sign the 'blood chit', and once again blew his top. Some of the way the old girl was praying and fiddling with her rosary. When we landed she told me that she had stopped this as she was not sure whether I could hear her prayers through the wires that led from my flying helmet to the R/T!

I spent part of the day at Bo Fai. As Don Finlay and I sprawled on the sandy beach, he confessed that as far as he was concerned he was single, but that in the eyes of the law he was a married man. I remembered what Dingle Bell had told me of Finlay's marriage. I believe he got divorced soon after returning to England.

At the beginning of November, a pilot turned up in a Sentinel aircraft. I learned that his job was to provide transport for some members of 136 Force. This was a special army unit that had been dropped into Siam during the war, with the objective of forming an underground army. This force had not been needed, though, as the war had come suddenly to an end. The officer in charge was a Colonel Smiley, nicknamed 'Colonel Grin' by the Siamese. Major Winn, another officer, was the son of a peer and had insisted on being dropped in full mess dress. He had landed in a bog, which had rather spoilt the effect of his formal attire. Yet another officer, Major Dumont, had spent the hostilities as a French peasant until the war in France had come to a close.

The pilot of the Sentinel was keen to see the sights of Bangkok, and when I offered to do his work for him he enthusiastically accepted. On 3 November I set off with Signalman Downs, otherwise known as the

'Spider'. Each officer worked with a wireless operator, and the 'Spider' was the w/op for Rowley Winn. He had got his nickname in Italy, through his manner of covering the ground when under fire. We landed first at Korat, an active Siamese Air Force station, on our way to the northern border. Our next stop was at a place called Udaun Thani, which looked deserted. I made a couple of circuits to attract the attention of the chap who was supposed to couple and refuel the Sentinel. We then landed and waited.

There was some time to wait. 'Spider', who had been in Siam for several months, told me that rice was their main crop; the Siamese did the work, but the Chinese were the businessmen who profited from the harvest and who were comparable to the Jews of the Western world.

A crowd of villagers collected round the Sentinel. It had a landing light that lowered from the wing by an electric motor and then turned itself on. I switched on the mechanism for this and the villagers were entertained. We communicated together in sign language until the official arrived with a supply of petrol, plus two army officers.

Signalman Downs left us then, and his place was taken by Major Winn and a Siamese army captain called Gunn. Winn spoke to Gunn in French, of the sort we learned at school and which I had no difficulty in following. At least he had the courage to make use of his French, which was more than I had. We flew on to Nong Khai, on the banks of the Mekong river, and called in on the Siamese governor of that part, who again spoke French as his second language. He had a large, comfortable house, where we had dinner at a table laid with cutlery and plates of a style that I had not seen for ages.

After dinner we went down to the centre of the small town, where a dance was in progress. The Siamese danced apart from their partners, which was a style unfamiliar to Europeans at that time. The partners would rotate around the dance floor in a similar style to ballroom dancing, but would remain separate, waving the hands and arms in a rhythmical fashion, which was supposed to symbolise something to the initiated. The girls were trained from childhood to hyperextend their fingers, so that they would arch backwards, and this was considered beautiful by the Siamese.

At one stage an auction was held. There was a girl wearing a wreath of flowers, standing beside the auctioneer in the centre of the floor. After several bids I asked my Siamese escort how high the bidding had gone. It was in fact a very low sum, so I put in a bid myself. At that point the auction concluded, and I found the girl coming over to me. Thoughts of

Peter Daw and his Siamese wife for £5 flashed through my mind. 'What's happened?' I asked my companion. He told me that I had won the wreath of flowers, that I got the next dance with the girl, and that it was customary to give the wreath back to her. So I presented her with the circle of flowers and had the next dance.

Later they started singing solos at the microphone and eventually they called on me to sing. I am a nervous performer, but they had been passing round some fiery spirit during the evening, so I stood up, walked over to the mike, and said: 'Ladies and gentlemen, l have been listening to you singing your sort of music this evening. Now I am going to sing to you in our English style.' They all sat around looking interested, so I took a deep breath and launched into the song, 'How Still is the Night', to the tune of some classical French composer. It appeared to go down well. There was a French girl in the audience who had been working with the 136 Force before the war ended, who seemed to like it. When the party broke up, I tried to make a pass at her, but she was expert at politely avoiding male advances. I spent the night at the hotel in the town. The bedrooms were approached by an outside staircase, and an outside covered corridor ran the length of the building, with the bedrooms leading off it.

Up in that province I was told they measured distance by how far away one could hear a dog bark, this unit of length being repeated as often as necessary.

The next morning a Frenchman arrived from across the river with a minor bullet wound. I gathered there was a lot of intrigue going on, with more than two sides fighting each other in Indo-China. I was taken across the Mekong in a long, shallow vessel with a canopy for shade, to have a quick look at the country separated from Siam by the river.

Major Dumont was a tall, thin man with spectacles, who probably looked very incommunicative and withdrawn in his role of peasant in occupied France. I returned with him in the Sentinel to Don Muang. As we refuelled before the flight, I could have sworn that the 'petrol' we were putting in the aircraft was the same stuff as the spirit we had the night before! Cases of blindness were being reported through drinking wood alcohol at that time.

A Mosquito squadron arrived at Don Muang to augment the army of occupation, which consisted of 20 Squadron only as far as the air force was concerned. A wing commander 'flying' also showed up, named Cox. He had made short visits to various theatres of war, and collected an impressive row of campaign ribbons as a result.

On 7 November I returned to the northern border of Siam with Ron Ballard in the squadron Harvard, as they were planning to have a party there that night. The function was held in the governor's residence and once again I was called on to sing. On this occasion I could not think of an appropriate song, and gave a rendering of a bawdy RAF ballad set to an Irish tune. Evidently I had been asked to sing on the strength of my previous performance. This time there was a more formal audience and my song was received without enthusiasm. I managed to find substitutes for most of the four-letter words, but one 'f' accidentally got through at the end. Later Ron pulled my leg about this, pointing out that the singing was being relayed down the main street by loud speakers, and was not confined to the governor's house.

There was a young Frenchman present, who had been awarded a DSO for his part in a raid, when he had been dropped by parachute close to some German installation, which his unit had to attack.

At the end of the evening, I was told that a good way to prevent hangovers was to drink a raw egg in a glass of brandy. I tried a couple of these, and fortunately was none the worse the next morning! We slept that night at the governor's house. During the evening, the 136 types informed me that the Siamese were very proud of their sexual prowess, and were capable of performing the act with many different girls throughout one night. I have heard similar stories about the Arabs.

Back at Don Muang, Wing Commander Cox had found a serviceable Jap fighter, an Oscar. He invited me to have the first flight in it, which I gladly accepted. There were two Japanese mechanics who told me all I needed to know in Japanese, and we then conversed in sign language. The aeroplane was obviously built for small men, as I was unable to close the cockpit hood because my head projected above its traverse. There were several petrol tanks, each with its own switch. The Japs pointed out the handles and showed me a gauge that looked like a fuel pressure gauge. Sure enough it registered once the engine was running. The writing on the instrument panel was all in Japanese, not surprisingly, but this meant I got no information as to the different devices. The air-speed indicator was probably in kph but I do not remember.

Anyway, I took off and flew perforce with the cockpit hood open. It handled quite well, seemed a bit heavy on the controls, was manoeuvrable, had a steeper gliding angle than I expected and was not so fast or powerful as the Spitfire. I stayed up for an hour and a half doing rolls and loops. At one critical point, the fuel pressure gauge started flickering back to zero, warning me that the tank I was using was running dry. I looked at all the different handles and tried to remember which one had been switched on originally. This was where 'on' and 'off' written in Japanese was not helpful. I made my choice and was relieved to find the fuel pressure gauge needle settled down again in its proper position. I landed carefully but, even though I had brought the machine in without drift, it showed a desire to turn to starboard on the landing run. I applied full port rudder and brake and in spite of this the plane veered to the right at the end of the run. I got out and warned Cox that the port brake was not working. He was going to fly next, followed by a Siamese group captain. I did not stay to watch. I heard afterwards that Wing Commander Cox ground-looped the machine on touch-down, and then the Siamese group captain crashed it when he landed. Cox got a raspberry from the Air Ministry as this was the only serviceable Jap fighter and they had hoped to ship it back to England for tests. Shortly after, Cox asked me if I would like to go on a course as an RAF test pilot. I had seen the circular about this, asking for names to be submitted, and I was not interested.

A few days later, I took the Harvard up to Nong Khai and brought Major Rowley Winn back to Don Muang. The following week our new Spitfires arrived. They were Mk XIVs with five blades to the airscrew, a ring and bead sight that allowed automatically for deflection, an automatic pitch control and a cartridge starter. The young ferry pilot told me to do up the friction nut tightly on the throttle before take-off, as he had not done so and the throttle had closed on him. This was wrong advice as the nut needed only normal tightening and I had some difficulty on my first take-off moving the throttle at all! So much torque developed that the port wheel flattened on lifting off. However, it was a beautiful machine, and it was child's play doing a roll where centrifugal force kept you firmly in your seat. If the nose was pointed upwards, the machine continued to climb in a way that was extraordinary after the old aircraft that we flew during the war. I compared it to the Mosquitoes but they were of course faster. On starting, one did the preliminary priming of the engine and then fired a cartridge, which started it. I found pleasure in diving the machine down to ground level, getting up a speed of 500mph and then levelling out. I would then look into the distance at the horizon and watch it coming towards me within a space of under a minute. We tried our hand at formation aerobatics, but most of the pilots felt that they had managed to survive the war and did not want to get killed now.

D.O. Finlay was due to be repatriated and we had a swim together on his last afternoon. We ran back to the mess. I was never a great runner but I was thirteen years younger than Finlay and managed to keep up with him. His feet were hitting the ground with force and I suspected that he could have forged ahead if he had wished. Later in the evening I was sitting in the mess with some of the squadron pilots when Finlay came in. I gave him a smile as he went by. The next morning, I was sent for to report to his office. I found him blowing his top. 'Where were you brought up, Millar?' he asked, looking at me with incredulous scorn. This was brought on because I did not stand up when he entered the mess. During my years in the jungle, I had forgotten that little custom.

I met Finlay twice more. Once at a 221 Group reunion in 1946 and again, years later in Oxford, when we had both taken our families to see the film, *The Sound of Music*. A few years after that, I heard that he had shot himself.

The ship carrying the squadron records had sunk on the way to Bangkok. The new group captain was unaware of the policy introduced during 1945, whereby part of the squadron was split into a separate unit called a servicing echelon, and was made independent as far as its administration was concerned. The new engineer officer replacing Dingle Bell was Flying Officer Dainty, but the group captain directed various enquiries to me on matters that were no longer my province and I had to explain this to him.

One day, carrying out an inspection, I came across three airmen lying in their billets. I told them to stay at ease. One of these, who was new to the squadron, said they knew what the squadron had achieved during the war but they did not know what I had done to get my DSO. He spoke insolently and I was not interested in informing him. The war was over and I made no comment.

We had a visit from the RAF historian, who said he had been given my name by one or two authorities and informed that he could accept what I disclosed. Ron Ballard took the opportunity of enlightening him about the day we found the Japanese tanks at the bridgehead on the Irrawaddy, and this appeared in the official RAF history, mentioning Ron and Jimmy's part, quite rightly. I felt some embarrassment at being asked to 'shoot a line', so the chap said it could wait until later in the day, and tackled me again after our evening meal. I told him about Wing Commander Carey taking off from Chittagong pursued by Jap fighters and of Guy Marsland throwing hand grenades out of the rear cockpit of my Lysander and that was all. I lost a golden opportunity to record the squadron's exploits in the official history.

I took a jeep into Bangkok to have dinner with Aage and Jackie Mork. We parked it in the yard of one of the main hotels. When we came out after the meal, the vehicle had gone. Unfortunately I had neglected to remove the rotor arm, which would have immobilised it. The thief turned out to be a paratroop deserter. He had accelerated out of the yard in reverse, hitting a tree – which luckily for him stopped him from going into the canal on the opposite side of the road – and had then driven off. I learned later that he had lived a hectic life before being finally shot by the army, carrying out robberies and running a brothel.

I returned to the Morks' house for the night. As I waited disconsolately at a bus stop the next morning, a carload of Japanese staff officers passed by and gave me a short salute from their open tourer.

Returning to camp I reported the loss to the group captain, who asked me whether I had taken out the rotor arm. I confessed that I had not. Later, talking to the M/T officer and others, I was informed that I should not admit this, so in my statement to the Court of Inquiry I said that I had removed the rotor arm. The group captain queried this point and I agreed that I had told him differently, but that I had been advised to say that I had indeed done so! As I was on my way out of the RAF they probably decided to do nothing about it.

I received a signal from SEAC asking whether I was willing to continue for a while as CO of 20 Squadron. Although I had missed the start of the academic year for my medical studies, I felt that I could not remain in the Far East any longer as I was truly 'puggled' by this time. Dai Lewis sent back a reply on my behalf, telling them to get knotted. A further signal from SEAC asked for a clarification of this signal, to which I replied that I did not, repeat not, wish to stay on in the Far East.

Finlay's replacement asked me whether there was anyone on the squadron suitable to take over from me, and mentioned Johnny Horrocks. I told him that Horrocks had only recently become a flight commander and that there was nobody on the squadron whom I could recommend. Johnny was still a flight lieutenant when he retired from the RAF many years later. Ron Ballard, like myself, was due for repatriation. My successor turned out to be Humphries, who had been CO of 60 Squadron.

When he arrived at Don Muang, I showed him round and then went through the drill that I had done two years before, when Peter Joel handed over the squadron to me. An inventory was drawn up of the unit's effects, which were checked by Humphries and myself. He then signed as having taken them over.

In the evening Humphries wanted to go into Bangkok, and I put him in touch with the squadron leader 'admin' of AHQ, who was going in with a jeep. Humphries accompanied him but, at the camp exit, the squadron leader took the corner too fast and put the jeep into the ditch. This squadron leader was unpopular. While both men were unconscious, they were taken back to the squadron sick quarters and the medical staff reprehensibly bound up the admin officer's hairy leg with sticking plaster and hoisted it from the ceiling by a pulley, so that when he came round they pretended that he had injured himself. An unethical 'leg pull'. Surprisingly, Humphries thought that I had engineered the whole thing and had let him in for the accident!

I remembered a very enjoyable meal at a Chinese restaurant in Bangkok called the Hoi Tien Lao. Soup had been served in a hollowed-out melon, and the French consul had plunged his chopsticks through the side of the melon so that the soup had gushed out, and we had held our plates so that the spouting soup had filled them. This had been followed by stuffed crabs' claws. Here the consul had indicated that we should dispose of the claws by throwing them over our shoulders out of the window. As we were four floors up, there were no repercussions from angry pedestrians below. The meal had been sufficiently memorable for me to feel that it would be a good place to have a squadron dinner and I went ahead and arranged this, financing it with money that had been given to me by pilots as they left the unit, and with a contribution of my own. In the end I departed a day or two before the squadron dinner, but heard that it was a success.

The officers each received a Jap officer's sword after I had gone, which I was sorry to miss!

On 1 December I flew Colonel Smiley to Korat in the Harvard and then back to Don Muang. In 1981 I met an ex-RAF officer called Geoffrey

Allan who since went to live in Spain. He told me that Colonel Smiley and Rowley Winn (later Lord St Oswald) also resided there. He was talking to Colonel Smiley about Siam, when the name of a Thai, which sounded something like Pawl, came up. Apparently he had managed to seize power soon after the war. Smiley became very worked up and said to Allan that he would kill the man with his own hands if ever he saw him. Pawl had invited to a dinner all the Siamese whom Colonel Smiley had trained as saboteurs. After the meal, the bearers had closed in from behind and garrotted every guest. It was like a tale from the dark ages in Europe.

It is said that the novelist John le Carré selected Smiley's name for one of the characters in his books, having known the name in his department, although there was no attempt to portray him in the fictitious character.

On 3 December I made my last flight with 20 Squadron. I was very conscious that this was the end of a long saga, and I savoured every moment of the trip, starting the engine by firing the cartridge, waving the chocks away after completing the cockpit check and enjoying my final hour of aerobatics in the Spitfire XIV.

In 1945 I had flown 89 operational sorties, with 150 hours 45 minutes' operational flying out of a total of 298 hours 30 minutes for the year. Altogether I had flown 204 sorties in 397 hours 15 minutes.

During my last few days in Siam, flags were hung up in the main street. This was not for my departure but to herald the arrival of the King of Siam, who was expected daily to arrive, for the first time since before the Japanese occupation.

On 5 December I heard that there was a Dakota due to take off for Calcutta, and at short notice I decided to skip the squadron dinner and catch the plane. It was piloted by a Frenchman called Laschennaie. We did the journey in a single hop, passing over the mountains to the Arakan coast, and I was able to make out Maungdaw and some of the other places where we had had adventures in 1942 and 1944, and watched as they receded out of sight.

After a few days in Calcutta, I took a troop train to Bombay. This was a very different experience from my original trip when I arrived in India. Now the train was packed and there were no luxurious touches like a compartment to myself with a bucket of ice to keep the carriage cool. The journey took a week, and at one point we were held up for most of a day, as the engine driver was arrested for theft and we had to wait for a replacement!

I spent seven days in Bombay, billeted in a flat at Juhu, which was a modern building with a nicely tiled squatter's loo. It was nearly Christmas when I boarded the boat for England. The Indian porter who had helped me with my luggage, asked for more when I gave him an adequate tip. I was suddenly filled with anger at the land I was leaving and the begging habits of its people. 'That's enough! Go away, you wretched man!' I shouted at him in troops' Urdu.

It took me a long time to get back to a normal state of mind. There were, however, still ten months to the start of the next academic year, in which to grow accustomed to being a second-year medical student and not an aviator. The war had made many changes, but soon my wings would start to wither and fade, and I would pick up the threads of everyday living again.

My flying hours were over.

Index